No Place Like Home:

Building Sustainable Communities

Marcia Nozick

CANADIAN COUNCIL ON SOCIAL DEVELOPMENT

OTTAWA

The analyses, views and opinions expressed in this book are those of the author and do not necessarily reflect the position or policies of the Canadian Council on Social Development.

Canadian Cataloguing in Publication Data

    Nozick, Marcia, 1952-
    No place like home: building sustainable communities

    ISBN 0-88810-415-4 (paper)
    ISBN 0-88810-441-3 (hardcover)

    1. Economic development. 2. Community development.
  I. Canadian Council on Social Development. II. Title.

    GF101.N69 1992   338.9   C92-090433-5

Cover design: Accurate Dezigns
Desktopping: Michel Henry
Printed and bound in Canada by Love Printing Service Ltd. on
    Canadian made recycled paper.

Published by:
Canadian Council on Social Development
55 Parkdale Avenue
Ottawa, Ontario K1Y 4G1
Tel: (613) 728-1865. Fax: (613) 728-9387

Dedication

In memory of Kent Gerecke (1937-1992), my husband, friend,
lover, teacher, and inspiration in life.

TABLE OF CONTENTS

Foreword --- ix
Preface --- xi
Acknowledgements -- xiii
Chapter One: For the Sake of Community -------------------- 1
No place like home --- 3
Organization and overview of the book --------------------------- 9
Sustainable development --- 12
Sustainable communities: A new future. -------------------------- 14
Chapter Two: Confronting the Global Economy ----------- 17
Cheaper goods — At what cost? ----------------------------------- 21
Global trade and the Third World ------------------------------ 21
Global trade and its impact at home -------------------------- 25
The new North: Rich and poor-------------------------------- 28
The alternative: An idea whose time has come------------------ 30
The transfer of Schumacher's ideas to the West ----------- 33
Popular movements confront the global economy ---------- 36
Choosing between two visions ------------------------------------- 38
Chapter Three: Working Toward Self-Reliance ----------- 41
The creation of local wealth -------------------------------------- 45
Making more with less--- 45
Making the money-go-round --------------------------------- 50
Barter credit --- 52
Making it ourselves -- 54
Measuring net gains --------------------------------------- 56
Making something new ------------------------------------- 57
Trading with equal partners --------------------------------- 59
Case study: Self-reliant development at Kingfisher Lake------- 61
Conclusion -- 62
Chapter Four: Harmonizing With Nature ----------------- 65
Forgotten nature -- 67
Loss of diversity --- 68
Ecology as a design for living ------------------------------------ 72
A bioregional perspective -- 75
Watershed report -- 77
Producing for life --- 78

Building green and healthy cities --------------------------------- 81
    Two eco-communities in Canada ----------------------------- 86
Eco-technologies and appropriate development ------------------ 88
    Ecological sewage treatment methods ------------------------ 89
    Tall Grass Prairie Bread Company --------------------------- 92
Conclusion -- 94
Chapter Five: Attaining Community Control ------------- 97
Personal power -- 100
    Personal power changes Alkali Lake community ---------- 102
Power with others -- 104
Community power: Lost and found ------------------------------ 107
Claiming power: Models for community control --------------- 110
    Control of land and housing — the community land trust ------ 110
    Community loan funds — gaining access to capital ------ 115
    Grassroots control of industry — small business to
        worker co-ops -- 118
    Neighbourhood/community development corporations ---- 120
Four examples of community control --------------------------- 122
    Evangeline, P.E.I. --- 122
    United Hands Community Land Trust, Philadelphia ------ 124
    Milton Park, Montreal -------------------------------------- 127
    Cedar Riverside Community, Minneapolis ----------------- 130
Conclusion -- 134
Chapter Six: Meeting Individual Needs ------------------- 139
Introduction --- 141
What do people need? --- 144
Nonmaterial needs -- 148
    Meeting the needs of autonomy ----------------------------- 148
    Meeting the needs of integration --------------------------- 152
Material needs --- 156
    Meeting the needs of survival ------------------------------- 156
        Feeding the people ------------------------------------- 157
        Making a safe place to live --------------------------- 162
        Housing the people ------------------------------------- 164
Three Housing Stories --- 165
    The story of Street City, Toronto --------------------------- 165
    Habitat for Humanity --------------------------------------- 169

Project for Pride in Living, Minneapolis ------------------ 172
Conclusion --- 175
Chapter Seven: Building a Community Culture ----------- 179
Discovering the culture of community -------------------------- 183
Reclaiming our social history -------------------------------- 183
Reclaiming our natural history ------------------------------- 187
The Forks-- 189
Cultural groups: The multicultural weave ----------------- 192
Building a neighbourhood culture -------------------------------- 196
Conclusion -- 201
Conclusion: The Way Back Home ------------------------- 205
Points for further discussion -------------------------------------- 210
What can we do? --- 212
Appendices --- 215
Appendix 1— Women's Economic Development Corporation,
St. Paul -- 217
WomenVenture -- 221
Appendix 2 — Aboriginal development in Winnipeg -------- 223
Select Bibliography -- 229
Index -- 235

Foreword

I believe that *No Place Like Home* is a work of quite exceptional importance. Its message is unequivocal and, to my mind, convincing: there is now sufficient experience of grassroots economic development to justify the claim that it offers an alternative to the conventional economic system, which is slowly disintegrating in the North, and has already proved to be useless, if not actually damaging, in the South. It is also now possisble to delineate the essential characteristics of sustainable local economic development, to show how and why it works.

While reading the book I was struck by several qualities it shares with Fritz Schumacher's classic *Small is Beautiful*. It is the product of an original and disciplined mind; it is both critical and constructive — its attack on "top-down" development and the emerging global economy is balanced by practical alternatives which, to borrow James Robertson's phrase, are sane, humane and ecological; and it is written in language that everyone can understand.

The similarities do not end there. One of the reasons why the message of *Small is Beautiful* is so powerful is that it makes explicit, gives form and content, to widespread but formerly inarticulate misgivings about where modern large-scale technology and centralized control were taking us: their destructive effect on people, the environment, and the world's resource base. Schumacher focused particularly on developing countries and showed that only a new kind of technology — small, simple, capital-saving and skill-intensive — could overcome their problems of mass unemployment and rural decay.

In this book, Marcia Nozick does something along the same lines for industrialized countries, by spelling out what it takes to achieve sustainable community development as an alternative to the prevailing top-heavy economic system. It is an alternative, as Paul Ekins has recently put it, informed by the recognition that human progress (even survival) means harmony with nature instead of an ever-expanding consumerism, and also that the nation-state is not the only form of legitimate authority.[1]

As unemployment, alienation, homelessness and crime have become pervasive in the North, a good deal has been written on the need to rebuild local economies, empower local people and foster self-reliance, and many remarkable instances of grassroots local development have arisen on both sides of the Atlantic and in developing countries. In the North much has been learnt, by hard experience, about the devastating impact of global free-market economics upon our urban and rural communities. But there is far less knowledge about how to arrest this damage and reverse it, about feasible alternatives.

Marcia Nozick makes a major contribution towards filling this knowledge gap. The book has five themes, each a component of sustainable community. They are: economic self-reliance; ecological development; getting community control over resources; meeting individual human needs; and building a community culture. Each of these five themes, which together comprise a new ethic of development, are analyzed and described with her rare combination of analytical skill and human insight. How they interact and reinforce each other in practice is illustrated by lively examples drawn from communities throughout North America. The result is a book that will be of value to community workers everywhere, and that cannot fail to inspire everyone who reads it.

George McRobie

ENDNOTES

1   In *A New World Order: Grassroots Movements for Global Change.* London: Routledge, 1992.

Preface

The other day I saw a professor from the University of Alberta interviewed on television, saying that the disappearance of "uneconomic communities" is a fact of life we have to accept. Small farming towns, rural fishing towns, are things of the past. He went on to say we should not put any resources into saving "places," meaning geographic communities, but into "mobility" — helping people to move to where economic pickings are greater, presumably to cities or "urban growth centres," as they are sometimes called. His expression "uneconomic communities" jarred me, but it is a telling statement about current values and myths. It says that people and places are expendable objects in a global economy, that economics, **as defined by the global corporate agenda,** takes precedence over people, local culture and history. It says that current economic forces erasing community life are **inevitable.** The professor's statement shows no recognition that community itself has inherent value, outside of economics, worth preserving for future generations.

There are fundamental questions raised by this expert's views on economy. The first that comes to mind is, who is in the driver's seat — people or a corporate-steered economy? Next, we need ask: what is economics for? Even more important, what are people for? Is the purpose of human life to serve the needs of an economic system? Or is the purpose of an economic system instead to serve the needs of human life, including the needs of belonging to a community? These questions need further articulation and much public debate before we begin to see more clearly the choices in front of us.

The economic-social-environmental crisis of today stems not from a lack of knowledge, resources or ability to solve problems, but from failing to ask the right questions. A problem needs defining before it can be solved. E. F. Schumacher once wrote, "There is no economic problem, and, in a sense, there never has been. But there is a moral problem, and moral problems...have to be understood and transcended."[1] We already have the capacity to meet everybody's material and nonmaterial needs: what we lack is an **ethic** to inspire and move us in a new direction. **Our problem is not one of economics but one of estranged values, where our economics is divorced from ethics.** It is this ethic we must discover, which must become the basis of development and must, in the end, guide a return to a society based on human and ecological values.

In this book, I have been on my own search for human and ecological values. I have immensely enjoyed writing *No Place Like Home* — what I have enjoyed most is learning about people's different communities and engagements in actions. Communities all seem to have their own unique personalities. Their stories are like good gossip — not the stuff they print in newspapers, but the juicy stuff of people's lives, often filled with personal and political intrigue. On a personal level, writing this book has affected my own way of responding to the world: I have become more sensitive to the subtle forces of domination which affect relationships in the family, school and work. I am much more aware of the need for all of us to develop our own citizenship.

ENDNOTES

[1] E. F. Schumacher, *Guide to the Perplexed* (London: Abacus, 1978), p. 160.

Acknowledgements

This book is the product of years of research, interviews, observations, writings, discussions and travels to different cities. Along the way there have been countless people who have contributed to the book through a sharing of their community experiences, ideas and support.

I first want to thank all the main characters in the book - all of the groups and individuals named in these pages, whose dedicated community work and creative practical solutions have shown me that real change is possible, that there are many things to feel hopeful about even in bleak times.

I owe a great debt to David Ross, my editor, who not only supported me throughout my writing, but had the very wise sense to recognize early on that what I *really* wanted to write about was something different than I had originally planned. He was able to help redirect my thoughts toward the vision that eventually became this book.

I want to thank all the readers of the early drafts of the book for their constructive feedback and generous encouragement: George McRobie, Katheryn Cholette, David Suzuki, David Witty, Michael Clague, Roberta Simpson, Ken Murdoch, Don Alexander and Art Stinson. Also, I want to thank all the people at CCSD who helped in the production of the book, Nancy Perkins and especially Bob Bisson who guided me step-by-step through the process. Virginia Smith did a teriffic job of copy editing.

My teenage children, Holly and Jacob Steele, must be commended for their enduring patience during the hundreds of hours I was glued to the computer and they were left to fend for themselves. They have been a real support to me.

Finally, and above all, I want to express my deepest gratitude to Kent Gerecke, my life partner in work, love and play, who died suddenly in May of this year. He was so looking forward to seeing this book in print. You might say he was a silent partner in the project. Kent was my inhouse editor, providing me with a running commentary on the chapters as they rolled off the computer printer. Our daily discussions about the world, about community, our work together as writers and activists, inspired most of the ideas contained in these pages. But mostly, I am grateful for the confidence he instilled in me. Kent was my biggest fan. He believed in my ability to write and, more importantly, he believed that what I had to say would make a difference in the world. This book is dedicated to his memory and our life together.

Chapter One

For the Sake of Community

As local community decays along with local economy, a vast amnesia settles over the countryside ... local knowledge and local memory are forgotten under the influence of homogenized sales talk, entertainment, and education. This loss of local knowledge and memory — that is, of local culture— has been ignored, or written off as one of the cheaper "prices of progress" or made the business of folklorists. Nevertheless, local culture has a value, and part of its value is economic.

Wendell Berry
What are People For?

1

For the Sake of Community

NO PLACE LIKE HOME

The Holiday Inn ad tells us "you can travel round the world and never leave home." Home, today, has come to mean the wide world at large, a "global home" which is both everywhere and nowhere. This global home we come to identify by the corporate images sold to us on mass media and repeated with regular sameness from city to city — suburbs of spaghetti design, shopping malls with glass peaks, McDonald's, Holiday Inns, domed stadiums. The shift from understanding home as a special place of origin — a community where we live, work, belong and feel a sense of social responsibility — to the perception of home as a World Class City such as New York or Los Angeles is a result of complex global forces promoting cultural uniformity.

In Winnipeg, on a cold winter day of minus thirty-five degrees Celsius, a typical youth can be seen wearing California sneakers and a light jacket as a replacement for winter boots and parka. Teenage girls are talking in a Los Angeles "valley girl" dialect, while boys are speaking black "rap" from New York City, and it seems that everyone is wearing American flags as emblems on clothing. These people were born and raised in Winnipeg, but, really, where is their home; where do they live?

Diversity and uniqueness of place is lost in the process of economic globalization (the replacement of local markets with global markets). We forget who we are and where we come from. Community identity dissolves into what Marshall McLuhan called the Global Village — a place defined by mass media and global corporate interests. The Global Village is everybody's but *nobody's* home: it is a familiar image among all those brought to us by mass communication — images of perfect Dentyne smiles with perfect bodies, of car chases, of suave men in business suits, of killings and bombings on the news, of Madonna in her latest rock video.

We cannot help but be tanatalized by these images, tricked into believing they represent what *our* life is all about. Yet by projecting and

3

focusing so much of our attention "out there," we lose track of what's going on "in here," within ourselves and our communities. The more we are subsumed by the Global Village, the more we lose touch with our own identities, our histories, our community roots, and our local ways and traditions.

Brian Fawcett, in his book *Cambodia,* tells the tragicomic story of what happened to one town when it hooked up to a TV satellite dish. The town of Huxley, B.C. is located sixty miles north of Vancouver and has a population of approximately 2,000, with most people employed in one way or another by the logging industry. When the satellite dish was put up, people discovered that they could tune their televisions into Detroit, Michigan and watch the same American TV programs as Vancouver, only *three hours earlier!* This became a source of community pride and one-upmanship. From then on the people of Huxley began to *live* in Detroit. Detroit became their home town, and Huxley disappeared from the hearts and minds of the people who lived there.

Within a few months the pub had lost almost all its local business as people stopped dropping in after work and in the evening. They chose instead to go straight home to drink beer and watch prime time TV with supper, followed by Johnny Carson at 8:30 P.M. The other stores in town started losing business as well in what used to be their peak hours. By 9:00 P.M. the town was dead. The principal of the local high school became somewhat concerned when kids began coming to school in black leather jackets with obscene words written on them and talking Detroit "lingo." Then race relations changed for the worse. The town had always lived amicably with the native people from the nearby Indian reserve. Then after the dish was erected, racial gangs began to form, and white and native persons no longer spoke to one another. It was as if people totally forgot where they were from and their history together. The school kayak team, which had always been a popular group on the local rivers, had no one sign up the next year — instead baseball and basketball became the town sports, and Detroit Tigers' hats were to be seen everywhere. All the Detroit Tigers' hats tipped off a journalist who happened to be passing through town that something strange was happening. Vancouver sent a TV news crew to Huxley and did a story on the town.

In an interview, one man, boasting he watched twelve to fifteen hours of TV a day since he'd been laid off his job, told reporters he was planning to look for work in the auto industry which "was looking up these days." Detroit, the auto city of North America halfway across the continent, had become more real to him than the town of Huxley, B.C.

where he lived. Then one day, the satellite dish was dynamited. Evidence pointed toward the pub owner as the perpetrator, but before charges were ever laid the man disappeared without a trace. The rumour was that he was chased out or possibly even murdered. The town got together to raise money, something people hadn't done in years. It took six weeks to replace the satellite dish, and everything was back to "normal."

By "tuning in" to the Global Village and "tuning out" of our local communities, we have become willing and happy participants in the destruction of our own communities, communities which we depend on for our livelihood and security. Community cohesiveness, economic viability and local autonomy are undermined in the process. Indeed, the roots of communities have grown so shallow that we seem not even to remember what it is we have lost — the values of community, of attachment, commitment, mutual support, self-reliance, self-direction. Instead we fill the empty spaces of our lives by shopping across the American and international borders for more and cheaper consumer goods produced outside our communities, thus contributing to the drain of wealth from our local economies.

In today's world "community" is fast becoming a thing of the past with urban neighbourhoods, small towns, whole regions and even third world countries being written off as bad investments, laid to waste in the economic restructuring of the world according to the dictates of global "economic efficiency." With all of the political attention and billions of dollars going to establish this "new world order" of corporate giantism, we seem to have forgotten our grassroots, the nonmonetary things that matter to people, and even people themselves, who are increasingly left out of the economic equation.

Rootlessness, transitoriness and dispossession are the fall-out of an increasing trend toward globalization and global competition. People move to find better jobs; corporations move to find cheaper labour; consumer products, including food, move thousands of miles to reach global markets; fashions shift with the change of seasons; neighbourhoods where people grew up have vanished within a generation. The notion of security, belonging and community are lost along the way and so is our connection with where we live, the people around us, nature and the things we consume.

The other day I was at a SuperValu store, a giant grocery chain, and the only sugar I could buy there was imported from London, England, on the other side of the globe. The irony struck me. Here I was standing in Winnipeg, the sugar beet capital of North America, just two miles from a major sugar processing plant, and I was having to buy sugar from England! If local stores don't support local producers, who will? Yet these are contradictions we live with all the time. They are an inherent part of the global economy's takeover of the distribution and production of goods, which used to be local. With global imports replacing local produce, our communities are losing their economic base and ability to sustain themselves. The survival of community depends, in large part, on whether we will be able to revitalize and resurrect our *community-based* economies.

Many industries are viable within their local regions, yet they are being shut down because of global management. The father of a friend of mine used to own an industrial rubber repair plant he started many years ago. When he retired he sold it to a transnational corporation with headquarters in London. Under current management, 17 per cent of gross monthly earnings is sent directly to support a head office in another city, and, though the local rubber repair business was once profitable, today it cannot carry the extra costs of its 17 per cent global "overhead" and is likely to shut down. There are thousands of examples like this one of profitable local businesses serving local citizens being systematically shut down as they are bought up by large national or transnational conglomerates. (Witness the closing of the Brandon, Manitoba airport and the closing of the Paulin's cookie manufacturing plant in Winnipeg, both profitable local operations.)

The point is that "globalization," as an economic development strategy and as a national government policy, is hurting rather than benefiting our local communities, by marginalizing them and making them dependent on imports and on powers outside their control.

Communities more than ever need to find the local means and wherewithal to survive the current forces of economic globalization threatening their existence. To this end, there needs to be an alternative vision to the global economy (which is being promoted by the powers-that-be as the only economic reality) — an alternative development strategy which has as its main purpose and goal, the preservation and revitalization of community "for the sake of community," as opposed to "profit for the sake of profit." If there is a single bias to my book, it is a belief that community provides something essential and vital to humankind which is worth saving and building further — a home base, meaningful relationship with others, a personal identity, a mutual support system for our life endeavours, and the values of caring and sharing.

This leads to the topic of the book — **building sustainable communities.** In contrast to the uniform Global Village or the World Class

6

City, this is a book about rediscovering the particularities of place, the reclaiming of home, community and local responsibility through **sustainable community development** (SCD). The goal of sustainable community development is to:

    (1) *build communities which are more self-supporting* and which can sustain and regenerate themselves through economic self-reliance, community control and environmentally sound development.

    (2) *build communities which will be worth preserving* because they are grounded in the life experiences of people who live in them and in the natural histories of specific regions. This calls for building local culture and meeting the full range of people's needs.

The breakdown of community and its capacity to sustain itself is a phenomenon which is occurring on many fronts. Communities in Canada and in the whole developed world are facing crisis because of:

- Economic de-industrialization, which is leaving thousands of people across the country in small towns and in urban communities unemployed due to plant closings.

- Environmental degradation of crisis proportion, which is poisoning our local water supplies and the air we breathe in major cities, through industrial pollution, consumer waste and auto pollution.

- Loss of local control over our communities, with major economic and political decisions made by higher levels of government or by companies whose head offices are elsewhere — by people who have no stake in the community except profit taking or managing people.

- Social degradation and neglect of basic human needs, so that increasing numbers of people in our communities are marginalized, alienated, homeless, jobless, hungry and living in unsafe situations.

- Erosion of local identity and cultural diversity as we conform to the homogeneous values of the Global Village, as we saw in the Huxley example.

The five trends above are the main pressure points of community breakdown; any one of these stress signals warns that community survival is under serious threat. Any plan to restore and revitalize community has to grapple with the whole ugly picture. Right now we have people dealing with the parts. Yet it is not enough simply to create more jobs, for example, through more economic growth. If we choose this route, we are as likely as not feeding into the problem of environmental pollution or overproduction, or, if we chase outside investments, increasing a community's vulnerability to outside interference. If we deal with social degradation by just providing more welfare and services in the inner cities, we are not allowing people to become self-sufficient or providing them opportunites to give something of themselves back to the community. People need a livelihood, and they need power to change their lives. Likewise, it is not enough to impose environmental restrictions on industries. We need to create whole communities which are environmentally sound — where people can walk, not drive to work and work at life-enhancing, not life-destroying activities.

The purpose of the book is to examine each of the five pressure points now triggering crises in communities and to see how they can be addressed through community action, bearing in mind the larger picture of connections among these pressures. The *reclaiming of community* is always the primary aim. The bulk of the book is devoted to exploring an alternative development which deals directly with these five aspects of community breakdown: declining economy, degrading environment, loss of political autonomy, neglected human needs, loss of community culture. One chapter is devoted to each of the five problems from the perspective of developing a counterstrategy to resist these destructive forces and also of seeing what actions various communities are taking. Together, the five themes create an action strategy for building sustainable communities and provide a broad framework of principles to tie together all the thousands of piecemeal community actions (often started in response to immediate crisis) into a purposeful and coherent *long-term* vision.

Before outlining the book's chapters, I need to inform the reader of three decisions which have shaped the research throughout.

(1) I have chosen to focus on the urban context (though not exclusively). One reason is that most people — 80 per cent of Canadians — live in cities. Another is that there is a growing literature about the crisis of single industry towns and declining farm communities, but little attention has been paid in that literature to the crises of urban communities from a sustainable development perspective.

(2) It is a well kept secret that there are thousands of successful community-building projects and activities emerging within our communities. Unlike the megaprojects — the domed stadiums and aquariums (the latest fad) of the World Class

City — these often underfunded, volunteer-based initiatives do not make front or even back page news. Yet quietly, invisibly, they are making their statement, transforming our communities from the inside-out. For this reason, I have chosen to tell the story of sustainable community development primarily through a myriad of examples. I hope to give the reader a sense of the diversity and multitude of alternatives which already exist or could be started in our communities.

(3) I began the research for the book on the topic of **community economic development** (CED) but discovered shortly that I was actually pursuing a broader and more inclusive subject area, which **sustainable community development** (SCD) encompassed. CED remains, however, an important theme, as will be seen from the many examples throughout the book.

ORGANIZATION AND OVERVIEW OF THE BOOK

The call for a turnaround, community-based approach to development is both an urgent emotional plea and a carefully thought out response to the increasing failure of the *global* economy to meet people's needs. Chapter Two, "Confronting the Global Economy," sets the background and context for the emerging sustainable community development. It paints a rather dark and frightful picture of the global economy, as the backdrop and *raison d'etre* for an alternative economic vision. What do we mean by global development? Who benefits from global development? — these are the key questions. The chapter looks critically at the effects of corporate concentration, international trade and large scale development on natural environments and the lives of local people in developing countries and in our own developed country. We see how global economic restructuring is creating a growing, permanent underclass of disenfranchised, dispossessed peoples around the world. The book's limited space unfortunately allows only a cursory introduction to these complex issues, but enough, it is hoped, to inspire further readings on the topic. Other recommended readings are included in the book's select bibliography.

With the need for an alternative development established, the second half of the chapter goes on to introduce the root concepts of an alternative economics, which have been percolating in various circles for a number of years. Most notable is the work of economist E.F. (Fritz) Schumacher, whose questions about development ethics and ideas about decentralizing economics, designing "appropriate technologies" for small scale industries and respecting the limits of nature, inspired others, such as those in the green movement in North America and Europe. The chapter explores how popular movements today are giving rise to a new consciousness and set of values signalling a quest for rediscovery of community and community values. It is within this new set of values that we find a place for sustainable community development.

With an awakening to new community values, we can move from criticism to positive alternatives. The core of the book, Chapters Three to Seven, focuses on the plans and actions of ordinary people in urban communities across North America who are out there doing it — taking charge of their lives and seeking control over their communities — from the homeless people at Street City building their own shelter in an abandoned warehouse, to the thousands of volunteers building houses for Habitat for Humanity. The chapters describe, through theory and examples, what it means to build sustainable communities.

Sustainable community development is a community-based approach to development which relies on self-help, community economic development and ecological principles. "Development" is seen as more than economic growth. To use the soft language of personal growth, development is a process of "coming into one's own" — for communities that means growing *qualitatively* and *ethically* as well as quantitatively. In the end we want communities which can be self-supporting, but also communities worth saving because they mean something to the people who live in them.

There are five major themes which constitute a framework of action for building sustainable communities. They are:

- **Working toward self-reliance** — Chapter Three
- **Harmonizing with nature** — Chapter Four
- **Attaining community control** — Chapter Five
- **Meeting individual needs** — Chapter Six
- **Building a community culture** — Chapter Seven

How can a community begin to disengage from dependency on global markets for imports and exports or dependency on large scale industries which are damaging the environment or threatening to close? How can a community with few resources begin to generate wealth within the community? These questions are taken up in Chapter Three, which explores economic self-reliance, which involves community use of its own physical and human resources to meet its own needs.

Urban development has been a major player in the destruction of our environment — bringing us smog, overflowing landfills and polluted rivers and watersheds. How can we rethink our cities and neighbourhoods to make them ecologically sustainable within a larger eco-system or bioregion? What are the guiding principles of "ecology"? Chapter Four, on **ecological development**, looks at the relationship of communities to nature and explores some of the new eco-technologies and experiments in creating green and healthy communities.

Communities, like people, need the power to plan and shape their futures. Chapter Five, on **community control**, introduces a political component into the development of communties founded on the beliefs that self-determination is the best way to look after community interests and that people have the right to manage their own affairs. The chapter examines the process of community empowerment through a discussion of personal power, the power of groups and community power. It also looks at a variety of alternative structures such as land trusts, worker co-operatives, community loan associations and neighbourhood corporations as models which give a community continuing control over land, capital, development and industry.

A community is only as strong as its individual members. If peoples' basic needs are not met — if homelessness, hunger, violence and alienation are allowed to fester — then a community can have no hope or future. Chapter Six examines the relationship between **individual human needs** and development. Human needs are seen as an integrated system including three types: the needs for belonging and relating to others (integration), the needs for personal freedom and self-expression (autonomy), and basic physical needs like food, security and shelter (physiological). The chapter ends with a number of examples of community self-help projects which are geared to meeting basic individual needs for food, housing, dignity and community belonging.

The Global Village is an insidious cultural force which is erasing cultural diversity and threatening the integrity of communities by bringing monotony, meaninglessness and more of the same. Chapter Seven introduces the fifth and possibly most important theme of the book — **developing a community culture**. Culture — as the collective expression of our shared history, traditions, values and ways of life — is the life force and soul of a community, the glue which holds our communities together. When we destroy a culture, we also destroy a community. The chapter looks at how social history, natural history and cultural diversity can be integrated into our development of cities and communities to encourage bonding among people and provide a sense of continuity and identity. Building a community culture requires us to create environments and opportunities for people to interact with each other in meaningful ways. Culture may seem like icing on the cake to some, but really it is the essence of our community roots.

SUSTAINABLE DEVELOPMENT

Building vital and sustainable communities "for the sake of community" is a right and worthy goal. Yet it is also part of a wider strategy of *sustainable development* for the world as a whole. Sustainable communities in themselves are nothing new. Tribal villages, medieval towns and intentional communities have sustained themselves and their land base for hundreds and even thousands of years. The idea of *sustainable development,* however, is very new applied to the modern industrial world, where, over the past fifty to one hundred years, industry has grown to such monstrous proportions that its daily intake of minerals, fuels, water, trees and air — combined with its output of chemical and natural waste — is causing alarming disruptions in natural cycles which affect climate and the sustainability of life on earth. Sustainable development in the global industrial context requires an analysis of the complex global connections among economics, environment and people's needs for survival.

In 1987, the United Nations' World Commission on Environment and Development published a landmark study, *Our Common Future,* calling for a world commitment to sustainable development. Sustainable development was defined as development which *"meets the needs of the present without compromising the ability of future generations to meet their own needs."* The threat to human survival was seen as encompassing a wide range of social, economic and environmental conditions, including mass poverty in the Third World, global warming caused by overuse of fossil fuels in the West, explosive urbanization, environmental pollution, armed conflicts and food shortages. The report showed how interlocking world economies and current industrial development are creating a greater polarization of world wealth, which is preventing large numbers of people from meeting their own needs and at the same time destroying nature's ability to replenish its own resources.

The UN report marked the beginning of an awareness by governments and the public of what environmentalists have long been saying, that our current path of economic development is leading us to the razor's edge of human survival. Since its publication, "sustainable development"

12

has become a popular phrase in all circles — from government, to business, to activist. Courses on sustainable development are offered in universities; conferences are being held around the world sponsored by governments and businesses alike. Winnipeg is now the location for a federally and provincially funded International Institute for Sustainable Development.

The difficulty comes when we look at the differing interpretations and approaches to sustainable development. The threat to human survival can be seen from many perspectives — as a problem of *under*development in poor regions and Third World countries; in other words, as a lack of economic opportunities. It can also be seen as a problem of *over*development and *over*exploitation of the earth's natural resources to accommodate Western lifestyles. Indeed, the word "sustainable" has taken on every shade of meaning, from conservative to radical, depending on the context. In large corporations, for example, sustainable development is being seen as an opportunity to "sustain" development by marketing new "environmentally friendly" consumer items and new technologies. For the business executive, as one article put it, "Sustainable development is long term defense of the bottom line. Sustainable development means sustainable profit."[1] For bureaucrats, sustainable development has become an exercise in planning resource management. Within conservative governments, it is being used as an excuse for cutting financial assistance to poor communities which are expected to sustain their own services and employment.[2]

The problem with these interpretations is that they come from big, top-down organizations which have created the environmental degradation and social inequalities in the first place. These organizations — centralist governments, top-down bureaucracies and large scale industries — are characterized by the pursuit of their own goals, which, when examined closely, are perceptibly related to *controlling* people (government), *managing* their affairs (bureaucracy), and *dominating* the marketplace (transnationals).

Sustainable development is becoming an endangered concept. Any serious discussion of sustainability must respect certain basic precepts. The first is that accumulating and concentrating capital, resulting in overproduction and overconsumption, is itself a major cause of our current state and that a "business as usual" approach will not bring about the radical reform needed in our fundamental relationships with each other and with the earth. The second is that a centralist, hierarchical approach to management, business and government cannot provide the plurality of solutions or the grassroots political will needed to deal with location-specific problems which are facing communities in crisis today. People need to define their own problems and find their own solutions.

SUSTAINABLE COMMUNITIES: A NEW FUTURE

This book looks at decentralized, self-reliant and human scale production methods as the most effective forms of sustainable development. *Think globally: act locally* — a concept of immense scope — is another key precept here. It means that while actions are always grounded in a particular place and time, their impacts are long-term and global. We need to understand these global connections and internalize them as part of a global *ethic* which will guide and inform our daily actions at home in our communities. In North America, for example, what we consume, how we distribute goods and services, and our development processes impact on the ability of people in the Third World to meet their needs. Our fax machines are produced in Third World "free trade zones" which have no regulations on workers' wages or environmental laws, so that people and nature are exploited to the fullest possible extent. In other instances, global corporations have moved into Third World countries and taken away local access to resources, such as forests, which were once held in common by villagers but are now owned and controlled by outside interests.

What we produce, and how, affects our *own* survival, since once we have destroyed nature's ability to replenish itself, we have killed our only source of food, energy, water and oxygen. *Think globally: act locally* instructs us to be aware of the wider impacts of our local actions on other people, other eco-systems and future generations. Permanence and security for all people are the goals. *Still the route is through taking responsibility for our immediate and local actions.*

A precondition to local responsibility is ensuring *local control* over resources and development. Local control can be achieved in a number of ways: by protective legislation and citizen action; by increasing local (both individual and community) ownership of industries; by democratizing management and decision making in the workplace; through pursuit of economic self-reliance, whereby local production is geared to meeting local needs.

An underlying premise of this book is that, to restore social and ecological balance to the world, we must shift our economic, cultural and political orientations away from global competition to a concern with local needs. The change makes sense both ecologically and economically. First, by concentrating on local production for local needs, we minimize the distances which products must travel for distribution, thus cutting down on transportation costs, wasteful energy use and pollution. Second, local demand for goods (community and surrounding region) can be met by smaller scale industries and technologies which can be more easily managed by the community. Decentralized development — using a scaled down technology to produce smaller amounts for fewer people — disperses the impacts of development more evenly throughout the biosphere, giving nature more time to absorb and reprocess the waste. Third, by decentralizing industry and creating more small scale businesses to replace megaprojects, we can increase the numbers of jobs and people's access to them, thereby creating a more equitable distribution of wealth. Fourth, at smaller scale enterprises, workers can have greater say over their work environment and therefore find work more meaningful.

For all these reasons, *community* engendered and controlled development contributes toward a sustainable future for all.

Building sustainable communities is an alternative which promises greater *personal* security and improved security for the *world as a whole*. People need a place to belong, a place they can call home. They also need to know that their communities will *continue to exist* and be able to provide for the present and future needs of themselves and their children. The relationships which make up a community are part of our human life support. We need to protect and sustain this life support system. Building sustainable communities is a good place to begin.

ENDNOTES

[1] Alan Scarth in "Sustaining the Bottom Line," *Business People Magazine*, June 1989, p. 11.

[2] The 1986 Provincial Report of the Royal Commission on Employment and Unemployment in Newfoundland recommended a "bold new course of development" aimed at self-reliance. It stated, "one of the major changes in western societies during recent years has been a dawning realization of the limits of the welfare state....we now know that the state is simply not able to satisfy all the needs of all its citizens [consequently] people will have to rely more upon themselves, their households and their communities to meet their economic and social needs." Critic James Overton, in his article "Building On Our Own Failures," in the *New Maritimes: An Independent Regional Weekly*

(Vol. 5, # 7, March 1987), called the report a Conservative government attempt to "relieve itself of the burden of supporting the poor."

Chapter Two

Confronting the Global Economy

Globalization is the new religion of big business. It is a Darwinian religion with the undemocratic standards and values of past centuries.

Mel Hurtig
The Betrayal of Canada

2

Confronting the Global Economy

The industrial age has burst its bubble. Big is not necessarily better; more is not necessarily satisfying; "having it all" may mean extinction in a finite environment. Still industrialism is extending itself into a new global order based on the free flow of international capital. How long can catastrophe be avoided?

When the idea of an alternative, community based development first emerged, it was in response to the destructive side effects of large scale industrial development in the Third World. This development was putting small scale producers out of work and forcing people to leave their villages for the overcrowded cities. At the time, the economist E.F. Schumacher wrote the book of essays *Small is Beautiful,* which promoted an alternative "new economics" based on small scale development using technology designed to meet people's local needs. This alternative model was contrasted to the Western model of large scale development. That was in 1973.

Since that time the world has undergone a global economic restructuring which has seen many of those industries grow from large scale to global scale in size and control of the world's market. Today, 25 per cent of everything produced comes to us from giant transnational corporations — 600 of them, each with sales of more than $1 billion annually — operating in countries around the world. The size of these global corporations is growing daily as conglomerates merge, buy out or put out of business their large and small competitors — including local producers.

The shift from a large scale industrial to a global economy is an attempt to create a new economic order which says that the world is no longer cities, regions or nations but is instead a Global Village. The new world order is built on free trade, world markets, competition, unfettered growth, trading blocks, level playing fields, harmonized national programs, transnational corporations and decline of the nation state. It believes that money can move faster than anything else, and so all else must follow its lead.

Where does the unrestricted flow of money lead?

My father had a business in Winnipeg. He owned a clothing wholesale operation for which he bought dresses made in Winnipeg and Montreal and sold them in small, selected amounts to retail stores in Manitoba and Saskatchewan rural towns. His profit was the markup between the manufactured price and the wholesale price to retailers. I remember as a child going out to some of the rural towns and meeting his customers. Some would come to visit our home in Winnipeg. My father worked in what is now known as the historic warehouse district with other wholesalers like himself — boys who had grown up in Winnipeg and built their businesses in the city. They were a network of mutual support for each other, and they had a community which extended into friendship outside of work.

Today, my father's business couldn't survive. The middleman was eliminated when chain stores like Woolco and Saan moved into the rural areas offering discounts to the consumer, with clothing supplied by a central distribution centre in Toronto or New York. This clothing was bought and shipped directly from factories in India, Korea and China. Not only were the little middlemen wiped out by the proliferation of chain stores, but so were hundreds of local retailers and also thousands of jobs in Canada's needle trade industries, which were forced to close down because they couldn't compete in the global economy.

Gone is a way of life in this country which used to rely on small and medium-sized locally owned and run businesses to provide for community needs. Some people would say, "And good riddance too. We have more choice of cheaper consumer goods now, and besides, we're helping Third World economies develop their export trade by importing their products." These arguments seem persuasive — they even have merit in certain cases — but when considered in terms of the wider impacts of global development, serious questions arise about who really benefits from large scale development and global trade. Are we really better off? Are people in the Third World better off?

To answer these questions let me give a brief overview of the impacts of global trade on the Third World and after that, on our home communities. The subject is vast and complex: my intent here is only to provide a glimpse into the workings of the global import/export model of development, to serve as a context for the following chapter which proposes quite a different approach — developing economic self-reliance.

Cheaper Goods — at what cost?

Global trade and the Third World

The nineteenth century classical economist David Ricardo advanced a theory of comparative advantage, which claimed that it would be in each country's interest to specialize in what it could produce at lowest cost and trade for products that it lacked or couldn't produce as efficiently. This theory still operates as the underlying justification for international trade.

In practice, the theory hasn't worked to spin off equal benefits for trading countries. What has been demonstrated instead is that trade between rich and poor countries entrenches patterns of domination and dependency. The richer nations, with the more advanced technology and access to capital, produce cheaper finished products — items like cars, TVs, computers or pharmaceuticals. Poor countries are left selling their natural resources like forests or primary commodities like coffee beans to pay for the finished products they import. The richer country benefits because it gets added value from product processing, which generates "spinoff" wealth in the form of extra local economic activity. The point is that there is no comparative advantage in trading coffee beans for computers.

Trading in the global economy has resulted in rising poverty for the masses of people living in the Third World. The United Nations Children's Fund (UNICEF) reports that "for almost 900 million people...the march of human progress has now become a retreat...into poverty." Average incomes in most of Africa and much of Latin America fell by 10 to 25 per cent in the 1980s, with dramatic declines in education and health.[1] The problem stems from an insurmountable debt owing to Western banks. It started when Third World countries were encouraged to borrow huge amounts of capital to import Western technology as the way to develop their countries' economies. Once caught in the global economy, they became vulnerable to fluctuations in world prices and interest rates. When interest rates rose and prices fell for their crops, they discovered they could not produce enough exports to pay off the debt and rising interest charges. By 1986, 35 per cent of export earnings in South America were going to pay off interest charges alone.

In the Third World, over seventy countries have undergone "economic readjustment" by the World Bank to pay off their debts. Economic readjustment means that stringent economic measures are imposed on the country to force accelerated production of exports. One of the measures is conversion of subsistance food crops into cash export crops. In Costa Rica, a typical example, family farm producers have been replaced by foreign-owned, industrial farm corporations.[2] Out of 2,400 rice farmers only 350 remain since economic readjustment five years ago. Lands which once grew corn and beans for local people are now growing strawberries, flowers and ornamental ferns for the Tokyo market. As one local put it, "We don't need flowers. We eat beans." To make matters worse, industrial farms have introduced pesticides and chemicals into farming practices, a practice which permanently destroys the natural land base and makes it forever dependent on imported chemical fertilizers. The pressures to pay off debts to the First World are forcing countries to overexploit their natural resources and turn them into quick cash, with resulting dangerous destruction to the world's rain forests. Costa Rica has the highest rate of rain forest destruction in the world because of economic policies imposed on it by the World Bank.

Earlier, the argument was made that importing products from the Third World is a mutually beneficial activity, which helps to develop Third World economies while it provides Western consumers with low-priced goods. Let's look now at where and how many of these goods are produced and judge who benefits.

Most industrial production in the Third World is carried out in free trade zones or export processing zones by giant transnational industries. These zones are land areas, usually near airports, organized to bring in foreign-owned industries — places where national laws and regulations governing working conditions and wages are usually suspended and where companies do not have to pay duty on the raw materials and equipment they import. The history of the zones dates back to the 1960s, when major international development agencies and financial institutions persuaded Third World governments to set up these areas to attract foreign investment. They were told that the zones would generate rapid economic development around *exports*, in contrast to the slow building of their economies around import substitution (i.e., setting up their own industries to produce locally what people are importing — an approach which would eventually make them self-sufficient and independent of Western producers). The major attraction of the zones to foreign industries would be the cheap labour the countries could provide, plus a host of other financial incentives such as tax exemptions, tariff exemptions, government-provided infrastructure and direct subsidies.

Many Third World nations bought heavily into this global strategy and borrowed from international banks to build the required roads, buildings, utilities, government offices and airports. By the mid-1980s there were more than 120 such zones around the world. Joyce Nelson, in *Sultans of Sleaze*,[3] exposes the history and frightful working conditions in these free trade zones. Minimum wage laws are by-passed. There is no job security, employment benefits, sick leave or paid holidays. Environmental regulations are lax or non-existent which makes the zones especially attractive to polluting industries such as the electronics industry. This industry uses Third World workers to solder lead and tin in the bonding of microchips (a process which gives off highly toxic fumes) and to test completed circuits in open chemical vats of toxic substances (causing liver, respiratory and kidney damage). With the "dirty work" completed in the Third World, companies can do their research, administration and distribution of products from headquarters in California and Japan.

Inside the zones, women (almost the total work force) are treated like slaves. They live in shanty towns or dormitory housing with six to ten people in a ten foot by twelve foot room, in some cases sharing a bed with two other workers on different shifts. Sterilization of young women is encouraged by companies for the least disruption of work — one company, Mattel Toys, awards prizes to women who get sterilized. At the Bic Pen factory in Bangkok, women must assemble more than 100,000 pens a day, and, if they do not meet their quota, they receive a *fine*. In the Philippines, women in the electronics industry display critical health problems within about four years (after which they are let go) as a result of exposure to toxic chemicals, working in extremely cold air-conditioned temperatures (to protect the semiconductors), straining their eyes staring into a microscope for ten or more hours a day, and being forced to work 100-hour weeks, often forty-eight hours at a stretch. Wages are so low that 100-hour weeks are needed just to make a subsistence wage in most zone areas of South Korea, Taiwan, Hong Kong, the Philippines, Sri Lanka and elsewhere. According to critics, "it is estimated that over the past fifteen years of zone proliferation some six million Third World women below the age of thirty have been summarily 'used up' and discarded by the multinational clients of the zones."[4] Among the hundreds of well-known names of companies which do their assembly work in free trade zones are Sears, RCA, General Electric, Sony, Lipton, Zenith, Singer, Union Carbide, Unilever, Bic and Mattel Toys.

Export-processing free trade zones have given birth to a whole new industrial process — the "global assembly line." Parts are assembled in different countries and then shipped directly to the West for distribution, by-passing local markets in the country which did the assembling. In other words, local businesses which might start as a result of the production are cut off from opportunities. What is particularly frightening is that transnational companies can shift their offshore operations to other zone locations at any time to follow a better tax deal and avoid interference by governments or worker unrest. Thus they play off country against country, worker against worker. Companies operating in the zones are truly trans(beyond) national, without loyalty to people or place — only to profits. One businessman in South Korea sums it up, "Free trade zones are like Hilton Hotels. When you're inside, you don't know what country you're in, and the hassles of the country don't touch you. It's a businessman's dream. And the workers are polite and obedient and most look alike — sometimes you wonder if they're Mexicans, Filipinos, Malays or Arabs."[5]

Certainly, working conditions were abominable during the Industrial Revolution in England, but at least they were visible and could be fought on political grounds in the home country where both workers and company owners held allegiance. The free trade zones of the Third World are hidden from sight (often built offshore and outside of cities), and owners of multinationals have no allegiance to the country which provides them with workers. Furthermore, because of the distancing and parceling out of assembly line processes to dispersed locations around the globe — Malaysia, Mexico, Africa, India, the Philippines, Thailand, Taiwan — Western consumers and smart shoppers, myself included, who pride themselves on getting the best deal, are cut off from any direct awareness of the human and environmental destruction which has gone into making many of the products so cheap and affordable.

To get back to our original question: who reaps the benefits from large scale industrial development in the Third World? Some beneficiaries are: Third World governments, many of them undemocratic and propped up by First World powers; banks lending the money; transnational companies which exploit a country's human and natural resources to reap huge profits; professionals in developed nations who export their expertise and technology; a country's rich elite who often have personal vested interests in development. The masses of people who are poor and getting poorer, who before could feed themselves and now cannot, certainly have not benefited. For the vast majority there has been no technology transfer, no improved living conditions, no upgrade of skills and knowledge, no "trickle down" development, no sharing in the enormous wealth the people have helped produce. The lesson we can learn from free trade zones is that as long as transnationals continue to own and control the technology that dominates the world, there will be few opportunities to redistribute wealth to the poor.

Global trade and its impact at home

The global economy also impacts on us at home in our cities and towns in North America — and not just by providing us with greater quantities of cheaper goods. Competition with Third World cheap labour has brought about the de-industrialization of the industrialized First World and with it the loss of thousands of manufacturing jobs. Whole sections of cities have become wastelands of abandoned industry which nobody knows how to handle. In many instances, whole towns and even cities have been laid to waste.

One city — Flint, Michigan — lost 30,000 permanent jobs in the space of a few months when General Motors decided, after seventy years, to close its auto plants and move production to Mexico for the cheap labour. Flint, once the automobile capital of the world, soon became the unemployment capital of North America and, as time passed and hope dwindled away, deteriorated into the crime capital as well. In fact, the biggest employer in Flint today is the new jail house, built to house all the former auto employees turned criminal.[6]

Something in our economics clearly isn't working the way we expected it would. We thought that as corporations grew and profited we would all benefit from more jobs and higher wages; this is called the trickle down theory of economics. What we didn't foresee was that as the globe opened up for business, our industries — upon which our jobs and standard of living depend — would have to compete with countries whose governments maintain the lowest wages and most exploiting environmental and labour practices in the world.

Maude Barlow, of the Council of Canadians, sums it up neatly:

A world without borders is a euphemism for a tightly controlled corporate system, where there is no power strong enough or international enough to protect the needs and rights of people. Those in control can play workers in one country off against workers in another, and governments will not be sufficiently strong to regulate on behalf of their populations. ...Because they are global, they can transfer money from country to country loading debt where they wish and avoiding costs. They do not have to consider the effect of their actions on a country, nor are

25

they in any way accountable to its population. In their world, the rules will come from the top down, not from the bottom up.[7]

In North America, banks and big businesses pushing for deregulation of industries and greater access to foreign markets have finally got a Free Trade Agreement between the U.S. and Canada, which may soon become a tri-level trading agreement with Mexico. Unfettered competition, deregulation of industries, privatization of public services and free trade are cornerstones of the global corporate agenda, which has been supported by the conservative Thatcher/Major, Reagan/Bush, and Mulroney administrations. The signing of the Free Trade Agreement marks a major step toward granting businesses the unrestricted right to shift production and profits to whichever location brings the highest rate of return, without government interference or answering to national, regional or community interests — it is like turning an entire country into a free trade zone.

The promise to the consumer is cheaper goods as industries rationalize toward greater efficiency through mergers, branching out across borders, and consolidating operations — urged on by the grow-or-die principle of capital competition. Cheaper goods perhaps, but at what cost? — the loss of jobs, the loss of local political control, the loss of cultural identity.

Already we see the effects as hundreds of smaller local businesses shut down, undercapitalized to produce for a large output and unable to compete with big U.S. corporations for a share of the world market. The Canadian Labour Congress estimated that 25,000 jobs were lost in the first six months of free trade. Canadian industries like the trucking industry, the furniture industry and the food industry have shifted their operations to the U.S. (where wages and taxes are lower) to survive. It is estimated by some that when Mexico enters the free trade pact our auto industry, which now accounts for the large majority of our exports aside from raw materials, will become a thing of the past, as plants relocate to where labour is cheap.

Some Canadian firms are moving just south of the border, relocating from Ontario to Buffalo, where they can get access to cheaper land, better tax deals and lower wages and still sell their products to the same Canadian market as before. In fact, 92 per cent of all new businesses in Buffalo in 1989 were started by Canadians. While some industries are leaving, others are simply closing shop. Hundreds of Canadian branch plants like Campbell Soup, Gerber Baby Food, Rowntree MacKintosh, Hostess, Kraft, etc., with parent companies in the U.S., have shut down because they were redundant when Canada became an extension of the U.S. market. A number of branch plants have been converted into warehouses for distributing U.S.-produced goods.

The import/export global model of doing business, as opposed to a self-sufficient home economy, is being waved in our faces as the only answer to a problem of rising national debt. If we just expand our export trade, if we just attract more foreign investors to our country, we could generate enough dollars to pay off our imported standard of living. It is a *dependency* model similar to what has been foisted on the Third World. Instead of developing a Canadian standard of living based on what Canadians can produce and afford, we are encouraged by the removal of tariffs to purchase even *more* imports, playing into the hands of transnationals who control the import market and can deliver the goods cheaper. At the same time, Canadian businesses — the few that are left after the free trade shake-down — are being forced to produce for export rather than local markets by the grow (meaning "go global") or die forces of competition.

The import/export orientation of our economy is a dangerous tread mill which can only lead to greater economic and social problems. Canada under free trade is at a comparative *disadvantage*, similar to a Third World country. Like developing nations, we have built our economy on selling our natural resources — lumber, wheat, minerals, hydro, water, natural gas — to the world in exchange for finished products. Today, our raw materials cannot pay for the imports we want. We have never built a self-reliant economy which extracts the greatest value from its resources by manufacturing them locally into finished products — instead we depend on imports from Japan or the United States. A prime example is the mining industry. While Canada is one of the world's largest producers of minerals, the nation produces no mining machinery of its own.

The more we get hooked on buying imports, the more we will have to pay for them by exporting our natural resources, since that is all we will have left to sell once manufacturing has shut down or left the country. That means more clear cutting of forests and more construction of hydro dams like Conawapa and the Great Whale project at James Bay, at a cost of irreparable destruction to the ecology of vast regions and destruction of native communities who live off the land.

In short, the above represents a brief overview of the global economy in action. It is a belief system, propagated by transnational corporations to the nations of the world, and the consequences for the majority of people are disastrous. A brief summary of impacts are as follows:

- draining away of local wealth to foreign owned companies;
- loss of local and regional employment opportunities;
- ecological destruction of the earth, as forests, waters and land are exploited in the over-production of consumer goods;
- colonization of people for their labour by transnational corporations;
- increased dependency on outside producers to meet our needs;
- economic efficiency becoming the greatest distance between producers and consumers (obviously ecologically unsound);
- mass culture imposed on us from above, designed to make us want to buy things;
- ethical entanglements: for profit we sell arms to countries our own governments do not support (e.g., Germany selling chemical weapons to Iraq), or we sell pharmaceuticals to the Third World which are banned as dangerous in our country.

The new North: rich and poor

Under globalization we have seen the transfer and concentration of wealth into fewer and fewer hands through a process of centralization (mergers, takeovers), expansion (franchising and expanding sales to China, Eastern Europe), and cost-cutting efficiencies (moving production from the First to the Third World for cheaper labour and resources or replacing workers with robots).

These economic forces have caused a major shift in work patterns and income of people in North America. Competition with Third World cheap labour has brought about the de-industrialization of the Western world and the loss of thousands of manufacturing jobs. In the southwest section of Montreal, 20,000 jobs were lost over the past twenty years. The loss of jobs has been compounded by a trend toward replacing workers with labour saving technologies — "jobless growth." The select new jobs being created by corporations are in management and high tech fields like computers and communications, which don't offer opportunities for the majority of people. Instead, the greatest number of new jobs being created are in the service industries — courier, fast food franchises — many of which offer low paying, part time work, mainly held by women, the poorest members of our society and the ones entrusted with bringing up our children — our country's future.

As wealth streams upward to an elite class of shareholders, professionals and executives who serve the interests of mega-corporations, poverty rates increase in our communities; this poverty appears in statistics which show a *widening gap* between rich and poor across North America and a shrinking middle class. In Canada, about one-fifth of the population is living below official poverty lines, while the top one-fifth of the population is receiving 41.3 per cent of the nation's income (1986 statistics)! The concentration of wealth within an elite is reflected in the country's corporate consolidations, which are occurring through mergers and takeovers. Here are some disturbing facts about corporate concentration in Canada (figures for 1987):[8]

- Twenty-five enterprises control 1,116 corporations and own 41 per cent of all assets;
- The top 1/100 of 1 per cent of all enterprises control 56 per cent of all assets;
- The top 1 per cent of all enterprises control 86 per cent of all assets and make 75 per cent of all profits.

With so few enterprises controlling most of the assets and making most of the profits, where does that leave the rest of us? And the situation is even worse today, after $57 billion in mergers in 1988 and 1989.

With the rise in unemployment, more people on welfare, more and more families becoming dependent on food banks, and increasing numbers of people living on the streets, governments are being pressed to do something. The result is that governments are squeezed between people crying out in real need for more income, decent housing, food and basics which are not being supplied by the economy, and a business community crying out for *cuts* in social programs to reduce the deficit, in order to make Canada more competitive in the global market. Conservative governments, visionaries of the global corporate agenda, have responded to the challenge by cutting back on social programs at a time when people need them most.

Obviously, cutting back on social programs is not going to solve the systemic problems of a polarizing global economy. But to be fair, government services are not going to bring back a disappearing economic base. What is needed instead is a whole new vision which aims at bringing our economy home again and developing our communities so that they can support and sustain local populations.

THE ALTERNATIVE: AN IDEA WHOSE TIME HAS COME

We are told that the forces of globalization are inevitable, that we can't turn back the clock. Our prime minister has gone so far as to say that any leader who resists the opportunity to "do the tough things" (like imposing free trade?) "should be shot."[9] Many people, including myself, do not believe the myth of inevitablity. Economic globalization is undisputably the most powerful and dominating force in the world today, but it is not the only game in town or the only vision. There is evidence all around us of grassroots resistance to globalization — in community movements, local actions and citizen protest against top-down political authoritarianism (e.g., the handling of the Meech Lake Accord and citizen protest against the GST).

E.F. Schumacher's pleas for an economics based on small scale local production, mentioned at the start of this chapter, have been drowned by the global restructuring of the last decade. Yet now that the crises of development are impacting on the whole world — the Third World and developed countries alike — the time may have finally come for an alternative. In this alternative we find the root of an idea for confronting the global economy. Let us now look at the origins of sustainable communities in the "new economics" of E.F. Schumacher.

E.F. Schumacher was the first Western economist to bring our attention to the destructive side effects of large scale economic development in the Third World. He was influenced by the teachings of Mahatma Gandhi, whose vision for Indian society blended spiritual ethics with an economics of self-reliance. Schumacher, over the course of his life, put together an alternative economic approach to Western, bigger-is-better style development. This approach is based on a human scale technology and organization and on a respect for nature and local culture. It puts human needs and ethics first, ahead of the economic dictates of efficiency and unlimited growth.

E.F. Schumacher is best known for his book *Small is Beautiful: A Study of Economics as if People Mattered*. The inspiration behind many of the essays came from what he saw when he was economic advisor in Burma and India in the late 1950s and early 1960s. At that time official government policy was promoting large industrial development.

Schumacher, a lone voice in the wilderness, warned against the importation of Western industries, which he noted were destroying the delicate balance of local cultures, while contributing to increasing disparities between the poverty-ridden masses and the rich elite. As well, it was causing upheaval and dislocation of the general population, as families left the rural areas to look for work in the new factories in the cities.

The problem was that the capital-intensive modern factory, designed to reduce labour costs in the West, could not provide the millions of jobs that were needed. Instead, the importation of Western technology created a split, *dual* economy composed of a small elite Westernized sector, on the one hand, and a rapidly deteriorating traditional sector on the other.

Since the primary problem was not enough jobs, the real solution would be to maximize job opportunities by supporting *labour*-intensive, smaller scale industries in the traditional sector. Schumacher could see that the effect of the modern factory was to put out of work huge numbers of small local craftsmen who couldn't compete with the lower prices of mass-produced goods. Instead of foreign factories putting people out of work and drawing them away from their communities and traditional skills, he proposed supporting the creation of local industries which would focus on producing for basic needs, using local materials and local skills to meet those needs.

Here, originating in an alternative development strategy for the Third World, lie the roots for community economic development in the West — the concept of local resources meeting local needs.

Over the course of his life Schumacher worked out a framework for development which would:

- **Rely on local resources** for material goods instead of on other countries.
- **Be compatible with peoples' values and culture.** "Development does not start with goods; it starts with people and their education, organization and discipline."[10]
- **Be decentralized.** People should be able to work where they live.
- **Place human needs first** (shelter, food, energy) thereby insuring a ready market for local producers while helping to meet basic needs.
- **Limit the use of nonrenewable natural resources.**

- Support the design of "appropriate" technology, which would make work easier and more productive, yet also be simple to operate, inexpensive and nonviolent against nature.

In 1965, Schumacher and others founded the Intermediate Technology Development Group, an international network of consultants and researchers working with at least twenty developing countries to design low cost, simple technologies which would enable local production, using local resources for needs such as water systems, building materials, cultivation tools, transportation, local energy production and factory technologies.

As an example of intermediate technology, Schumacher tells the story about meeting an unhappy farmer on a road in Zambia. He asked the farmer what was the matter. The man said he produced eggs for a living but couldn't get his eggs to market because he hadn't any egg crates to carry them. The factory which made the egg crates was on a long strike, and there was a shortage of crates. Schumacher, inquiring further into the matter, found out that the factory which made the crates, the factory on strike, was located in the Netherlands! Refusing to let go of this matter, Schumacher arranged to meet with the company president in the Netherlands to whom he explained the sorry predicament of the peasant farmers — that their survival depended on getting their eggs to market. He suggested that the company build a factory in Zambia to supply the farmers there. The president found the suggestion outrageous — an impossibility. His factory was optimally sized, he contended, and anything smaller would be *inefficient*. Optimum size was one that served the entire continent of Africa!

Although Schumacher knew nothing about the production of egg crates, the situation didn't make sense to him. So, through his Intermediate Technology Group, he contacted different universities and with the help of graduate students soon came up with a new design for egg cartons and a new chemical production process which, within a year and a half, led to a new production facility in Zambia which produced 120 egg crates per hour as opposed to the 7,000 crates that the Netherlands factory considered optimally efficient. The unit cost turned out to be *identical*. What they had done was invent an intermediate technology which employed more labour and much less capital and which in terms of cost was equally efficient.[11]

By the 1970s, more people were catching on to the idea of local development geared to self-reliance, particularly as the world became more aware of the destructive ecological and social impacts of large scale international development. In 1975, the UN report, *What Now?*

Another Development, was published, calling for a unified approach to world development which would incorporate specific processes and structures aimed at decreasing Third World dependency on industrial nations. It pointed its finger at Western nations for their dominant role in maintaining a system of unfair economic benefits and encouraging unsustainable consumer lifestyles which lead to *overconsumption* of world resources. The report called for a new approach to development which would be pluralistic, *locally controlled* and an alternative to global economic dependency. In many respects *Another Development* was more radical and less compromising in its recommendations than the later but more widely recognized UN Brundtland Commission report, *Our Common Future* (1988), which also called for an integrated world system of sustainable development. The earlier UN report, *Another Development,* took a stance in favor of *limiting* growth and pursuing *bottom-up* as opposed to top-down development. This bottom-up development which would grow out of local culture was termed "endogenous development" in the report.

The transfer of Schumacher's ideas to the West

While the decentralized development approach was gaining legitimacy in international development circles, it was not yet understood as having any application in the Western hemisphere. The turning point in the transfer of ideas to the West was marked by the publication of *Small is Beautiful: A Study of Economics as if People Mattered,* a best selling collection of essays by E. F. Schumacher on the "new" economics, and a book which still continues to be a solid foundation for understanding the principles of sustainable community development. In 1974, *Small is Beautiful* gave focus to a growing force which was spreading across Europe and North America — a grassroots alternative movement which brought together peace activists, environmentalists and community activists. At the same time, the 1973 world energy crisis, brought on by the industrialized world's dependence on oil from the Organization of Petroleum Exporting Countries (OPEC), gave credence in even the most established circles to Schumacher's ideas about the need for self-reliant economies and renewable energy sources. In the mid-seventies, Schumacher lectured extensively across Europe and the United States to large audiences who were coming to believe that the only solution to the world's current ecological and economic crisis rested in a complete turnaround of the industrial world's development strategies towards small scale, nonviolent technologies, decentralization and local control.

There were similarities between what was happening in the Third World and in parts of North America as a result of mass corporate development, such as increasing polarization of the rich and poor, increasing disparity between growing metropolitan centres and declining rural areas, and increasing disparity between wealthy suburbs and decaying inner cities. A community-based development strategy could help the poorest, most disadvantaged and dependent communities toward becoming self-sufficient, self-sustaining and self-determining.

Schumacher's impassioned speeches asked audiences to rethink economics:

> What is the meaning of democracy, freedom, human dignity, standard of living, self-realization, fulfillment? Is it a matter of goods, or of people? Of course it is a matter of people. But people can be themselves only in small comprehensible groups. *Therefore we must learn to think in terms of an articulated structure that can cope with a multiplicity of small-scale units* [my italics]. If economic thinking cannot grasp this it is useless. If it cannot get beyond its vast abstractions, the national income, the rate of growth, capital/output ratio, input-output analysis, labour mobility, capital accumulation; if it cannot get beyond all this and make contact with the human realities of poverty, frustration, alienation, despair, breakdown, crime, escapism, stress, congestion, ugliness, and spiritual death, then let us scrap economics and start afresh.[12]

Of each and every development Schumacher insisted we ask ourselves: *Development of what? Development for whom? Development how? Development with what side effects?* These questions force us to a new consciousness regarding the practice of development, one that acknowledges our global and social responsibilities. They open up discussion of the new economic agenda to include items such as meaningful work, definition of human needs, the ecological effects of development, the interrelationship between Third and First World development, democratization of the work place and empowerment of local communities.

Although Schumacher died in 1977, his work has been carried on by a growing network of groups and individuals in Europe and North America committed to furthering the "new economics." In 1981 George McRobie, one of the original founders of the Intermediate Technology Development Group, published the book *Small is Possible*, a practical follow-up account of *Small is Beautiful* which provided a comprehensive survey of the mushrooming alternative networks across Britain, Canada, the U.S. and the Third World.

The legacy passed on to us by Schumacher is also being carried forward by an emerging political green movement in Europe and North America, whose agenda includes community-based, decentralized economics linked to social justice and a global concern for the environment. In Germany, where *Die Grunen* built the support of millions of voters,[13] Greens have created their own banking system which finances community economic and social development projects. The "new economics" promoted by Greens includes the following principles:

- small scale industries;
- decentralization;
- distribution of wealth based on both formal and informal work (home, community);
- shift from the economics of more to the economics of enough;
- international equity;
- sustainable development bearing in mind the needs of future generations and the planet's health;
- participatory approach to the generation of wealth.

In North America, some of the main spokespeople pushing for an ecological, decentralized and self-reliant society are Murray Bookchin (social ecologist, author of many books, including *The Ecology of Freedom*), Herman Daly (*Toward a Steady-State Economy,* coauthor of *For the Common Good*), David Morris (founder of the Institute for Self-Reliance, author of *Self-Reliant Cities*), Hazel Henderson (author of *Creating Alternative Futures*), and Amory Lovins (founder of Rocky Mountain Institute, author of *Soft Energy Paths*). One group active in promoting the "new economics" is The Other Economic Summit, known as TOES. Since 1984 TOES has organized its own conference annually to meet in the same city alongside the traditional Economic Summit conference. Participants have included economists and theorists such as Susan George, James Robertson, Johan Galtung, Paul Ekins and Herman Daly, among others. The Human Economy Network in Britain and North America, through conferences, newsletters and computer networks, helps link together people in the field/movement of "new economics." Its focus is on furthering analysis, policy development and economic practice, based on the values of: sustainability, decentralization, equity and justice, voluntary simplicity, co-operation, respect for nature and life, qualitative aspects of economic life, empowerment, human development and individual responsibility.[14] More specifically relating to the urban environment, we find a growing interest in the "healthy cities" and "green cities" movements in Canada and the U.S., which are taking many of these same concepts and applying them to urban communities. (There is more about these movements in Chapter Four.)

Popular movements confront the global economy

While the corporate world attempts to force its competitive agenda on mainstream society, there is a growing revolution in life values occurring outside the system. Popular movements have been gaining momentum since the mid-1980s. Three, in particular, have had a profound influence on changing values in society — the ecology movement, the movement for self-determination and the women's movement. Each in its way has been a counterforce to the top-down powers of globalization and an agent for grassroots change and reclaiming communities.

Ecology: The ecology movement has helped focus public awareness on the irresponsibility of large corporations about caring for our water, air and soil. Exxon's massive oil spill, the mining industry's pollution of water and air, the clear cutting of forests in B.C. by MacMillan Bloedel, are direct results of cost cutting for profit and capital efficiency. Ecologists, on the other hand, are calling for *ecological* efficiency. How can we reduce consumption, conserve resources, waste less and recycle what we now throw away? The study of eco-systems and of the human relationship to the natural environment has given rise to a social ecology movement which looks at how principles of ecology — the study of natural relationships between living and nonliving things — can form the basis for a new model of social relationships — political, economic, personal — to replace our corporate model based on hierarchy and domination.

The ecological model of relationships is cellular: each cell has an integrity of its own, is self-organizing and self-determining, yet bonded to other cells to make up larger organic structures which are in themselves self-organizing and self-determining — like the cells of our body and the interrelationships within eco-systems. The ecological vision of society calls for communities to operate on the basis of:
- co-operative instead of competitive relationships;
- decentralized processes of production and decision making;
- the creation of autonomous and self-reliant communities;

- respect for differences and cultural diversity while recognizing our interdependence with one another.

Democracy movement: Another major shift in values is coming from a revival of grassroots politics which is part of a growing democracy movement worldwide. People are disenchanted with big government bureaucracies, professionals and self-serving politicians deciding what is best for them. In Canada, the majority of people cheered when native Manitoba MP Elijah Harper stopped the passing of the constitutional Meech Lake Accord. People were fed up with the federal government's undemocratic processes, in which Prime Minister Brian Mulroney tried to push the deal through using threats, manipulations and behind-closed-doors dealings with other premiers, all the time ignoring the public will. The failure of Meech Lake was celebrated around the country as a victory for democracy against the government. (Polls showed that 71 per cent of Canadians supported Elijah Harper.)

The Meech Lake fiasco focused attention on the government's neglect of the aboriginal community: since then there has been a growing momentum within the aboriginal community. The blockades at Oka, the Montreal Mercier Bridge and in other parts of the country, while disruptive, have helped to gain public awareness and support for native self-government and settlement of outstanding land claims. According to the 1991 Citizens' Report on the Future of Canada (Spicer Commission), most Canadians now support efforts to have land claims settled and the right to native self-government. Canadians are beginning to view the Canadian government itself as the major problem. The Citizens' Forum showed that "most often the government was singled out for destroying the institutions and symbols Canadians identify with." The report directly states that Canadians are "cynical and mistrustful of their political leaders."[15]

The native self-government movement is one example of a general increase in grassroots activism. Citizen action groups, environmental groups, feminist and women's groups, heritage groups, neighbourhood and community groups, and the general public outcry over the government's Goods and Services Tax (GST), are all part of growing revolt against bureaucratic government policies which fail to protect people, nature and history from the ravages of our economic system. Popular movements over the past decade, in particular the women's movement and the environmental movement, have done more to affect social change than organized political parties.

What we are seeing is the rise of pluralism and minority power through special interest groups, splinter groups, affinity groups, and the proliferation of subcultures within society. This rise of citizenship is a force against globalization — it is the reclaiming spirit of community power.

Rediscovering the Feminine: The women's movement has had a major influence on changing values and social structures in society. Acting on the slogan "the personal is the political," women have brought personal life concerns to the forefront of politics — rape, wife and child abuse, daycare, safety in the streets, the quality of food and recycling of our wastes. Women are active in the ecology and peace movements and operate a network of diverse women's groups including consciousness raising, mother support, eco-feminism, women's health clinics, incest survivors, women's shelters, and political parties like the Women's Party in Iceland — each in some way furthering the goals of co-operation, security and nonviolence.

Perhaps the greatest contribution of the women's movement has been a raising of consciousness to appreciate feminine, life-affirming values, long neglected by Western culture. They are values similar to those held by aboriginal cultures and the ecology movement. They include:

- co-operation, empathy and nurture stemming from a relational, nonhierarchical view of the world;
- a focus on process rather than end results: ends and means are one;
- a belief that social change begins with personal transformation;
- the valuing of intuition, subjectivity, creativity and spontaneity.

These feminine principles are forming the foundation for an alternative vision of society which is influencing how we work, organize and make decisions — smaller, more personal structures and processes, co-operative work situations, consensus decision making and reliance on community supports and the informal economy. They are values which support the building of sustainable communities.

CHOOSING BETWEEN TWO VISIONS

A Community Directions Conference was held in Vancouver in 1990. A vision statement was drawn up which outlined *two* visions for the city, two choices — the Executive City and the Inclusive City. The Executive City was described as the architect's model or poster picture which views the city as a sculpture from a bird's view on high, with skyscrapers, mountains and sea all rolled into one scenic vision. It is the city of bright lights, world fairs, tourist attractions and executives who travel on Lear jets, live in luxury condominiums and "do lunch" with each other on company expense accounts. What we *don't* see in the picture are all the thousands of ordinary people at street level, breathing pollution fumes, scurrying through wind tunnels and shadows of highrise cement walls which block out the view of the beautiful mountains. Many of the people left out of the picture live in dilapidated single rooms and are lined up at food banks. The Executive City is an investment playground for international capital — an exclusive city designed to benefit people with power, money and prestige.

There is another vision which we can choose — the vision of the Inclusive City or the City of Choice, designed to meet the needs of *all* people, not just an elite few. It is the livable city of green, clean neighbourhoods and human scale communities which offer security, work opportunities, comfort and companionship. It is a dynamic city in which ordinary people have an active voice in shaping their communities, and where the histories of neighbourhoods and people count.

The two visions are *mutually exclusive.* The global corporate vision aims at taking over local neighbourhoods and local economies: the local vision answers the crises created by the global corporate vision.

We have a choice. The following chapters outline a direction for how we can begin to take back control of our communities from the global economy or — in a catchy metaphor I heard in a talk given by David Morris — to move from the "global village" to creating a "*globe of villages.*" It is a community movement already partly happening, which can only be fully understood by looking at examples. Whether this myriad of community efforts is evidence of a new dawn is too early to tell. But something is happening, and we need to put a name on it. Let's call it sustainable community development and look at what it is.

ENDNOTES

1   Rick Salutin, *Waiting for Democracy: The Canadian Election* (Ontario: Penguin Books Canada, 1989), p. 284.

2   From the CBC Radio program, "Sunday Morning," 13 July 1991.

3   The facts on free trade zones come from the chapter, "Multinational Free Lunch" in Joyce Nelson's *Sultans of Sleaze* (Toronto: Between the Lines, 1989).

4   Ibid. p. 106.
5   Ibid. p. 96.
6   For the complete story of Flint, Michigan, see the award winning documentary movie, *Roger and Me*, available on video.
7   Maude Barlow, *Parcel of Rogues* (Toronto: Key Porter, 1990), p. 20.
8   Mel Hurtig, *The Betrayal of Canada* (Toronto: Stoddart, 1991), p. 159.
9   Francis Russell editorial, *Winnipeg Free Press*, 20 July 1991, p. 7.
10 *Small is Beautiful* (London: Abacus, 1974), p. 140.
11 "New Ideas in Ecology and Economics," from the CBC Radio program, "Ideas," May/June, 1986.
12 Schumacher, *Small is Beautiful*, p. 62.
13 In the 1990 unified election of East and West Germany, the West German Greens lost all their federal seats, while the East German Greens won eight seats. Previously, the West German Greens held 8.3 per cent of the popular vote; today they hold less than 5 per cent. The party is undergoing restructuring, becoming a less radical, more middle-of-the-road environmental organization. Greens are still well represented at the municipal levels of government.
14 These are the values of New Economics as defined in the leaflet/prospectus of the Human Economy Network. The address of the organization is Don Cole, c/o Economics Department, Drew University, Madison, N.J., USA 07940.
15 *Winnipeg Free Press*, 28 June 1991, p. 17.

Chapter Three

Working Toward Self-Reliance

3

Working Toward Self-Reliance

Self-reliance means that each community relies on its own physical resources and human capabilities for production to meet its own needs instead of depending on outside economic forces.

Self-reliance starts with the idea of people in communities producing the things they need for themselves, rather than getting them through exchange. A self-reliant economy is the antithesis of a global import/export economy which relies upon *external* producers to supply localities with mass goods and far flung markets to purchase items which communities *specialize* in producing. The global economy, with its trend to specialization, concentration and mass production, may generate high productivity and output, but it is costing dearly in the accelerated destruction of *local* economies, community culture and degradation of the environment. In contrast to the shifting and footloose development of a global economy, a self-reliant economy aims to give roots to local economic activity by tying it to local markets and production to serve community needs. It also strives to capture and retain the wealth produced in a community.

Self-reliance is an approach to development which looks inward rather than outward, building on internal strengths and resources. As a direction and process, self-reliance can be applied to all levels from the individual, to the household, community, city, region or nation. At each level self-sufficiency is the goal or ideal. The world is thus viewed as a network of s*elf-contained systems* within other larger self-contained systems. Within this cellular network the one rule of thumb for self-reliant development is that we should never assign to a larger entity what can be produced by a smaller one. Or, as David Morris, author and director of the Institute for Local Self-Reliance, might say, "If we can produce it ourselves we probably should."

Generalization, not specialization, is the aim of self-reliant development — producing a diversity of goods and services at a community scale to meet local needs. Obviously this approach contradicts the economic othodoxy of large scale efficiency and global specialization — a myth needing to be challenged. Large is not always most efficient.

As economist Jane Jacobs has pointed out, large structures and organizations require *extra* added expenditures because of complicated coordination and administration, of supervisors supervising supervisors.[1] We need to open our minds to new concepts about how wealth is created. Rather than seeing wealth as created by mass output of centralized industries, we need to see that wealth is generated by the thousands of economic exchanges which occur within a community and focus on increasing these local exchanges.

One of the indicators of a community's vitality is its active level of exchange among community members. In economics, this level of exchange is represented by our consumption and production activity — how much we produce to meet our own needs and user demands. Just as a nation measures its productivity through its Gross National Product, so too a community can measure the flow of goods and services it produces. One aim of community economic development is to increase the level of productive interchange among community members and to contain the flow of money within the community.

Imagining a self-reliant neighbourhood in our homogeneous and externally dominated city of today is a difficult task. It is made more difficult by the fact that a self-reliant neighbourhood would be characterized by diversity, making all the parts and their relationships hard to convey in one vision. One may think back to medieval times, along with Lewis Mumford:

> [The] decentralization of the essential social functions of the city not merely prevented institutional overcrowding and needless circulation: it kept the whole town in scale....In a sense, the Medieval city was a congeries of little cities, each with a certain degree of autonomy and self-sufficiency, each formed so naturally out of common needs and purposes that it only enriched and supplemented the whole. The division of the town into quarters, each with its church or churches, often with a local provision market, always with its own local water supply...was a characteristic feature.[2]

The self-reliant neighbourhood is like a medieval city organized to provide its citizens with basic goods and services using local production and local resources — only the technology is modern and the walls are invisible. With banking, education, shopping, living, working and recreation in close proximity to each other, the self-reliant neighbourhood reduces the necessary use of the automobile. Next, we could imagine local production to include growing most of our own food, producing our own energy with solar plants and biomass fuels, making much of our own clothing, furniture, housing and so on. These enterprises would occur gradually through a lot of inventiveness and experimentation. The resulting increase in local exchange and face to face dealings with our neighbours would help to rekindle community spirit and identity.

The self-reliant "inside-out" approach to development is a radical shift in direction from the conventional model of "outside-in" development imposed on our communities. Self-reliant development requires a total re-examination and reassessment of the resources and wealth contained within our communities and surrounding region. It makes us much more aware and appreciative of the geographic region where we live and work because this is where we get our sustenance. It makes us much more aware and appreciative of the people who inhabit our communities because we rely on them/us to produce for our needs. Self-reliant development thus helps to bond people in communities together and to connect them with the natural region where they are situated.

THE CREATION OF LOCAL WEALTH

The goal of a self-reliant community is to enhance the pool of local wealth through discovery and development of a community's existing resource base. Yet where do you begin in a community which seemingly has nothing to start the process? All communities, even the poorest, have some means to produce wealth, but often the resources may be hidden or lying dormant. Specific action strategies are needed to stimulate the creation of wealth from the inside-out.

Local wealth is generated in five basic ways:
1. Making more with less.
2. Making the money go around.
3. Making it ourselves.
4. Making something new.
5. Trading with equal partners.

Each of the above approaches and strategies requires further elaboration and will be discussed in the following sections of this chapter.

Making more with less: conservation, prevention, recycling

"Reduce, reuse and recycle" is a catchy logo for how we can all live more ecologically within the limits of nature. Yet it is also a prescription for how communities can create local wealth through reduction, reuse and recycling of their resources. Lucrative savings are to be had from using our resources more efficiently, particularly through **conservation.** That is because *new* wealth is created when we produce more using the same or less amount of energy and materials. Energy conservation is a good example. In the town of Osage, Iowa, population 4,000, the municipal hydro company has helped people to save electricity and gas in their homes through simple technologies. The result over ten years was that the utility saved so much money that it paid off all its debts and had an interest bearing surplus; it cut the tariff five times in five years, a reduction which has attracted two new employing industries to the town; it saved an average of $1,000 per household per year in energy costs which were going to outside suppliers of energy but are now being spent in the town, helping to make it more prosperous. Local independent businesses are thriving because of their cost savings which enable them to compete with chain stores in neighbouring towns. The bank has seen a 10 per cent per year increase in deposits, of which 10 per cent is due directly to energy savings.

We tend to believe that we profit more by selling more of a given resource. But in truth, if we can make a resource stretch further, extract more energy out of it by applying efficient technologies, the amount *saved* is almost always cheaper to produce than mining more of the same resource. The billions of dollars now going to build and operate nuclear plants and giant hydroelectric dams could be saved with energy efficient technologies. According to research by the Rocky Mountain Institute in Colorado, three-quarters of all electricity used by factories could be eliminated with equipment now on the market.

Because most of our energy is imported, the dollars we spend on it drain out of a community (only thirteen cents out of the dollar remains on average). A self-reliant community would put the money saved by conservation to *productive* use within the community, helping to support local businesses.

There are several key areas to target for energy savings, such as the use of more energy efficient transportation (public transit, rapid transit or even smaller cars); programs to retrofit older homes and buildings for increased energy efficiency (the corporate plan for the city of Sudbury, Ontario has targeted retrofitting 5 per cent of the housing stock per year); building codes requiring energy efficient construction of new buildings (e.g., the city of Davis, California); use of new technologies in factories; an integrated approach to land use planning which brings in closer proximity the places where people live, work and spend their money, thereby reducing the distances people need to travel by automobile. The city of Portland, Oregon figured out that by reviving neighbourhood grocery stores alone, it could save 5 per cent of the city's energy consumption now spent on trips to shopping centres for small items.

Prevention is another way to save local dollars by eliminating wasted expenditures on treatment and aftercare. Preventative health care is an example. Many other social expenditures — welfare, jails, treatment centres — could be reduced if we invested in the physical and psychological well-being of all people, who are our primary resources, and particularly in the security and well-being of our children, who are our future.

Prevention can save millions of dollars expense on physical infrastructure such as roads and sewers. In Chicago, the problem of clogged sewers during heavy rainfalls was solved very simply by removing drain pipes around buildings and replacing them with splash blocks which slowed down the raindrops. By investing in public rapid transit, our cities can save on future road expansions and freeways. By making the most efficient use of *existing* urban infrastructure to accommodate increasing populations — filling in vacant lots, sharing resources, restoring older buildings — we can prevent millions of dollars from being spent on new construction and services to suburbs. At the same time, by containing urban sprawl we can prevent the loss of scarce, rich agricultural land to new development.

The suburban municipalities around Toronto, known as the Greater Toronto Region, are facing a projected population growth of 1.2 million by the year 2011. Planners know there are no services to accommodate this growth — sewers and water supply are already at capacity. There are no landfill sites to take present garbage. Highway movements are grinding to a halt with traffic congestion and the rivers are dead from pollution. The question is, how can further costly deterioration of the environment be prevented? How can the quality of life be restored? The solution touted by planners and many politicians is to curb urban expansion by making more efficient use of existing developed lands and resources — intensify residential suburbs; make them more self-sufficient in terms of social services, work opportunities and cultural activities; discourage use of cars by investing in public transit; refuse to allow construction of any more shopping malls (in fact, it is recommended that multiple family apartments be built on existing mall parking lots). Prevention sometimes costs more initially, but when all impacts are accounted for, it yields savings.

Recycling of resources is another method for generating local wealth. Every community has a rich supply of garbage — glass, paper, aluminum, rubber — from which to recover raw materials for production. By mining our waste we recapture some of the energy we have thrown away. By disposing of less, we pollute less. At the same time, we gain a product of value which was previously considered worthless. We can produce methane gas from our own organic wastes. (Los Angeles, New York and Vancouver are drilling wells directly into landfill sites.) We can manufacture all of our paper products from recycled paper. We can build houses out of discarded building materials. We can reuse the waste heat from factories and incinerator plants to heat our homes and businesses, as is done in Sweden.

What about old buildings? With de-industrialization there are growing numbers of abandoned warehouses and plants which can be reused for social and commercial purposes. Currently, 16 per cent of our landfill sites are taken up with demolished buildings. By recycling old buildings we are not only being ecologically creative and finding needed space, but in many instances we are also helping to preserve our community's heritage, which is all too rapidly vanishing from our midst. Heritage conservation is a complex and messy issue in the urban context, where buildings belong to a community's identity and history, yet property is privately owned. Land values and taxes may actually encourage owners to demolish rather than redevelop. The old movie theatres of our inner cities are prime cases in point. Many are the finest examples of well done, historical architecture we have in this country and yet they are being torn down for high-rise developments or else left to deteriorate by absentee corporate owners who are shifting investment to shopping malls.

Only some communities have been successful in saving their old buildings. Success depends on the political will, organization and strength of a community's identity. The Cedar Riverside neighbourhood in Minneapolis has, for example, targeted the renovation and revival of its six or seven older theatres as a major component in its community revitalization program, resulting in the creation of new businesses and renewed cultural life for the area. It is not widely known, but, according to Marc Denhez, Canada's leading heritage consultant, the rehabilitation/renovation of buildings in Canada has overtaken new construction — it is an industry which makes $30 to 40 billion annually, with a growth rate of 12 per cent.[3]

Recycling vacant buildings is one thing, but what do we do with our abandoned towns? Here is one solution: in British Columbia there are plans to resettle an abandoned forestry town by turning it into a support community to help rehabilitate young prostitutes and runaways from the streets of Vancouver. Similarly, a group of Sudbury citizens got the idea to resettle an abandoned prison farm thirty minutes outside of the city. The Burwash prison farm and village, spreading over 26,000 acres of forest and grasslands in the 1970s, had been self-sufficient in vegetables, meat and dairy production. The government had renovated sixty-nine houses, a gymnasium and several barns and shops before the centre was abandoned. The citizens planned to create a community, using the existing facilities to establish worker co-operatives in dairy processing, organic farming, construction and tourism. They also wanted to establish a group home for children in foster care. Their plans were dashed, however, when after two years the government decided instead to sell to the Department of National Defence to turn the property into a rifle range.[4]

In May 1991, Winnipeg's Habitat Re-Store opened. Habitat for Humanity is a nonprofit organization which builds houses for the poor, using volunteer labor (see Chapter Five for more on Habitat). The organization found that it was getting offers of donated used building materials which it couldn't use in its construction work. As a result, it decided to set up a giant warehouse/depot which would collect and recycle donated building materials (new and used) gathered from building sites, individuals, manufacturers and demolitions. The items (lumber, windows, doors, cabinets, paint, electrical, plumbing, etc.) would be sold to the general public at reduced prices, about 50 per cent retail. The extra money earned by the recycling depot would go into a fund to construct more Habitat houses. The idea has worked. Since it has been open, the Re-Store has surpassed all expectations, bringing in $28,000 in the first two months. The benefits of the Re-Store are numerous:

- by recycling building products locally, the store reduces the amount of money which leaves the province to pay for materials produced elsewhere;
- by providing low cost materials, the store is encouraging more activity in home renovation, thus improving living conditions and maintenance of existing homes;
- by recycling building materials the depot is reducing the amount of new resources consumed and is helping to divert waste which would otherwise end up in landfills;
- the money raised in selling the building materials is kept circulating in the community, going to pay employee wages and building affordable homes in the community.

Making the money-go-round

Every time a dollar changes hands it becomes a new dollar for somebody else to spend. In this way dollars in circulation *multiply*. As long as money circulates within a self-contained system, it generates wealth within that system, but when money leaves the system the multiplier effect stops. In a healthy economy a dollar gets spent six to eight times before it leaves a community. By contrast, in a poor community money falls out of local circulation almost immediately and out of the community. As a step toward self-reliance, a community can take measures to plug the leakage of dollars from its local economy and thus retain the local wealth which already exists. First, one needs to determine the ways money flows out of a community and where it is going.

There are two main sources of money leaks. The first is via imports. Whenever we purchase imported products from another country or region, our local dollars are exported to outside suppliers. When we shop, eat or spend our leisure dollars at national or transnational chain businesses, a large portion of that money usually leaves the community to support head offices in other cities. The same applies to subsidiary branch companies. A friend of mine who manages a small Winnipeg subsidiary business of a large transnational corporation told me that *over half* his company's earnings in 1990-91 were sent directly outside Winnipeg to headquarters in Montreal.

Every community has a source of income, even the poorest, welfare dependent communities. By consciously applying strategies to keep local dollars circulating and multiplying *inside* community boundaries, much can be achieved to alleviate local poverty. The case of the Kingfisher Indian reserve presented in this chapter shows how this process can work.

The second source of money leaks is bank savings. Every time we put money in the bank it is taken out of circulation. This need not be detrimental to a local economy if, in return, banks use these savings to invest in community projects — but they don't. Except for a few community investment funds, banks have consistently invested our billions of dollars of personal savings and pension funds *outside* our communities in large scale, global developments, many of which have unethical employment practices and/or very bad environmental track records (cutting down rain forests, supporting apartheid, constructing nuclear plants and hydro dams).

On the other hand, since it is *our* money, it is entirely possible for us to insist that banks and credit unions reinvest our savings at home, in our communities. For example, the millions of dollars we pay into union pension funds could be targeted for community economic development. Special bank accounts could be set up for individuals to support local initiatives directly, such as is carried out by the SHARE community loan program in New Hampshire. The way SHARE works is that individuals go into a specific bank and open up a passbook savings account which is a joint account with the nonprofit SHARE organization. By opening the account, individuals agree that their savings can be used as collateral for loans which SHARE makes to local businesses.

In another example, in the Evangeline region of P.E.I., residents have used their decision-making powers in their local credit union to invest in worker co-operatives and local businesses, with the result that their local economy has been completely revitalized in a short span of years. (Refer to Chapter Five for a more detailed account.) Then in the U.S., because of disinvestment in the inner cities and the costs associated with urban decay, the government has passed a *Community Reinvestment Act* requiring banks to reinvest a certain percentage of their earnings in poor communities.

The point is, if we are aware and have the will, there are any number of vehicles for directing both our savings and personal consumption toward community reinvestment. How we choose to spend our money determines whether that money will stay to be recirculated or instead leave the community.

After plugging the leaks, a self-reliant community tries to get the most value out of every dollar by intensifying the level of exchange among community members. Manufacturers use local raw materials, hire local workers who spend their paychecks at local retail stores which, in turn, stock their shelves with local produce and employ local people. In Minneapolis, a neighbourhood construction company, set up in co-operation with a nonprofit development corporation, trains local native people to become carpenters and hires them to build and renovate houses and apartments in the inner city neighbourhood. The community captures added value for the dollars it spends by paying these local residents to build, repair and renovate local housing.

More and more communities are catching on to this idea of the "money-go-round" — keeping dollars circulating locally. As a consequence, many communities are now setting up their own local currencies to promote spending at local stores. One example is the community cash program being started in rural towns of Saskatchewan and Manitoba, which is popular at Christmas time. Local credit unions there are issuing community cash (a type of coupon) to individuals who then are able to spend it like regular money at *stores within their community.* The attraction for consumers is that they have three months interest free spending before they have to pay the credit union in dollars what they have already spent in "community cash." Local businesses pay the intervening interest — but local businesses also benefit because the scheme captures a local market for them and increases sales.

Local currencies are not something new. In Austria, during the 1930s depression, the mayor of the town of Worgl issued a local currency to be used for spending in the town. The only cost to the consumer was a two cent stamp, a tax attached to the currency. In this way, the town was able to stimulate local spending, generate public revenues and pull the community out of economic stagnation in less than a year. It is reported that during the first month of issue, the money circulated twenty times, creating employment, business prosperity and tax revenue.

A similar experiment was tried in 1972 in the town of Exeter, New Hampshire, when a local bank agreed to sell a local currency, the "constant," for one dollar — a currency which was honoured by local merchants. Buoyed by its statement of independence, the "constant" became a popular item — a symbol of local pride and status in the community. More recently, a new local currency has been established, again in New Hampshire in the town of Great Barrington, which exchanges real dollars for tender which buys food at two local farmers' markets. This system, the Berkshare Farm Preserve Notes, helps to stimulate the local economy by capturing a direct market for local farm producers, and it pays farmers the cash they need at various times of the year when they are short. People purchase the notes or certificates in winter for nine dollars and redeem them from June to September for ten dollars worth of vegetable produce. Locally owned businesses and restaurants which buy from the food stands are being encouraged to accept these notes, thereby helping to keep money circulating locally.[5]

BARTER CREDIT: THE LOCAL EXCHANGE TRADING SYSTEM

Perhaps the purest example of a self-contained system of local exchange is the Local Exchange Trading System (LETS) developed by Michael Linton of B.C. In the LET system trade occurs among community members without the use of money through a system of *barter credit.* Members advertise their services and wares in a monthly newsletter and "sell" them to each other for a "green dollar" price which they set themselves. The "green dollar" is the local currency of LETS. Each member has an account like a bank account at a central computer which keeps track of all transactions. What is unique in the LET system is that "green dollar" credit is unlimited from the start and issued without interest. In other words, one can purchase items at any time, even without "green dollar" credits on one's account.

To understand how the system functions it is perhaps easiest to follow an example: Mary enters the system and for her first transaction wants to buy some children's clothing. Having not yet earned any "green dollar" credits, she begins her account at zero. She notices Shirley's ad in the LETS newsletter for children's sweaters at fifteen green dollars. She calls Shirley and makes the purchase. Then she phones in the transaction to the LETS office where it is recorded on a computer. Mary's account now is minus fifteen dollars while Shirley's account rises fifteen dollars from what it was previously.

In LETS, one person's purchase (negative green dollars) is another person's gain (positive green dollars). A healthy system shows many exchanges among members, with individuals' accounts moving back and forth between the plus and minus sides of the ledger. Unlike money in the bank, positive balances are not assets in LETS because there is no interest paid on savings and individuals can purchase from a negative account. The only value to members of any credit received comes in the form of purchases — an impetus to continue spending which keeps dollars flowing and helps to create more work and more income for all. As long as members of a LETS community have products to offer and matching needs to be met, the system works to create jobs and keep wealth circulating inside a self-contained community.

The collective barter system is built on the premise that capabilities to produce tend to remain constant despite scarcity of money in a community. One of the serious flaws of our current economic system is that consumer demand for goods and services — the engine of economic growth — depends not on what people need but on how much money people have (or are worth on bank credit cards). Communities rich in dollars generate high levels of exchange and become even richer, while communities scarce in dollars suffer from low levels of exchange and become even poorer. The collective barter system counteracts this dilemma by allowing people to meet their needs without money and without borrowing on credit and paying interest — in effect, by trading their own skills for needed products. Otherwise, the situation is of a group of people with needs to meet — clothes to buy, food to eat, houses to furnish, teeth to fix — and owning the skills and abilities to meet those needs, who are standing around with their hands in their pockets, idle, because there are not enough "dollars" to create activity. In the end, the strength of LETS is its potential to facilitate the creation of *new* employment and purchasing power — new wealth — through a trading structure which works by closing the circuit of goods and services within the community. For example, in the Comox Valley, B.C., LETS generated some $250,000 worth of goods and services in the first twenty months of operation which would otherwise not have existed. In Winnipeg, the Community Circle barter network has generated some $15,000 over three years.

LETS has some flaws that need attention. As an alternative money system — a local currency — it only works well when there is a short supply of real dollars in the community. If people are employed at traditional jobs for traditional pay, they will have little time to contribute or "need" for an alternative money network. Disuse of the system is deadly and spreads a loss of confidence in the network, whose success depends on the members' commitment to use the system. On the positive side, LETS is a way of putting a value on work which is not valued by the formal economy. Because it operates on the principle of "give and take," it helps to build a symbiotic, interdependent relationship among community members.

Making it ourselves: replacing imports with local products

If we take stock of all the things we purchase and use in our daily lives, most, we will find, come from other cities, regions or countries — the clothes we wear, the gas in our cars, the food we eat, the toothpicks we use. How many of these items could we produce in our own community? By replacing imports with locally manufactured products, we are generating new community wealth through new businesses which in a chain reaction will result in the start of even more businesses. For example, the production of local jam could lead to the start up of businesses to produce jars, lids and berries. According to urban economist Jane Jacobs, *import replacement* is the major mechanism by which cities can expand and develop their local economies. Import replacement is also another way to make the dollars go around.

In Eugene, Oregon, ten diverse businesses were analyzed to find what they bought from outside the region. Then they were put together with *local* suppliers who could do the job more cheaply, but whom they had not previously known. One hotel was importing order forms from Boston when local printers could provide them 40 per cent more cheaply. Another business, which made airline meals, was importing chicken broth from Arkansas. A consultant for the project went to local poultry growers and asked if they could produce chicken broth more cheaply. They said yes, if they had $1 million dollars worth of equipment, which they didn't. The consultant asked, "Supposing you did, how much would you have to charge to make a profit on your broth?" She took that figure over to the airline meal company and asked how much broth they would buy for that price. She asked them to sign a letter of intent, which she took to the bank and helped set up a loan for equipment to the poultry growers. Eighty-five local jobs were directly created plus hundreds more for the building and installing of equipment.

One of the keys to successful import substitution is setting up local markets for local products through matchmaking and prearranged agreements, as the consultant did in this case. A community development organization can do the same task and can also help by researching the money flow within a community — what money is being spent on imported products? What existing local suppliers could do the job just as well? What new businesses could be started to meet market demands and the local community needs? Governments can be effective catalysts in community renewal through their local spending. For example, if governments required their departments to use only recycled paper, a local paper reprocessing plant could be set up on the basis of a guaranteed market.

Import replacement, like energy conservation, is an important tool for "plugging the leaks" of a local economy. The same concept can be applied to housing. For example, in poor inner city neighbourhoods, rent paid to absentee landlords usually accounts for a major outflow of local dollars. Government programs and nonprofit development groups which enable residents to purchase their own homes, either privately or co-operatively, keep money from leaving a neighbourhood. As one woman explained, "We're all of us paying one way or another to own a home — the question is whose home are we paying for — ours or our landlord's?"

Local credit unions or community banks can play an important role by holding mortgages on local properties, thus pumping money back into the community. The Chicago South Shore Bank is a good example.

This community bank, which has concentrated on investing in local businesses and housing in a badly deteriorated neighbourhood, has had fewer bad debts than most banks. In 1983 the bank had deposits of $60 million and ranked in the top 12 per cent among American banks.

If new homes need to be built or existing homes renovated, then a community-based construction company employing local people and using local or recycled building materials should be hired in order to reduce spending leakage. The Minneapolis-based Project for Pride in Living (PPL), a nonprofit community corporation, has generated $21.7 million in revenue and services for that city's poorest inner city neighbourhood, mostly through housing rehabilitation and low income housing development tied to home ownership, sweat equity and use of a construction firm which employs and trains local people. One of PPL's activities has been to convert low rise apartments from absentee to co-op ownership, which promotes owner occupancy. A revolving loan fund pays for the renovation of abandoned houses which are then sold at minimal cost to local residents. Mortgage payments revert back to the revolving loan fund to help finance other neighbourhood housing projects. Over fifteen years, the work of PPL has altered the face of the neighbourhood, reversing the outflow of both dollars and people from the community. (See Chapter Six for the full story of PPL.)

MEASURING NET GAINS: PRICE DOES NOT EQUAL COST

In Eugene, the ten businesses researched all found cheaper local products to replace imported ones. Still it is important to note that it is not always the cheapest price tag which nets the most gains for a community. Sometimes a local product may cost a bit more initially, but because of the local multiplier effect, the actual pay back to a community in terms of jobs and local exchange more than compensates for the extra initial outlay. David Morris, cofounder of the Institute for Self-Reliance, estimates that a higher price of up to 20 per cent for local products still achieves net gains for a local economy.

We need to broaden our economic vision by considering the whole picture of costs and benefits for a community. In 1988, the city of Winnipeg undercut its own economy when it by-passed a bid from its own bus manufacturing firm, New Flyers Industries, to purchase buses from a Québec manufacturer for a price only 5 per cent cheaper. A purchase at home would have provided much needed local employment and spinoffs for the rest of the city. Similarly, when the city decided on the basis of direct costs alone to close its central steam plant downtown, it did not consider the impact on the city's famed heritage warehouse buildings. Many of them which were vacant would be left unheated and subject to deterioration. The 1990 closing of the steam plant has resulted in the abandonment of several more heritage buildings now left to withstand the minus thirty degrees Celsius winter temperatures. As the heritage warehouses deteriorate for lack of maintenance, millions of tourist dollars will be lost. (Studies have shown that the majority of tourists come to Winnipeg to see its old buildings.) The same principle holds true for the ferry from Victoria, B.C., to Seattle. Its private owners announced that the ferry would shut down because it was losing $20 million a year. The ferry was initially owned by the government but then sold to private interests. The result of the ferry closure will be a loss of $30 million tourist revenue to Victoria each year.

Making something new: the importance of invention

Successful import replacement requires a business to be flexible, adaptable, innovative and inventive in improvising with local materials and new production methods. Entrepreneurial inventiveness and creativity are two of the most important human resources we have in creating new wealth for local communities. It is through the power of invention that we learn how to extract more from the resources we already have and so create wealth which hadn't existed before. Creativity is needed in community economic development projects to stretch scarce resources to their limit and to make more out of less. It is also needed to discover unconventional market niches for businesses which are themselves often unconventional in structure and social aims.

The Great Western Brewery, started up in 1990, is an example of local ingenuity at work in import replacement. After Carling O'Keefe merged with Molsons, the company decided to close down one of its Saskatoon breweries to streamline its operations. In response, fifteen workers banded together and decided that if they pooled their skills and resources, they could take over the plant themselves. They were able to finance 25 per cent of the company and borrow the rest from the bank. Yet the major problem they faced was how to compete with the multimillion dollar ad campaigns of the large corporations, given their own limited budget. The solution was to develop a uniquely local product — a beer with a distinctive western flavor, using more malt. Now, instead of paying for ads on TV, the company promotes its product, nicknamed "The little beer that could," at the grassroots level through community pubs. According to co-owner and company President Peter

McCann, what they are selling is local identity, and the beer is catching on like wildfire. In just over one year Great Western captured 21 per cent of the Saskatchewan beer market — more than they need to profit and 300 per cent more than predicted. The worker-owned company is testing to see if its beer will sell in Manitoba and Alberta.

Invention and creativity are what powered the success of a community business started in 1978 by a group of women from a Kingston learning/counselling centre; their enterprise is a clothing industry employing low income single parents. They lacked experience in the industry and had to discover how to compete with the established needle trades. Their solution was to find a niche in the market which wasn't being filled by the traditional trades through the design of a line of attractive, but easy-to-put-on clothing for handicapped people and seniors, using velcro and special fastenings. Today, Comfort Clothing Services employs thirty-five workers (many of whom own shares in the company), and operates a profitable manufacturing and mail-order business. In another example from Toronto, a group of homeless men have come up with an attractive and unique design for lawn furniture which is especially targeted to people with back problems, but which can be used by everyone. The Community Business Centre in Toronto is assisting them toward getting this new product produced and distributed.

Making something new calls for creativity and inventiveness — but it also calls for a belief in our own local and personal uniqueness. For so long we have been accustomed to relying on professional experts to solve our local problems that we have lost the belief in our own capabilities and knowledge. Typically, we hire consultants from other cities to tell us how we should manage our local affairs. For example, in inner city Winnipeg, one hundred acres of old railway yards are located at the scenic junction of the Red and Assiniboine Rivers. This land, known as "The Forks" was turned over to public ownership by the CNR in 1987. As people began to reacquaint themselves with the heretofore hidden rivers, they discovered that the site was not only probably the most beautiful in Winnipeg, but was also steeped in 6,000 years of aboriginal history and hundreds of years of western Canadian history. Camp sites, trading posts, Métis settlements, early white settlements and railroad history can be discovered in artifacts buried on the site. Winnipeggers, through the media and presentations to city council, have expressed their desire that the land be developed as a historical/cultural park and a site for local outdoor events.

Instead of following local peoples' ideas, the corporation charged with developing the land hired architects and consultants from Vancouver and Toronto. As a result, The Forks has modeled itself after the Granville Island "festival market" in Vancouver, while Toronto consultants at one point proposed building a state-of-the-art tourist centre with a million dollar spaceship simulator as the central attraction, like Toronto's "Tour of the Universe." The irony and absurdity of imposing these high tech, commercial theme concepts on a local historic site derives from a corporate mind set which wants to emulate the World Class City by borrowing formula developments. It would be more appropriate, and likely more attractive to tourists and local residents, if development of The Forks evolved as an expression of the site's unique cultural and natural history.

Festival markets are one of the popular theme developments of the World Class City. They cost millions to build, and in city after city they have gone bankrupt after a short span of years. *Newsweek* has reported that, "...as waterfront chic spreads, more and more cities are finding that it's not so easy to keep the fancy developments afloat. Crowds often clear out after business hours and on weekends, and high rents scare away store owners. Festival markets in New York, New Orleans, Toledo, Ohio and Richmond, Virginia have all lost money."

In contrast, Cleveland's people have developed its river bank area in a small scale, natural way. The area along the Cuyahoga River called "The Flats" has now "become the centre of city night life without public money, master plan, or cute tourist attractions. Young entrepreneurs simply started opening restaurants and nightclubs. Now developers are converting warehouses, just to the east, into loft style apartments. Unlike the massive projects in places like Toledo, says Richard Shatten, head of a local development group, 'The Flats just plain old happened.'"[6]

A self-reliant community, then, is one that defines its own problems and finds its own solutions through relying on its own uniqueness as a community and drawing on the inventiveness and creativity of its own people.

Trading with equal partners

Self-reliance is development from the inside-out, starting with needs, starting at home. It is an approach which helps to *minimize* exchange with the outside but does not exclude it. Since few communities will ever achieve complete self-sufficiency, there will always be a need for some degree of trade with other communities. This is where *collective self-reliance* comes into play. Collective self-reliance is a trading strategy which sets guidelines for what, when and how exchange can best be arranged to avoid exploitation and unequal advantage of one partner over another. It is a strategy of exchange among equal partners for the *purpose of building collective strength and wealth* among a block of co-operating communities.

It is now known and coming to be widely accepted that trade between *unequal* partners tends to benefit the stronger, bigger partner over the smaller, weaker one. While in the short run a trade deal may seem like a good exchange for both parties, countless examples have shown that over time trade between rich and poor countries, or even rich and poor regions within a country (urban centres and rural hinterlands), has led to dependency and greater impoverishment of the poorer party. It is what is known as the centre-periphery trade dilemma. What happens is that less developed regions, the *peripheries,* tend to export their raw materials and primary products, such as lumber, wheat, fish and minerals, in exchange for imported finished products, such as machinery, chemicals and technology, from developed regions — the *centres.*

Because the process of finishing a product creates so much spinoff wealth for a community — through supporting industries, research and the addition of value through processing — the developed region ends up with a long-term advantage in the trade deal. This is why communities need to learn how to process their own materials to meet their own needs. Where trade is necessary, it should be arranged to benefit all parties in the spirit of collective self-reliance. Collective self-reliance occurs through (1) making trade alliances with parties at about the same level of development, and (2) by trading primary products for primary products; manufactured products for manufactured products. Trade between rich and poor regions creates dependency of one upon the other, but trade between equals for items which cannot be produced locally can help build collective strength through *interdependence*, as opposed to dependence.

Canada's Maritime provinces, victims of regional disparity, are working to set up a trading bloc among themselves as a step toward collective self-reliance. Trading blocs, however, will build self-reliance only if local production is first and foremost geared to basic community needs — food, shelter, clothing, education, health and energy.

One product can be exchanged freely without limit — knowledge. David Morris says that a self-reliant community "defines its own problems, asks its own genius to solve its own problems, and then exports the solution it found to its own problems." In this way, cities can begin to *share* their experiences with other cities, and small communities with other communities. Within this context there may be a whole new agenda and reason for "twinning" cities and making new alliances based on common themes, such as the 1986 Livable Winter Cities Conference in Edmonton. By sharing our own solutions to our own problems we avoid imposing inappropriate solutions on other people who can best decide on solutions for themselves.

Case study: self-reliant development at Kingfisher Lake

Over the past ten years, a small native community of 350 at Kingfisher Lake in northern Ontario has turned a poor, dependent community into a thriving economic concern and in the process has gained economic control over future development.[7] The native band used to be a self-sustaining community which lived off the land and produced its own food, clothing and shelter. In recent years many factors, including government restrictions, forced the band to purchase its basic needs commercially at the local Hudson Bay store. By 1979, 80 per cent of the band's income was being spent at the store, and almost all of that money was leaving the community. That was when the band decided it wanted to buy the Hudson Bay store and keep the profits at home. After eight months of negotiations a deal was struck — but not before the band threatened to open its own store if the Bay refused. The purchase was the beginning of a series of economic developments leading toward self-reliance.

Since the store opening in 1980, the band has used the revenues for other community projects. It started a laundromat which has been operating for over eight years, despite initial objections from the Federal Department of Indian Affairs. It bought a house in Thunder Bay, a place where band members can stay at nominal cost when they travel to the city. To lower the cost of travel to Thunder Bay, it bought two vehicles for band members' use, asking only that drivers cover the cost of gas and maintenance. The vehicles are stored in another community eight hours away, because Kingfisher Lake is accessible only by air and roads during the winter.

Because the community is so dependent on air travel, the band joined with six other native communities to buy a 49 per cent interest in a local airline (Kelner Airways), which gives the band a share in profits as well as some control over operations. The bands sharing the airline have since purchased together a two-thirds interest in First Nations Petro, a company supplying fuel to communities as far north as James Bay. These last two initiatives are functioning examples of collective self-reliance, where northern communities are pooling wealth and mutually investing in industries geared to the special fuel and travel needs of people in the north.

Having built substantial wealth by keeping local money circulating within the community, the band is now able to construct a $1.3 million arena and an electric generating system, thus greatly improving living conditions at Kingfisher Lake. It has also created a loan fund and acts as a bank for band members who cannot get capital from conventional institutions because of lack of collateral.

Kingfisher Lake owes its success to a clear and focused strategy for community self-reliance. One of the principles of self-reliance evident in the Kingfisher Lake example is that community economic development starts by meeting people's basic needs — food, clothing, fuel, travel — instead of pulling development ideas out of the air in the hope of developing an "export" market, which is so often the approach. The example of Kingfisher Lake also illustrates peoples' power to define their problems and find appropriate solutions grounded in local culture and ways of life. It is unlikely that the Indian Affairs Department could have come up with the economic plans which have worked so well.

CONCLUSION

A self-reliant economy is one that uses its own resources and inner strengths to meet its needs. Every community has wealth and the potential to generate more — the job is to discover these resources; use them to their greatest efficiency and advantage, always with an eye for community gains; wherever possible, reclaim the wealth which belongs to a community but has been appropriated by outside interests. Import replacement, recycling money and resources, plugging the leaks and encouraging invention are strategies for self-reliance.

The benefits of self-reliant development extend beyond economics. They are political: a self-reliant community has greater autonomy and freedom to decide its priorities and determine its future. The self-reliant community also has ecological benefits. A community with local production and consumption has close links to development's direct impact on the environment. By producing what we consume and consuming what we produce, we are forced to live with our own waste by-products instead of shipping them somewhere to become some other community's problem. What better way to ensure environmental responsibility?

Finally, the benefits of self-reliant development are cultural. Community relationships, community identity and sense of place are lost as we move in cars through wastelands of thoroughfare strips lined by repeated patterns of chain stores. We could be anywhere. By reviving community-based businesses we begin to restore trust and personal accountability between consumer and producer and also to re-establish a community's home identity and rootedness.

ENDNOTES

[1]   Jane Jacobs, *Canadian Cities and Sovereignty Association*, CBC Massey Lecture (Toronto: Hunter Rose Co., 1980), pp. 32-33.

[2]   Lewis Mumford, *The City in History* (New York: Harcourt, Brace and World, 1961), pp. 308 and 310.

[3]   Figures are based on combining residential and commercial/institutional building renovations. The Canadian Home Builders Association (CHBA) statistics show residential renovation to be $22.4 billion a year, and, while no formal statistics are kept on commercial and institutional building renovations, the accepted figure in the industry is that commercial/institutional renovation is roughly the same. The two figures combined total $45 billion dollars. It should be noted that the CHBA definition of renovation includes additions, repairs, restoration, maintenance and life style changes to the structures (kitchens, bathrooms). These figures were quoted in interviews with Marc Denhez, a heritage lawyer and Ottawa consultant, in January 1992.

[4]   A short account of the efforts by the Sudbury Citizens' Movement to reclaim the prison farm is told by Joan Kuyek in *Fighting for Hope* (Montreal: Black Rose Books, 1990), pp. 55-56.

[5]   Information on local currencies comes from "Redefining Development" on the CBC Radio program, "Ideas," 25 April 1991. More examples of local currencies are discussed in an interview with Susan Witt in "Deli Dollars, Trash Cash, and Local Loans," in *Green Business: Hope or Hoax?* Christopher Plant and Judith Plant, eds. (Gabriola Island, B.C.: New Society Publishers, 1991), pp. 95–104.

[6]   Joshua Hammer and Todd Barrett, "Rough Sailing on the Waterfront," in *Newsweek*, 27 March 1989, pp. 44–45.

[7]   The story of Kingfisher Lake was written up in the *Winnipeg Free Press*, 20 September 1990, p. 22.

Chapter Four

Harmonizing With Nature

Nota: Man is the intelligence of his soil,
The sovereign ghost.
...
Nota: His soil is man's intelligence.
That's better. That's worth crossing seas to find.

Wallace Stevens
The Comedian as a Letter C

4

Harmonizing With Nature

Ecological development: autonomous, locally based development must also be ecologically sensitive — that is, fit within the greater eco-system of which it is a part — thus contributing to a pattern of sustainable development for the planet as a whole.

FORGOTTEN NATURE

Sustainable development places economic growth within the natural limits of the biosphere. The Western world's *over*consumption and *over*production have resulted in global environmental destruction including acid rain, holes in the ozone layer, lead in the air, pollution of water by factory wastes, nuclear leaks and explosions, pesticides and preservatives in food, oil spills in the sea and so on. Instead of adapting to the processes of nature we have expected nature to adapt to the industrial processes of modern humanity. It can't be done. There is a limit to the amount and concentration of waste which nature can absorb and reprocess through its cycles.

Cities, as we have created them, are anti-natural places. The sheer numbers of people and industries located in cities create traffic congestion, auto pollution, strain on resources, large scale industrial pollution, paving over of agricultural lands, elimination of wilderness and scaring away of wildlife. What do we do with our human waste in the city? We flush it away down the river and then import our water from somewhere else to drink. What do we do with our leftover dinner? We throw it in the garbage and then cart it off to a landfill site to mix with all types of incompatible solid wastes and take up more precious agricultural land. At the same time, farmers who could be fertilizing their soil with human organic wastes produced by city dwellers — wastes which now pollute our rivers — are instead depleting the soil of its nutrients by applying chemical fertilizers imported from outside producers.

Loss of diversity: oversimplification of the environment

Underlying these destructive actions, and perhaps most threatening of all, is a trend toward *oversimplifying* our environment, resulting from the centralizing processes of production. Through a process of corporate takeovers, capital concentration and the pursuit of highly centralized control over resources, there has been a noticeable and systematic elimination of diversity from the face of the earth. Every city is beginning to look like every other, with company franchises, uniform architecture and a mass advertising culture.

Single industry towns are another example of oversimplification. We can see the disastrous effects on the long-term survival of communities where industries have closed and left behind a shattered community with no source of income, which eventually becomes a ghost town. Many of these single resource communities are now turning to community economic development (CED) as a way to diversify and so minimize the risk to their economies.

Monoculture or single crop farming is yet another example of dangerous oversimplification of the environment resulting from expanding agribusiness (industrial farming) and the elimination of the small family farm. Small farmers used diversified farming methods, grew a variety of species and harvested and experimented with their own plant seeds, but industrial farms require large open fields of *single* crops, *uniform* in size, shape and time of maturity in order to maximize efficient use of expensive machinery. Single crop farming uses chemicals and hybrids to achieve product uniformity and so reduces the diversity of plants grown. While the large choice of foods on grocery shelves may provide the *appearance* of widely diverse plant species providing our food, the opposite is actually true. We are *eliminating diversity* from the food chain. Where once our global food derived from three to four thousand different crops, today the global food system is dependent on only twenty-nine or thirty crops, whose seeds are genetically engineered, manufactured and distributed by a few large corporations.[1]

Why is this transformation threatening? The practice of growing many crops or different species of the same crop in the same field has traditionally been an insurance against famine — against the sudden destruction of crop by an unforseen pest or change of climate. Diversity is an essential health safeguard; it is part of the ecological web of life.

Elimination of diversity extends to the genetic material of nature itself — corporate and centralized control over plant breeding (production of seeds) and seed patents has resulted in a shrinking gene pool of plant life. It is estimated we are losing some two hundred strains of genetic material every year due to centralized control of the plant breeding industry by giant food and chemical companies. Genetic engineering of plants has resulted in *specialization* and *reduction* of varieties grown. For example, just two varieties account for 96 per cent of peas grown in the U.S.; in Canada four varieties account for 75 per cent of wheat crops. Out of 2,000 species of potatoes, one is grown commercially in the U.S. The reduction in seed species and variety is furthered by the loss of small independent seed companies to large competitors, who now have a cartel-like control over the market. Of 230 companies inventoried in Iowa in 1984, fifty-four were out of business in 1987.[2]

What kind of specialized plant species are being engineered by biotechnology (genetic engineering of biological material using molecular techniques)? The answer is: vegetables designed to profit large corporations — easy to transport, process and sell on the store shelves because they are durable and uniform in shape. Tomatoes, for example, are engineered to withstand long distance shipping. By increasing the solid content of tomatoes, producers can save dramatically on transport costs — $80 million a year per 1 per cent increase in solids.[3] The end product is a tasteless, plastic tomato. There have even been tomatoes designed to grow a square shape (efficient for packing) and so tough they won't break when dropped from a building.[4] Are there any tasty tomato genes or species left? Will our children and grandchildren never know what a "real" juicy tomato tastes like? Hybrid species are the most popular seed types being developed by agribusiness because the seeds from the mature plant are unable to reproduce themselves, guaranteeing that farmers will purchase *new* seeds each year from the company, as opposed to harvesting seeds themselves as they used to do. Here again, we see how centralized control of the food industry is limiting the farmer's choice of plant variety/species.

Animals are also disappearing from the earth at alarming rates, hunted to extinction to meet consumer greed for furs and other luxury goods. Experts estimate we are losing from one to as many as forty-five species of plant and animal life a *day*, globally, as a direct result of human interference with the environment. The rain forests are home to millions of diverse plant and animal species which are little know to us. Some 70 per cent of new cancer drugs are made from plants native to tropical rain forests. Yet the forces of global trade and Third World debt encourage companies to cut down the forests, snuffing out the life and future of hundreds of thousands of plant and animal species. Some of these may have proven to be the cure we awaited.

Diversity is an essential ingredient to all life. In nature the ability to adapt and survive depends upon the diversity of a species' collective gene pool. Evolution of nature over millions of years has always been toward achieving a greater *complexity* and *flexibility* through diversity. In the last hundred years, modern industrialism with its emphasis on increasing specialization and uniformity has undone the work of a million years of evolution. It has systematically eliminated the key element of *choice* from our surroundings. Diversity is what gives us choice: elimination of diversity, both in nature and in human society, marks the end of our freedom to choose.

We cannot speak about environmental destruction and the loss of diversity without also speaking about root causes — the ingrained attitudes and social and economic institutions which have led to the ecological crisis. An example is the supposition that money can solve all problems if there is enough of it and that therefore we have to generate more through accelerated "development." This attitude has created more ecological problems. Vandana Shiva, Director of the Research Foundation for Science, Technology and Natural Resource Policy in Dehradun, India, sums it up:

> You can't have cash flows that will suddenly create soil fertility, money that will bring to life dead streams or bring water to dead wells. ...Nature doesn't get created by money but it can get destroyed for generating money. That is where the logic of the banker is collapsing. They think they can play God, that they can restructure nature, and they think that all the problems of scarcity today, which are problems of the scarcity of nature to produce food and scarcity of humans as part of nature to take care of her needs, are problems that they will be able to solve as bankers through money, cash flows, investments, and returns on investments.[5]

The problem is that we believe humans are *superior* to nature: that nature is an object *separate* from ourselves, a "resource" to be used, conquered, harnessed, tamed, measured, distributed and owned. In essence, we believe nature belongs to us, not that we belong to nature. Our culture has taught us that human life is a struggle *against* nature, that if we did not dominate nature, nature would dominate us. For example, the bible teaches that God gave humans "*dominion* over nature;" Sigmund Freud, that the *repression* of our natural animal instincts is what gives rise to higher civilization; Karl Marx, that human liberation depends on the technical *mastery over* nature to free us from the realm of material necessity. Given this legacy, the thrust of scientific research, technical innovation and economic development has been to ever more *control* over nature and ultimately, as Murray Bookchin says, "to crack open the mysteries of matter and life itself," through nuclear physics and genetic engineering.

What we have forgotten in our frenzy to control and dominate nature is that *we too are nature.* Any perception of the essential *unity* and connection which underlie all natural relationships is lost. By splitting ourselves off from nature we have alienated ourselves from our deepest roots, our supporting structures. It is rather like the cartoon which shows a person merrily sawing away at a tree branch — while he is sitting on it.

In his in-depth analysis, author and social ecologist, Murray Bookchin, pinpoints *domination,* both of humans over nature and of humans over humans, as the root of the current ecological crisis. Domination takes different forms. It is codified in the *hierarchy* which forms the basis of our many social institutions and organizations — churches, the military, government bureaucracy, court systems, schools, unions, corporations and family structures which historically have placed men as "heads" of households. Hierarchy is a pyramid model of social organization which operates by assigning certain people positions of power and authority to control and dominate others.

How does hierarchy relate to the loss of diversity and domination of nature? Hierarchy separates and specializes various functions by dividing up a whole into different parts. Under hierarchy the different parts are assigned *unequal value* — a set-up which, in the history of the Western world, has given whites superiority over people of color, men privileges over women and all humans superiority over nature. Differences, instead of being valued, are evaluated on a scale of one to ten. The "things" on the bottom — animals, nature, women, "other" people different from ourselves — don't count; they can be used or disposed of by the higher levels of the hierarchy (workers fired, women paid lower wages, mountains blown apart). This is harsh language, but it makes the point. The important contribution of Bookchin's critique of hierarchy and domination is to show the connection between our social attitudes and institutions, and our attitudes toward nature. Both have to change.

To sum up, our anti-nature behavior is characterized by overconsumption, oversimplification, domination and hierarchy. We certainly won't find a future ethic to guide development of a new society in this model. Instead, we need turn to ecology.

ECOLOGY AS A DESIGN FOR LIVING

A new understanding of all relationships is needed, which will help heal the alienation between people and nature and also among people themselves. Ecology gives us this new perspective — a framework and design for living.

But what do we mean by ecology? There seems to be some confusion. Often, the word is used loosely to refer to the state of our environment — the air we breath, the water we drink, the forests, the mountains and the oceans. This, however, is *environment*, not ecology. The difference is that environment refers to a physical world around and *outside* of us, an objective world out there to be managed with what we call "environmental management." Ecology, on the other hand, refers to a *dynamic system of relationships* of which we are all a connected, living part.

Ecology is the study of relationships between living organisms and their living and nonliving environment, between plants and animals, between humans and nonhuman nature, and between humans and other humans. These interactive relationships form a multitude of systems, in which each system is *self-contained* like cells or organs in a body, while at the same time, *connected* to and a part of larger systems. Ecology, then, is about more than trees, air and water — it is a complex of processes, relationships and natural systems of integration, which together make up a holistic model of human and non-human development.

From an ecological perspective then, the solution to human-created environmental problems will require a fundamental rethinking and restructuring of human processes, relationships and systems, including our social, political and economic systems. To illustrate this point, *Clouds of Change,* the forward looking 1990 report by Vancouver's Task Force on Atmospheric Change, begins with the statement, "Atmospheric change means *we* have to change." The overriding message is that in order to reduce levels of ozone-depleting chemicals, sulphur dioxide and methane released into the atmosphere, people in Vancouver will have to radically alter their present patterns of living, working and relating to one another.

Clouds of Change contains thirty-five recommendations, starting with an environmental focus banning the use of specific chemicals and expanding into an ecological perspective with suggestions for redesigning cities and workplaces to reduce the need for transportation, especially by automobiles which are major polluters. Included in the policy report are recommendations to:

1. Decentralize work back into the home, using telecommunications to tie businesses and people into information networks;
2. Introduce energy efficient land use policies by creating self-contained communities where social services, shopping, working, recreation and housing are within walking or bicycling distance of each other;
3. Intensify residential neighbourhoods, thereby reducing urban sprawl;
4. Implement an urban reforestation program;
5. Set up community councils to develop ecological neighbourhood plans;
6. Give incentives to ecological enterprises;
7. Implement an energy conservation by-law for new and existing buildings;
8. Institute a composting program out of schools and community centres;
9. Design urban space to encourage bicycle transit;
10. Step up drilling for methane gas from landfills;
11. Expand programs for recycling and reducing solid wastes.

As we can see, when ecology, as opposed to environment, becomes the measure for development, *all* relationships between people, nature and the built environment come into question. It is in the nature of ecology to be holistic. What *principles* of ecology derived from nature could we follow in order to redefine human social and economic relationships? I will mention four. They are:

- unity in diversity;
- process: means over ends;
- qualitative development;
- ecological efficiency.

To begin with, nature is made up of an integrated network of self-contained systems related to other systems. This complex web of "systems within systems" is like a human body in which each cell operates as an autonomous entity, capable and active in processing its own food, energy and waste, yet is not isolated, but connected to other cells which make up larger systems — blood circulation, lung, heart, renal systems. **Unity in diversity** is the key ecological concept here where the smallest "part" is understood to be an autonomous, living system in itself (our diversity) yet part of a greater whole (our unity).

As a principle for human development, unity in diversity leads to an understanding that the health of the planet depends on the health and integrity of the smallest community — the fate of the people in Brazil is in some way connected to my own fate. Acknowledging the value and contribution of *all* people including children, women and minority groups, will lead to a more balanced and sustainable society. To make this happen we need new institutional structures and processes which respect difference and minority opinion. These *non-hierarchical* structures would be based on co-operation, partnership and consensual decision making.

From an economic perspective, unity in diversity translates into community support for a diversity of small local enterprises as the way to achieve long term economic stability. Economic diversity, like ecological diversity, provides a natural protection against the kind of sweeping disaster which can occur when a large scale industry shuts down in a single industry town. To help foster economic diversity, communities can offer a range of technical and financial supports to small scale owner-operated or co-operative businesses and encourage initiatives in the informal economy of home and community. Support might include an incubator facility for new businesses to pool information and resources, a community loan fund or a community development corporation, which brings together a wide cross section of people in the community — known as the ABCDE group — administrators, businesspeople, community groups, decision makers and experts.

In nature, growth is a process of becoming. Human development can likewise be viewed as a **process rather than an end product** — a coming into one's own or realization of an individual's and a community's potential. From the point of view of "process," the main concern of development is *how* we interact with each other. Does the activity respect the limits of nature? Is the process of development integrative and empowering, or is it dominating and hierarchical? Nonhierarchical, partnership organizations such as co-operatives and community groups help to ensure grassroots, democratic participation. Growth is understood as more than bottom line profits or employment statistics; it has to do with a *learning process, an empowering process* and *an improved quality of life.*

74

The focus on growth from an ecological perspective is **qualitative** as opposed to quantitative. Herman Daly, proponent of steady-state economics, compares the sustainable economy to an eco-system in which the earth's physical stock — people, capital and resources — remain constant yet are always changing. Births replace deaths; production replaces depreciation; raw materials are used and expelled as waste, but only as much as can be regenerated by the natural environment. What *does* change and develop are nonphysical things like culture, knowledge, technology and the distribution of artifacts.

Finally, ecological development distinguishes between economic and **ecological efficiency**. For example, where traditional economics views long distribution lines — airports, railroads, highways — as the most efficient methods for distributing goods, sustainable economics considers them to be inefficient since they consume more energy and resources than would be necessary if the goods were produced locally. As Schumacher said: "The necessity of goods transport is a sign of failure." From an ecologically efficient point of view, instead of shipping lettuce from California, we should be growing our own lettuce in greenhouses fertilized by our own organic compost and heated by the energy of the sun, wind and the waste heat of nearby factories.

A BIOREGIONAL PERSPECTIVE

If the city, with its polluting industries, concrete structures and high concentration of people, is the enemy or opponent of nature, perhaps we can get a healthier view of cities if we see them as part of natural regions, in particular, of *bio*-regions. A bioregion is a geographic area usually identified by its watershed catchment area and common features such as landforms, elevation, vegetation and animal life. Human history and culture connected to the land also figure into the definition of bioregions. A bioregional perspective, then, views a specific locale in terms of its *natural* and *social* systems, whose dynamic relationship help to create a sense of "life place," rooted in both natural and cultural history.

The Bioregional Congress of North America defines bioregionalism as the *local* connections among:

Land
Plants and animals
Springs, rivers, lakes, groundwater and oceans
Air
Families, friends, neighbours

Community
Native traditions
Indigenous systems of production amd trade

Bioregionalism, which looks at each region as a living, organic system comprised of people, culture and nature, is an aspect of ecology, the study of self-contained systems and their relationship to other systems. For example, humans are autonomous beings — systems in and of themselves — yet are at the same time part of a larger network of systems — family, community and nature. Likewise, communities are self-contained systems belonging to larger systems — cities and surrounding bioregions. Bioregions together make up our earth.

The total bird's-eye view provides us with a local/global perspective in which human activities, bound by the particularities of time and space, are seen to fit within a greater pattern which includes all of creation. Knowing our place within the earth's eco-system is a humbling insight, one that forces us to see ourselves as *stewards* of and not masters over nature. Within this new perspective, development and technology must find their most appropriate scale so as to not impede the health and security of other people, natural systems and future generations. We can best accomplish this task by, in Wendell Barry's words, "learning to live at home," by developing our communities from within to become self-sufficient through self-reliance.

It has been argued that self-reliance, looking inward, is a form of isolationism which encourages attitudes of unconcern about sharing — "I have mine so why should I be concerned about you," or else the NIMBY syndrome (Not In My Backyard), prevalent in Toronto and Vancouver neighbourhoods where booming land values turned ordinary homeowners into land developers. The necessary counterbalance to self-reliance, therefore, is an ecological consciousness which makes clear that every local initiative is part of a greater world pattern of sustainable development requiring co-operation, caring and ecological sensitivity to other people and nature.

One way to see the relationship of local development to the larger environment is to visualize our homes and communities as part of a bioregion, a natural watershed area made up of connecting rivers, lakes, land, air, plants, and the human and animal life living within the region. How do our towns and cities relate to this eco-system in terms of transportation, sewage, solid waste disposal, air emissions, use of water, energy production, building development and settlement patterns?

This eco-systems view of development is the focus of the recent planning report, *Watershed*, by a joint federal/provincial Royal Commission on the Future of the Toronto Waterfront, headed by David Crombie. The strength of the report is its *bioregional* concept, an idea capturing the imaginations of many people and changing the way local municipalities see themselves in relation to the "whole." For example, the town council of Aurora put development plans on hold when it found out it was sitting on top of a specially designated natural area called the Oak Ridges Moraine. The report is the first of its kind to put forward ecology as the measuring stick and overriding consideration instead of the short term economic and political goals of local jurisdictions and government departments. For this remarkable contribution alone *Watershed* warrents further consideration.

Watershed report

The report begins with the statement, "Everything is connected to everything else." What started as an inquiry into Toronto's harbour front soon grew into a study of the entire *Greater Toronto bioregion*, an eco-system stretching forty miles east and west of Toronto and inland thirty miles defined by a watershed of sixteen rivers rising in the Niagara Escarpment (west) and the Oak Ridges Moraine (north and east) and flowing into the Great Lakes Basin (south). It is impossible to separate the lakefront waters from the waters flowing into it or from the human activities of work and play which affect the water's flow and quality.

An environmental audit has shown that the Greater Toronto bioregion is an eco-system under stress. The Don River, thirty years ago a place of natural beauty teeming with wildlife, is today a dead river — an open sewer filled with industrial discharge, effluent from the sewage plant and sewer overflows. The Great Lakes Basin, the source of drinking water for half of Canada, is considered to be the most polluted part of all North America. Toxic chemicals and bacterial contamination make the lakes dangerous for swimming and fishing.

While people in the region are upset that their quality of life is diminished by environmental degradation, the question remains how to co-ordinate ecological restoration of such a large bioregion, one that crosses the boundaries of five regional and thirty local municipalities including 6,000 industries, plus numerous government departments, agencies and ministries intent on pursuing their own, often conflicting, interests. The problem is compounded by the diversity of human activities contributing to environmental stress — population growth, water and sewer systems at capacity, dispersed settlement patterns eating up the best farmland in the country, lack of landfill sites, consumer driven lifestyles, commuter dependency on the auto, polluting practices of industry.

What *Watershed* offers is a new planning tool to help sort out the environmental chaos — a bioregional reference point that acts as a bench mark or map underlay against which human development and settlement patterns can be measured and guided within the larger system of natural relationships. The commission stresses the need for an eco-system approach which brings together social, economic, ecological and political systems within the bioregion. Local municipalities and administrations are asked to work together for the sake of the whole, since air and water know no political boundaries. Through *partnerships* it is hoped that people will be able to transcend narrow interests. For example, the commission has recommended that the elevated Gardiner Expressway, which runs along Toronto's central waterfront, be dismantled because it blocks visual and physical access and creates noise and air pollution. Transportation engineers, who created this monstrosity in the first place, are part of the ecological restoration project, thus becoming part of the solution instead of part of the problem.

The eco-system, bioregional approach to development is a radical idea which could transform how we understand and deal with the interdependent relationships of people to place.

PRODUCING FOR LIFE

Under traditional development models, economic growth of *any* sort is interpreted as a sign of health. Growth is quantified by the GNP — the measure of total consumption and production of goods and services formally exchanged within a nation in one year. The fallacy of looking at growth as a measure of health is that many of the goods and services produced are actually causing illness, depleting the earth of its nonrenewable resources and potential to sustain life over the long term. Other renewable resources, like water, air and soil, are being poisoned by industry and recycled through the eco-system, killing wildlife, forests and humans — yet the GNP does not account for the costs associated with these life-taking "production" activities. In fact, the hospital care, research, clean-up squads, etc., created to deal with the fall-out of pollution are accounted for in the GNP as more healthy growth! Dollars spent on welfare, police and social services because of poverty, community disruption and social alienation are entered into the GNP as "productive" growth.

What is needed is a new perspective on economic health which distinguishes between *life-producing* and *life-destroying* activities, an approach to development that encourages life creation over life destruction. Ecological feminists are calling for a holistic, women's perspective on development which acknowledges the true value of life-producing, life-sustaining activities in the home, community and village, generated by traditional women's work. These activities of the informal, household economy — rearing children, caring for the elderly, helping in the community, organizing and running a household — are unaccounted for in the GNP, yet they produce from fifty to sixty per cent of the total goods and services we use.

In the Third World, women are likewise the main producers and providers in the village, subsistence economy. Their knowledge of local eco-systems is invaluable. Experience has taught them the intricacies of plant and animal life and the wealth produced by living forests and running waters. In recent years, industrial development, what Research Foundation Director Vandana Shiva calls masculinist *maldevelopment*, has destroyed the sustainable resource base of the village economy. Large lush regions of India, such as the district of Uttar Pradesh, have in just thirty years become deserts. Hundreds of villages have been abandoned because of commercial forestry, the introduction of monoculture and overexploitation of water for cash crops — all part of the Green Revolution, which was supposed to modernize agriculture and improve living conditions. The opposite has occurred; there is less nutrition today than thirty years ago.

Women, as the food providers, have always known the relationship between forests and food. A group of women in the northern hills of India have formed a movement called Chipko (meaning "tree-huggers") to fight against the destruction of the sacred forests. They hug the trunks of trees to prevent loggers from destroying their forests. They are prepared to sacrifice their lives for the future of their communities. The women have succeeded in halting numerous developments, with the result that the Chipko movement is spreading across India. Their message is: forests produce soil and water. The Chipko women sing, "Give me an oak forest and I will give you pots full of milk and baskets full of grain." Where industry sees only productive value in *dead* forests — timber and resin for export — the women see only productive value in *living* forests. Trees produce a continuing supply of food, medicine, clothing, shelter, fodder, soil and water, which are necessary for survival. The point is clear: there are fundamental differences between *producing-for-life* and *producing-for-death* which must figure in any theory of sustainable development.

In another example, "production-for-life" is occurring in the city of Maputo, Mozambique, amid the disaster of civil war, by a group of women known as the Green Zones Co-operative. These women organized themselves in 1986 to do market gardening on vacant tracts of land in the capital city. After the first year they were able to feed their families with their fresh vegetables. By the end of the second year, with more people involved, the group had a surplus to sell. Every year the co-operative has grown to the point that today 900 families are involved. Their fresh vegetables, chickens and other food fill the city's market, providing fresh produce that would otherwise not be available. A grant of $5,000 for hoes and rakes got them started. Today the co-op is self-sufficient in its own operations and active in helping others to set up similar co-operatives in other places.

In Japan, a highly successful food purchasing collective, called the Seikatsu Club, has attracted the participation of 220,000 families.[6] (It ranks ninth in size out of Japan's 700 co-ops.) The collective had its beginnings in 1965 when one housewife organized 200 others to purchase milk directly from local farmers as a way to cut costs. Since that time, the Seikatsu Club has grown in size, investment capital and social/ political influence, promoting life-affirming ecological values through its purchasing activities. The club is a network of housewives who believe they can bring about ecological and social change by taking action from the home. The co-op operates through thousands of small autonomous local groups, called "hans," comprised of six to thirteen families who work together to purchase, distribute and decide on policy issues. As one of its principles, the co-op purchases products which are environmentally safe and organically grown. By buying directly from local farmers through advance purchase orders, instead of from the grocery shelf, co-op members (mainly urban housewives) have become active and aware participants in the food production process.

Members even help in the harvest if needed. The co-op is more than self-supporting — it has built up 7.5 billion yen (nearly $7 million) in investment capital which it uses to invest in its own food operations, such as the organic milk production facilities it runs with local farmers, and the more than forty worker collectives, owned and operated by women, that it has helped start in the food service industry. The Seikatsu Club has inspired several housewives to become active in local politics with the result that thirty-three co-op members have been elected at the municipal level.

In a similar vein, but on a much smaller scale, the movement, Community Supported Agriculture (CSA), is taking hold in North America. It works by city people buying "shares" in local farming operations through payment in advance for organic produce which will be grown and delivered to them at a drop-off in the city. The capital advance helps farmers to finance their operations without having to depend on bank loans: at the same time, the direct relationship between urban consumers and local producers helps to keep money circulating in the local economy by eliminating food chain representatives such as corporate retailers. CSA helps to create a better understanding about urban/rural issues by letting people experience their interdependence first hand. (Examples of Community Supported Agriculture, including a recently started Winnipeg project, are provided in Chapter Six.) CSA and similar projects demonstrate an emerging ecological perspective which places the *ethics of life and nature* as the working criteria to screen and guide development for a sustainable future.

BUILDING GREEN AND HEALTHY CITIES

There are two billion people, 40 per cent of the world's population, living in urban areas today, with the numbers increasing at alarming rates. In Canada, 80 per cent of the population lives in cities. This fact, combined with the reality that cities are our major producers of pollution and consumers of natural resources, has resulted in the emergence of two important urban ecological movements — "Healthy Cities" and "Green Cities." Both movements are aimed at bringing health and balance to our urban communities.

"Healthy Cities" was a project initiated in 1984 by the World Health Organization (WHO). In Canada, it was spearheaded by a doctor named Trevor Hancock and its ideas adopted and promoted by public health organizations and the city planning profession. The purpose is to promote a holistic concept of health which includes social, economic, psychological and environmental well-being and to develop programs and policies for cities to achieve this goal. A healthy city is defined by the WHO as "one that is continually...creating those physical and social environments which enable its people to mutually support each other in carrying out all the functions of life and achieving their full potential."

Toronto's Board of Health in 1988 completed the 180 page "healthy communities" report, *Healthy Toronto 2000,* which has since been adopted by City Council for implementation. Figure 1 shows the mandala (symbol of symmetry and wholeness) of health which has become the model for developing healthy communities. At the centre it depicts the individual, whose total health is represented by the integration of body, spirit and mind and the influences of larger systems of which the individual is part. These larger systems are the family (genetic and environmental influence), the community (health care system, workplaces, schools and neighbourhood environment), the general culture and the biosphere.

The report calls for *reducing inequities in health* through:

- housing policies which address affordability, occupant control and eliminate homelessness;
- food policies which improve nutrition, access to food and eliminate the need for food banks;
- economic development strategies to create healthful workplaces and a more equitable distribution of income;
- programs for adult literacy and health education in schools.

Next, it calls for *creating physical environments supportive of health* through:

- environmental legislation aimed at reducing pollution, implementing energy conservation and recycling;
- city plans which encourage public transit, walking and cycling.

Thirdly, the report calls for *creating social environments supportive of health* through:

- community development and community empowerment backed by government grants and contracts;
- community-based health services;
- "safe city" planning guidelines to reduce violence in communities.

Fourthly, the report calls for *increasing health expectancy* through:

- preventative community health care programs including dental care, fitness, substance abuse, self-help groups and support for seniors.

"Healthy cities" was an idea inspired by the community health movement; "green cities," a similar concept, has emerged in recent years out of the bioregional movement. Green cities has a definite ecological focus. Bioregionalism is a philosophy which attempts to integrate human *culture* with *nature* by rediscovering and redefining the meaning of

THE MANDALA OF HEALTH

A Model of the Human Ecosystem

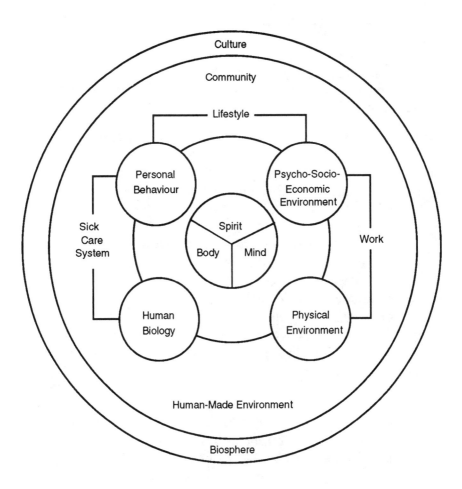

"community," "place" and "home" within specific regions. From a bioregional perspective, human settlements, including cities, need to develop within the capacities and resources of their own "life-spaces" as opposed to eating up other communities' "life-spaces." The green cities movement explores new patterns for production and consumption to make cities self-sustaining on the natural resources of the bioregion. It looks at new forms of transportation, food production, concepts of work, energy sources, waste renewal and the restoration of natural watersheds and wildlife within the city itself. The concept is not a utopian vision but a reality which urgently needs addressing. Cities are not going to stop growing. If there are no alternatives, cities will continue to pollute the atmosphere, spread out and pave the topsoils, and poison the waters with toxic waste.

The green city calls for a fundamental shift in how we view urban form. Rather than setting aside special areas for parks, we view the *entire* urban area as parkland and set aside areas for housing and industry designed to harmonize with the natural surroundings. The city is viewed as a living organism complete in its own survival capacity. It is made up of smaller cellular units — neighbourhood villages, each active in processing its own food, energy and waste. Some of the main concepts for a green city design include:

- self-sustaining: meeting its own needs from its own resources;
- non-polluting;
- recycling of waste for utilitarian purposes;
- conserving by minimizing waste and material consumption;
- ecological transportation: bicycle paths, walking, electric cars, rapid transit, sharing automobiles;
- urban planting: gardens and orchards woven into the urban fabric on vacant lots, street dividers, boulevards, front lawns;
- urban food production: using converted warehouses, greenhouses, empty lots;
- development of renewable energy sources — solar, biomass, other;
- ecological treatment of waste at the neighbourhood level;
- creation of wildlife habitats in the city by reclaiming marshes, lagoons, creeks and urban forests;
- learn about the indigenous plants and animals in our bioregion;
- awareness of the history of human cultures in our bioregion;

- restoration of the local rivers and watershed so they can be utilized safely for drinking, swimming and fishing;
- provision of a wide range of cultural and recreational activities which help bond people to place and community, and build local identity.

A useful tool for the green city is the ecological audit. The ecological audit takes stock of all the resources and potentials within a community and measures them for ecological efficiency. It might ask: what goods are being produced in the community? Are they "life-affirming" (healthy food, recycled materials) or "life-destroying" (overpackaged junk food, dangerous chemicals)? What chemicals are used in production and how are they disposed? What do we import and from where? What local opportunities exist for producing similar goods at home? What goods do we export and how far away are they shipped? How much money saved locally is reinvested in the community? How many businesses are locally owned? How many are franchises? How much money leaves the community? Where does our food originate? Can we grow locally what we now import, using new technologies? Is the food organic or chemically grown? What are the impacts on the soil of using these chemicals? What is the economics of the food we eat — are local farmers able to sustain themselves?

How much waste does our community produce, and what do we do with it? Can it be reprocessed locally through recycling, ecological water treatment? Where does our drinking water originate? What is the condition of our rivers and lakes? How can they be protected or restored from pollution? Where do building materials come from and what chemicals are used in their manufacture? What nonpolluting alternatives exist? What vacant buildings need to be restored or recycled for other uses? What are the costs of our transportation systems — counting auto pollution and energy depletion as well as capital costs? What renewable energy sources could be developed in our community?

The ecological audit is a tool to help communities see where they stand in relation to the goals of ecological efficiency and bioregional self-sufficiency. It helps a community determine areas for future development.

The green city movement is a recent phenomenon initiated by Peter Berg of Planet Drum Foundation in San Francisco in 1986. Some key references and follow-ups since then have been *A Green City Program* (1989); *Ecocity Berkeley* (1987); Green City Conference, Toronto (1989), which resulted in the book *Green Cities; Ecologically Sound Approachs to Urban Space* (1990); the International EcoCity Conference, Berkeley,

California (1990). Further references appear in the notes at the end of this chapter.[7]

Two eco-communities in Canada

On the steep forested slopes overlooking the Saanich Inlet, thirty-two kilometres north of Victoria, B.C., lies an old abandoned cement works known as Bamberton. It is here, at Bamberton, that plans are in progress to build an "eco-village" for about 12,000 people, using ecological principles and design guidelines to harmonize the built environment with nature. Covenants and by-laws will restrict the removal of trees and topsoil, and prohibit any use of pesticides or herbicides. Buildings and roads will be laid out in such a way as to least disturb the existing landscape and plant and animal life. Storm water will be treated through a natural purification system and the tertiary treatment of sewage will produce compost to be recycled back into the soil. Nearly 50 per cent of the 1,560 acre site is to be kept as green space with walking trails, nature sanctuaries and protected areas for native plants.

A consortium of trade unions has invested its pension funds in this development through South Island Development Co-op. The project also has social and economic goals built into the design. It is intended to be a *community*, complete with an interactive cultural life and a local economy which will provide jobs for at least one person per household. (Home-based businesses, telecommuting through a fibre optic grid set up in conjunction with BC Tel and light industries which produce and use environmental technologies, are envisioned.) The site layout is being developed through public workshops, a design charrette (a group of design specialists assembled to examine a problem) and a team of architects, engineers and planners including Andres Duany, who is noted for his pedestrian friendly, "traditional" town plans. (Refer to Chapter Seven for more about Duany's work.) The site layout will have village-type neighbourhoods linked to a vibrant town centre, all within walking distance. Narrow, windy roads are designed to encourage walking over driving. A minibus will pick people up at neighbourhood centres to further discourage use of cars.

Bamberton will have shops, hotels, plazas, restaurants, office space, light industry and an organically maintained golf course. The idea is to create a community which will provide a quality of life that meets people's daily needs and reduces the need to travel away from home; there is a conscious effort to cut down on carbon dioxide emissions in the atmosphere caused by cars. These are just a few of the hundreds of features being planned, including a Bamberton Nature Preservation Trust, energy efficient buildings, a variety of housing types and much more.

One aspect which seems underdeveloped is affordable housing — an issue which, in my mind, ought to receive high priority, given the high cost of housing in Victoria (third highest in Canada) and the inflationary pressures on the real estate market. The South Island developer's response to the need for affordable housing was to say that, by not needing a car (presumably he meant a second car), families will save some $5,000 a year in disposable income which could be applied to housing; also "granny flats" will be allowed to bring in extra income.[8] An innovative project such as this one, where building community is a key aim, ought surely to consider community-based models of housing (e.g., community land trusts, discussed in Chapter Five) which would keep house prices affordable for varying income groups. Nonetheless, Bamberton is a very interesting experiment to watch unfold in coming years. Will its ecological and social goals be fulfilled?

A second, very different, eco-village is being planned by a team of architects, planners and engineers from the University of Calgary, in cooperation with the city of Calgary and community residents. It is to be a demonstration project on a city-owned site — Inglewood — in east Calgary, close to the downtown. Inglewood is an urban residential neighbourhood adjacent to a bird sanctuary and across from a vacant Petro Canada refinery site. The project will be much smaller than Bamberton — about thirty-five to fifty units, compared to 4,900 units. There are interesting comparisons, however. Inglewood is part of the continuing research project Affordable-Sustainable-Community (ASC), which has a strong focus on community development, user design and community-based models for housing geared to affordability. Combining the goals of *affordability* and *sustainability* makes the project particularly interesting. The ecological components of the community design will include aqua-solar sewage treatment, separation of gray water, minimized energy consumption, composting, recycling and community gardens. A mix of housing types is being planned: cluster housing, cohousing with common living spaces and townhouses with energy conserving features. Meetings are proceeding with the City, private developers, interested private organizations such as the Rotary Club, and residents in the Inglewood community, with the purpose of establishing a partnership to see the project through.

Eco-village demonstration projects are occurring throughout Scandinavia. Some are new developments; others involve older urban districts which are being renewed ecologically using new technologies. Sweden,

Denmark, Norway and the Netherlands have all established national programs to provide financial and technical assistance to municipalitites for action research on urban ecology projects. A "Town Ecology" section at the Danish National Planning Laboratory monitors over 100 local urban ecology initiatives.[9]

Eco-technologies and Appropriate Development

With a bit of creativity we can find many opportunities within our own neighbourhoods to integrate the combined goals of sustainable production, local economic revitalization and community development. Alternative technologies are already providing a stimulus for the creation of new ecological enterprises — producing solar energy, converting biomass into high energy fuel, processing Canola grain into fuel oil, selling environmental household products and recycling businesses, to name a few. In Vancouver, Elson Hanson discovered he could mine the garbage sites of that city and make a profit. He drills for methane gas produced by rotting garbage in huge landfills. One landfill site alone has sixty gas wells.

Still we can go further. For example, the New Alchemy Institute in Cape Cod has developed a diversity of biotechnical systems for the decentralized and miniaturized production of local energy, food and sewage treatment. The systems are designed to work in remote communities as well as in urban neighbourhoods and could transform the total organization of cities into ecological organisms. The eco-city is comprised of diverse, connecting, small neighbourhood villages, each one reliant on decentralized, internal systems for waste disposal, waste renewal, energy and food production based at the urban street level. Old warehouses and factories are converted into centres for growing vegetables and raising poultry. Each street has a common collection tank for reprocessing organic waste into compost for neighbourhood farmers to use as fertilizer. Wet sewage is pumped into local greenhouses where water hyacinths and other plants feed off the nutrients while purifying the waste water for reuse by local residents.

Eco-technologies are based on knowing how natural systems integrate with each other to their *mutual* advantage. For example, lettuce, when irrigated with water in which catfish or tilapia fish live, produces 120 per cent higher yield, because nitrogen fish waste is highly nutritious for lettuce. Applying this knowledge, we can design urban farms to provide neighbourhood food which combine fish and vegetable farming within a closed, self-sustaining system. One proposal uses a converted three story warehouse fitted with solar panels on the roof to power inside lights for growing vegetables. On the main floor chickens are raised and allowed to roam freely among the catfish tanks. The fish water from the catfish tanks is pumped up to the next floor where it feeds tomatoes, peas and other vine plants growing hydroponically in the nutrient rich water which, in turn, is being purified by the plants growing in it and pumped back down into the fish tanks. Composting of animal and vegetable waste takes place in the basement where mushrooms are also grown.

One of the most interesting and promising experiments in local food production is in the northern Manitoba town of Flin Flon. Nearly 2,000 feet below ground level, flowers and vegetables are growing productively in abandoned mines which have been converted into greenhouses by the use of artificial light. The greenhouse mines do not require any extra heat, maintaining a constant temperature of seventy-three degrees Fahrenheit during the day when the lights are on and fifty-four degrees Fahrenheit at night when the lights are off. The plants love it — tomatoes are ripening in a short six weeks and roses are blooming beautifully. The success of this experiment could mean that northern Canadian bioregions will become self-sufficient in fruits and vegetables year round.

Ecological sewage treatment methods

A sustainable community looks for avenues where human development can be integrated with natural systems. A working example which I witnessed was the sewage purification greenhouse in the town of Sugar Bush, Vermont, which combined the ecological processing of human waste with an aquafarm enterprise (e.g., fish farming).[10] In the greenhouse, plants such as pussy willows, swamp alder, irises and water hyacinths were growing hydroponically with their roots reaching into the contaminated water pumped into the facility from sewage lagoons. Through a natural process the plants break down the poisonous pollutants in the water, such as ammonia and nitrogen. Within three to five days the water was purified to a higher standard than water treated with chemicals. Fish were being raised commercially in the clean water to produce added income. The project, monitored by Dr. John Todd, co-founder of the New Alchemy Institute, showed that sewage can be purified *simply, ecologically, locally,* and *inexpensively* compared with the millions spent on chemical treatment facilities, and the water is more pure than water treated with chemicals. In addition, an aquafarm attached to the greenhouse can provide an extra source of income for a community.

The success of this new eco-technology has attracted a write up in the October 1990 *National Geographic* and interest by a number of communities to set up their own systems. In 1989, Providence, Rhode Island, built a similar solar aquatic sewage treatment greenhouse to treat its industrial urban wastes.[11] The sewage is funnelled by gravity through a series of six foot diameter vats which are at different stages of the purification process. The sewage begins in the algae room where bacteria digests organic matter and converts ammonia into nitrates, upon which algae then grow and thrive. Zooplankton and snails feed on the algae/bacteria which is treating the waste. In the next phase, sewage runs through a marsh of grasses and rocks to take out the heavy metals. In the fish room, striped bass and tilapia eat/clean up the zooplankton and other microscopic animals in the water. A diversity of floating plants feeds off the remaining contaminants. In the final phase, the water goes through a polishing marsh to remove sand and fine particles.

In just four days, contaminated, carcinogenic industrial sewage has been converted into purified water by plants and animals feeding off it (and each other), and no chemicals have been added! The technology is so simple. Purification takes place the same way it does in the wild. Only instead of releasing phosphate laden sewage into our rivers and lakes, a system which only encourages algae to grow and choke off the oxygen supply to the fish (a major environmental problem), we encourage algae to grow in the sewage in the *treatment plant*, soaking up the phosphates they love — and then release *purified* water into our lakes so the fish will thrive. There are other spinoff benefits. At the sewage plant in Providence, plants at the end of the cycle are being harvested and composted. Other plants are being tested for their content of heavy metals such as mercury, cadmium, lead, copper, zinc and silver extracted by the plants' roots from the industrial sewage, with the hope that soon it may be possible to mine the precious metals collected in the roots. In Harwich, Cape Cod, another solar aquatic greenhouse has been built but this plant treats *septage* waste, the highly toxic output of septic tanks that is fifty to one hundred times more concentrated than sewage. The results show that this method is cheaper and more effective than conventional tertiary sewage treatment methods.

Some of the major advantages of the solar aquatic technology are that it can be used in northern climates; it is easy and quick to build; it can be flexible is size; it can be decentralized for use in neighbourhoods. Amazingly, the sewage does *not* stink (I can vouch for that) and even looks quite beautiful with all the flowers and vegetables blooming in the midst. The treatment plant in Providence services 150 households and is approximately eleven metres by forty metres in size — a small building. Cities could have this same technology in neighbourhoods, using the existing sewer system and pumping the sewage into dispersed greenhouses throughout the city. We could imagine indoor or outdoor swimming pools with greenhouses attached which would not only bring natural beauty to the surroundings, but could also grow food for a neighbourhood and kill contaminants from the pool water at the same time, instead of our current chlorination treatment which is damaging to people and the environment.

Another waste water treatment technology is currently being tested in California. In this case a special glue compound is dropped into waste water where it pulls together and coagulates all the heavy chemical pollutants and virus wastes into a solid ball, which then sinks to the bottom of the pond. The ball with chemicals attached is then filtered out and fired up in 2,000 degree Fahrenheit kilns. The end product is a concrete aggregate material which can be sold competitively for construction purposes. In contrast to the previous example, the process of waste water treatment is chemical, not biological. Still there are ecological advantages because waste is being recycled into usable materials, and water is being purified. In addition, the technology is designed especially for use at a small scale; a neighbourhood of 20,000 to 30,000 user households is the optimum size to achieve the highest benefits per cost.

The eco-technologies described above could be called "appropriate technologies" in the sense that Schumacher described — small scale, decentralized to the neighbourhood level, environmentally safe and geared to meeting community needs. Other "appropriate technologies" include simple, affordable machines which enable local people to produce cost efficiently on a small scale. A prime example is the small, eight inch diameter flour mill sitting in the window of the Tall Grass Prairie Bread Co. in the Wolseley neighbourhood in Winnipeg. This unobtrusive machine has sparked major changes in the bread production process which, in turn, have impacted on the local urban community *and* the local farm community. Ray Epp, part owner of the co-op bakery, describes the flour mill as being the prairie equivalent to Mahatma Gandhi's spinning wheel. By turning raw wheat into bread, local bakers gain control over both the quality and price of the flour they use and capture for the local economy a portion of the value added to bread, which is currently being drained into the coffers of large corporate milling companies.

Tall Grass Prairie Bread Company [12]

The bakery grew out of the vision of two women who loved to bake and cook, one having learned her skill while growing up on a Hutterite communal farm. The women were part of the Grain of Wheat church community which began baking bread out of a church basement and selling it on Saturday mornings to the community. A few years later, a group of families pooled their resources to purchase a neighbourhood bakery which was closing. What makes the Tall Grass Prairie Bread Co. unique is its commitment to local Manitoba farmers and local neighbourhood needs. From an ecological perspective, the bakery is an expression of the group's deep spiritual commitment to supporting sustainable land stewardship. Tall Grass Prairie Bread purchases only organically grown wheat, which it then grinds into fresh flour daily and bakes into wholesome bread.

Besides providing the neighbourhood with fresh, organic baking, the small scale flour mill has enabled the company to pay local farmers *triple* the going rate for their wheat — about six dollars a bushel. This fact introduces a further story about wheat prices and the milling industry in Canada.

Prior to the Canada/U.S. Free Trade Agreement there was a two price system for wheat operating in Canada: the Canada Wheat Board sold milling wheat to domestic mills for a price roughly double the export price. In exchange, domestic millers were protected from foreign competition. In 1988, in preparation for free trade, the two price system was abolished and the price paid to Canadian farmers for domestic milling wheat dropped to the world market level, about two dollars to two dollars and fifty cents a bushel. It also opened domestic mills to foreign competition — the Canadian mill, Robin Hood Multifoods of Canada, could now compete against its U.S. parent company, International Multifoods Incorp., based in Minneapolis. (Is this real competition, we may ask?) The abolition of the two price system resulted in a $250 million loss to Canadian farmers (and another $24.8 million loss as of January 1991), losses which taxpayers are now subsidizing through government safety net programs.[13] Milling companies might argue that *they* were subsidizing farmers before free trade by having to pay a higher than world price for wheat. Yet what is the true cost of growing wheat? Farmers can't make a living at current prices. It might more accurately be said that farmers are subsidizing the profits of milling companies. Milling companies have been expanding, merging and extending their control over the market, buying up bakeries and vertically integrating production activities. In 1988, in preparation for free trade, Maple Leaf Mills, one of the largest mills in Canada (owned by Canada Packers), formed Corporate Foods, a company which set about buying bakeries in Ontario, Quebec and Atlantic Canada. In three years the company has grown to be the 175th largest company (in terms of rate of profit) in Canada. This has been accomplished without incurring any debt. Where did all the capital and profits come from?[14]

With farmers receiving *one-third* what they got before free trade for their milling wheat, one might expect a similar drop in the price of flour or bread. This has not happened. Large milling companies are not passing on their cost reduction to consumers — flour and bread are being sold at about the same price as before free trade. In the meantime, farmers cannot sustain a livelihood on two dollars to two dollars and fifty cents a bushel and so are being subsidized through tax dollars.

This background on the milling industry and the price of wheat explains why a major goal of the Tall Grass Prairie Bread Co. is to pay farmers a fair price for wheat and do it without jeopardizing its business. The small flour mill has enabled the bakery to do just that. With its own flour mill, it can buy wheat *directly* from farmers, rendering large scale transportation systems and commercial flour mills unnecessary. This simple, affordable technology has allowed the bakery to direct the money it pays for grain and flour to *local* organic farmers, who are paid six dollars a bushel — three times the going rate! The bakery makes its flour for less money than it costs to buy flour from a commercial mill, and after it pays out fair wages for seven full-time job positions, it *still* makes a profit. With an initial investment of $30,000, the bakery has managed in one year to gross $200,000 in revenues and pay out $100,000 in wages. The bread is sold at comparable prices to similar breads sold in supermarkets, but when you buy it from Tall Grass Prairie Bakery, you know it is fresh from land to mouth and supporting organic farmers. Consumers are happy, farmers are happy and the workers at the bakery are happy. The success has attracted national media attention and an interest in starting similar businesses elsewhere, in both urban and rural areas.

In summary, the Tall Grass Prairie Bread Co. is a shining example of how a simple but appropriate technology can trigger structural changes in our economic, social and ecological systems. The lessons are fourfold. First, the small flour mill helps to cut costs to local bakers, making their operations viable in the competitive global market. Second, it builds connections between rural farmers and urban producers of food, while keeping wheat-flour-bread production within the bioregion. Third, the bakery is an example of community economic development creating seven new full-time jobs in the neighbourhood by meeting local needs with local resources. Last and most important, the bakery points to a future way for struggling organic farmers to become self-sustaining through linking with urban producers directly and *sharing* in the wealth produced, to the mutual benefit of all.

CONCLUSION

In summary, ecological development can only truly be embraced within the context of a community-oriented, bioregional model of decentralized, human scale development which respects the balances of nature. There are five points to note in this regard.

First, the self-reliant community — which consumes what it produces and produces what it consumes, which replenishes itself with its own reprocessed wastes and which extracts the maximum work out of its own existing resources — is contributing to the sustainability of the planet by reducing pollution and depletion of the earth's resources.

Second, a decentralized development which uses a scaled down technology to produce smaller amounts for fewer people also disperses the impacts of development more evenly throughout the biosphere, giving nature time to absorb and reprocess the waste.

Third, a neighbourhood village economy, which provides employment and goods for people where they live, cuts down on traffic in the city, just as local production reduces the need for transporting goods, thus saving on fuel and reducing auto pollution.

Fourth, sustainable growth focuses on expanding the household or informal economy, since this is the level most committed to nurturing and *life-sustaining* activities — child care, care of the elderly, recreation, schooling, health, food consumption and distribution, recycling garbage.

Fifth, the informal economy composed of co-operatives, volunteer activities, and small, owner operated businesses, has an ingrained feeling for people and place and therefore is the sector most compatible to sustainable development. Profits of businesses in the informal economy, though needed to maintain operations, are often secondary to social goals or the gaining of personal fulfillment from meaningful work. Large corporations, in contrast, are dedicated to the grow-or-die ethic, to making money for money's sake by compounding capital and competing for control over local, regional, national and world markets.

Ecological development reminds us, perhaps more than any other theme in this book, that we cannot continue with our current way of thinking — a global ethic has to enter into all our local affairs.

ENDNOTES

1. Brewster Kneen, *From Land to Mouth* (Toronto: NC Press Ltd., 1989), p. 60.
2. Ibid. pp. 59–60.
3. Ibid. p. 39.
4. Reported by Pat Mooney at a lecture, University of Manitoba, 1986.
5. Kneen, *Land to Mouth*, p. 59.
6. For a more complete story of the Seikatsu Club, refer to *Green Business: Hope or Hoax?*, Christopher Plant and Judith Plant, eds. (Gabriola Island, B.C.: New Society Publishers, 1991).
7. Further publications on Green City include: *Home! A Bioregional Reader* (1990); *Raising the Stakes,* a journal published by Planet Drum (1991 issue on Green City); *The Urban Ecologist* newsletter (P.O. Box 10144, Berkeley, California, 94709); *Green City* quarterly (published by the Ottawa-Carleton chapter of the Green Party); article "Green City" in *The Canadian City*, Kent Gerecke, ed. (Montreal: Black Rose Books, 1991); the report, "Eco-villages and Sustainable Commumities" (see Endnote 9 below).
8. From a report on a public meeting in the *Bamberton News* (Vol. 1, no. 2, November 1991).
9. For more information on eco-communities refer to, "Eco-villages and Sustainable Communities," a report written for the Gaia Trust, available from Context Institute, Box 11470, Bainbridge Island, W.A., 98110.
10. The waste treatment greenhouse was a pilot project set up in 1987 by Dr. John Todd and associates to test the viability of solar aquatics greenhouses in cold weather. It proved successful and has since been dismantled.
11. An interview with Dr. John Todd by David Cayley on the CBC Radio program, "Ideas" tells about the Providence solar aquatic sewage treatment plant described in *Green Business: Hope or Hoax?*, pp. 124–132.
12. Information comes from interviews with Ray Epp, media coverage and newspaper clippings.
13. "Wheat Prices Forced Down," in *The Manitoba Co-operator*, 10 January 1991.
14. *The Globe and Mail Report on Business Magazine*, July 1991, p. 66.

Chapter Five

Attaining Community Control

No organic improvement [of the city] is possible without a reorganization of its processes, functions, and purposes, and a redistribution of its population, in units that favor two-way intercourse, I-and-Thou relationships, and local control over local needs....*It is not merely the pattern of the city itself, but every institution, organization and association composing the city, that will be transformed by this development.*

Lewis Mumford
The City in History

5

Attaining Community Control

Community control means that the decision-making processes and organizational structures within a community are especially designed to give all members of a community the power and means to manage their own affairs. Since society is primarily organized on a top-down basis, community control will necessarily require a transformation from hierarchical to nonhierarchical structures so as to allow for the maximum participation by community members in the decision making and development process.

The goal of community control introduces into developing sustainable communities a political component, founded on the belief that people have the right and capacity to manage their own affairs. This goal deals directly with the issue of power in society — who holds it, how is it distributed among the people, and what is its impact on the community's long-term security. An important precondition for a community's ability to affect its future and meet the needs of its members is control over the allocation and development of community resources. Because power in today's society is centralized and concentrated at the top, local control will require major changes in our institutions to facilitate a transfer of power from top to bottom, from central to decentralized control, from bureaucracy to grassroots management, and from outside ownership and control of capital to local ownership and control of capital.

I have argued the need for communities to become economically self-reliant. A decentralized, community power base is the political structure needed to support a community-based economy, much the same way that centralized power is now used to support national and global economic goals. The role of central government, particulary since the Second World War, has been to pave the way for the accumulation and concentration of capital by big corporations through measures such as Canada Mortgage and Housing Corporation programs, tax incentives and national subsidies for industry, free trade agreements, and, when necessary, through military force, such as in the recent war on Iraq initiated in part to protect oil supplies for the West. So tied to the global economy and big business is the central government and its bureaucracy that to propose a power transfer to local communities is tantamount to calling for the overthrow of the status quo power structure. It is no wonder that aboriginal people, women and other groups meet with such resistance when they begin to assert demands for self-determination, for equal pay, or for rights to their traditional lands.

There is a widening gulf between what communities need and want for their long-term security and what central government is pursuing for its global agenda. The massive James Bay hydro power project may serve the interests of the Québec government, but its effect on the sustainability of the environment and communities in the region has been devastating. Likewise, the Free Trade Agreement may benefit some large corporations which can enter the American market, but for thousands of formerly profitable local businesses, the competitive grow-or-die ethic forced upon them by free trade has resulted in bankruptcy.

More and more we are witnessing a distrust of and grassroots re-action against the actions of big government. The fiasco surrounding the Meech Lake negotiations was a case in point, when it became clear to a majority of Canadians that the federal government was playing a self-serving, mean-spirited game of divide and conquer politics, manipulating negotiations and closing its ears to the public will. Eleven men deciding the fate of a nation behind closed doors appeared an arrogant abuse of power which angered most Canadians, according to polls. The government's action showed how far we have strayed from the goal of participatory democracy and community involvement.

This chapter looks at the development of community power from the inside-out, starting with the individual, moving outward to the group, the community as a whole, and finally considers some organizational models for community control. These perspectives are presented in a sequence with the headings: (1) Personal power; (2) Power with others; (3) Community power: lost and found; and (4) Claiming power — models for community control. The chapter concludes with accounts of three specific communities and their struggles for control over local resources and future development.

PERSONAL POWER

Power in society takes many forms. Authoritative powers are granted to those who hold exclusive claims to expert knowledge, wealth and privilege — professionals, political elites, corporate owners. These persons, mainly white middle-class males, are propped up by our social, political, and economic institutions (family, schools, churches, workplaces). The majority of us are always under threat of being fired from our jobs, being ordered to behave, or being forced to bear the negative effects of development imposed on our communities by outside interests. In contrast, there is a different kind of power residing in communities — a power which finds expression in bonding, in history, in community identity, and in pooling resources.

The first kind of power is what feminist psychologist and author Starhawk calls *power-over-others*, a coercive power based on structures of hierarchy and domination. The second type of power manifests itself as a *power-with-others*, generated by people acting together and identifying with a common purpose. Underlying this collective power is yet another type of power, a "power within," a *personal power* residing within each of us as self-awareness and the power to act for oneself. These two non-hierarchical powers — the *personal* power within and the *collective* power of acting with others, are fundamentally different from the hierarchical and dominating powers which govern society. Where domination humiliates, dehumanizes and engenders feelings of helplessness and dependency in people, empowerment through self-knowledge (power within) and active participation with others (power with) liberates people from feelings of dependency. The difference is between the bottom-up and top-down exercise of power, beginning with individuals and their feelings of self-worth.

The process of *community* empowerment draws on both the power within and the *power-with-others*. But there are difficulties in bringing these powers to the surface. The downtrodden, who have been marginalized, alienated and told they are lazy and worthless, become resigned to conditions of dependency, unwilling to take risks, believing they are unworthy of a better life. At that point, the structures of domination have been internalized as low self-esteem and a lack of belief in one's own ability to affect positive change in life; access to the power within is blocked.

Personal empowerment starts with an awakening to *self-knowledge* and the realization of the value of the individual's life experience and potential to affect the world. This self-knowledge seldom emerges in isolation, but is usually sparked by an interactive process of *identifying with other people in a common struggle*. Others of like mind and like situation serve as a kind of *mirror* to reflect back images of who we are and what we might become. In this way, a group process which allows members to interact and participate with one another on an equal footing can help to facilitate "self-discovery" and the realization of one's own potential to act and affect change in one's life.

The dynamics of power within and power-with-others is the basic working principle of *self-help*. To better understand how self-help works to empower and transform, it is instructive to look at the model of Alcoholics Anonymous (AA), the largest self-help group in the world with over twenty million members. Prior to the founding of AA in 1930, there was no successful cure for the disease of alcoholism, which led its victims into insanity or death. The turning point came when psychiatrist Carl Jung noted that, in rare cases, the craving for alcohol disappeared *after there had been a personal spiritual transformation* in the alcoholic, or, in terms of this discussion, when the alcoholic had been inspired by a "power-within." It was later discovered that this power within could be evoked by a collective process of identifying with other alcoholics. Identifying with others is like seeing oneself in a mirror for the first time — alcoholics became *aware* of their own condition, a first step toward change. Where many alcoholics had failed in efforts to quit drinking in isolation, they gained power to do what they could never do before by joining with others in a *common struggle*.

An important discovery of AA self-help was that, for the power within to be replenished, it must be shared. It is a basic principle of self-help that in helping others we help ourselves, otherwise known as the principle of *mutual aid*. Thus by reaching out to aid others (an action involving self-sacrifice), individuals can gain a sense of belonging which is a wellspring of transforming power to change the conditions of their *own* existence.

Personal power changes Alkali Lake community

A community relies on the strength of its individual members. Personal empowerment is, therefore, a necessary precondition to community development. The story of the Alkali Lake Indian Band in northern British Columbia gives us a dramatic illustration of the relationship between personal and community empowerment. After suffering years of humiliation and mistreatment by whites, the native people had turned to alcohol as an escape. By 1960 there was 100 per cent alcoholism on the reserve, along with rampant crime, murders and mass unemployment. The elders had left the community because of its deteriorated and demoralized state. Then in 1971 one woman made a decision to quit drinking. Five days later her husband also quit, and after a while he persuaded someone else to quit. Together they started an AA group.

With new found confidence rooted in sobriety, the woman secured a government grant to set up a store on the reserve, replacing a white man's store which was siphoning off the band's welfare money. Soon afterward her husband took over as chief and food vouchers were disbursed instead of welfare money in an effort to stop people from spending their income on alcohol. The changes sparked resistance, but gradually the ones who had quit drinking persuaded others to quit, until one by one the residents turned dry.

In 1975, 40 per cent of the band's members had quit drinking; by 1979 over 60 per cent were sober; finally, by 1985 the band had reached 95 per cent sobriety! Transformation had become a *community process*. Every time a member left the reserve for three weeks of alcohol treatment, the others would paint and repair the new AA member's house for the return to a new life. All the while, the reserve's economy was developing. The band built its own school and hired its own teachers, who spoke the Shuswap language; they founded an agricultural co-op, a logging company, a horticultural collective and a carpentry business. Over time unemployment turned around from 75 per cent unemployment to 75 per cent employment!

What happened at Alkali Lake was the linking of personal and social empowerment to revitalize an entire community — spiritually, morally, culturally and economically. Personal empowerment had to come first, and, from that, community economic development followed. A holistic model for development based on native traditions has evolved from the process, which the band is now sharing with other native communities.

Holistic Development Model of the Alkali Lake Indian Band

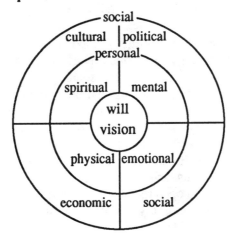

The model illustrates that at the centre of development is individual will and vision — the powers within needed for the spiritual, mental, physical and emotional development of the individual. These qualities together make up the cultural, political, social and economic resources of a community. Community or social development, thus, is a natural outgrowth or extension of personal development, built upon the well-being and maturity of individuals and their collective will and vision.

POWER WITH OTHERS

Community power is different in essence from the hierarchical power which runs our society. Where the pyramid structures of bureaucracy are designed to take power away from the many and give it to the few, community power gains its strength by *power sharing* among as many community members as possible — broadening its power base through bonding, networking and coalition building. Active citizen participation occurs, not in the voting box once every five years, but in the continuing efforts and struggles of thousands of community groups. The true power cells of a community are its movement and pressure groups (e.g., women's groups, peace activists, residents' groups); community service organizations (e.g., daycares, drop ins, transition centres, shelters); single issue groups (e.g., fighting to stop a freeway, mosquito spraying or destruction of an historic building).

Through co-operation at crucial times, by networking and forming coalitions and alliances, these energies multiply and take on a life of their own to become a major force in the shaping of communities. For example, after a Toronto hotel fire killed ten residents, over thirty organizations came together to form the Rupert Hotel Coalition, an advocacy group for securing, upgrading and appropriately managing rooming houses in the core area.

In Winnipeg, a broad coalition group called "Choices" organized in early 1991 to voice the angry concerns of hundreds of groups and individuals committed to fighting for social justice. The coalition has staged guerrilla theatre-type actions and protests over such things as the province allowing construction of a high-rise seniors complex under a flight path close to the airport; the granting to Ducks Unlimited a permit to build a head office and commercial centre at the ecologically sensitive and "protected" Oak Hammock Marsh; government cutbacks in education, social programs and inner city funding. The coalition holds meetings weekly for an open membership steering committe, while larger meetings are planned monthly. There is an action line which informs people about all upcoming "events." So far, the coalition is growing in numbers, energy and grassroots power.

Every city can tell similar stories of collective community action for different situations — poverty groups joining with housing groups, women's groups joining with ecology groups, and so on. The town of Sudbury, Ontario, faced with economic and environmental crises, formed a group called Sudbury 2000 made up of dozens of community organizations, union groups and local politicians to create a vision and action strategy for Sudbury's future. A sustainable development plan for Sudbury was one of the results. In ten years, because of broad, grassroots community involvement, the town has significantly revitalized its economy and environment.

Behind nearly every successful community struggle lies a wealth of collective energy drawn from a coalition of residents, volunteers, activists and community groups. Looked at this way, community power is a power shared among many. Its strength lies in the horizontal connections among many people and many groups. The key processes are networking, partnerships, co-operation and interdependence. The structures are open, shifting, spontaneous, and nonhierarchical. Contrary to the belief that power sharing means giving up power, power sharing means gaining *more* power by building solidarity, vision and community purpose.

To this point, we have been speaking about power shared at the community level. Within individual groups, power sharing calls for new nonhierarchical structures and group processes for decision making. The structure which best encourages equal sharing is the *circle*; the decision making process which best encourages equal power sharing is *consensus*. Circles and consensus are complementary to each other. They are widely used by women's groups and native groups as an alternative to hierarchical organizational models, and they deserve serious attention and analysis.

In a circle everyone faces each other. No one is above, below, in front of, or invisible to anyone else. Meetings held in a circle give a clear message that everyone counts; everyone's thoughts and opinions are of equal value. The circle is an important structure for empowering people to participate in group discussions, particularly when the group is a mix of those who, on the one hand, have been conditioned to value their own ideas and take charge (people with money, whites, men, professionals) and those who, on the other hand, have been conditioned to think their ideas are valueless and who therefore withdraw (poor people, women, minorities and lay people).

Using a circle, discussions can take place in a round where each person is given the opportunity to speak in turn, uninterrupted. Native sweat lodges use a variant of this model when they pass around a rattle and let the various holders have the chance to express themselves in whatever way inspires them. How we listen and pay attention to each other in a circle is as important as what we say; it reflects our respect and regard for the other person.

Consensus decision making further serves to put into practice the idea that everyone's opinions are of equal value. Consensus is founded on the traditional Quaker belief that each person's experience holds a *piece* of the truth and that only by welding together the *differences* of opinion (even when they seem to contradict) can we arrive at a greater truth, a unified vision. Consensus is the most democratic, grassroots form of decision making because it allows all people, whether they are in a majority or a minority, an equal say in the political process and its outcome. Compared to majority rule, which allows 51 per cent of the population to impose its will on the remaining 49 per cent, consensus strives toward a solution supported by all. In a consensus model, if individuals have a strong objection, especially an ethical one, they have the power to block a decision from proceeding. In most cases, however, individuals will "step aside" and let a decision go forward as long as they do not feel that the decision is wrong and fundamentally damaging to the group itself.

Consensus has its challenges — it takes time, flexibility and creativity to work out a solution satisfactory to all. Yet once made, the decision has the best chance of being implemented effectively because it is backed by community support, commitment and an understanding of the issues. When worked at in earnest, consensus has a return which binds a group together with a common vision lasting beyond the issue of the moment. It is the *process* of working through conflict which builds unity, not any particular outcome. Where majority rule works by suppressing conflict and by ignoring or denying minority positions, consensus brings conflict to the surface to be debated openly and worked through to a resolution.

Consensus is used in large and small groups, but to work well, relies on participants' common understanding about helpful ways of relating. These are:

1. Respect for differences and other points of view.
2. Honesty and openness in dealing with the issue at hand.
3. An ability to listen well and not be defensive or rigid in one's own position.

4. Courage to express what one honestly believes.
5. Commitment to working in good faith toward a shared common goal.
6. Willingness to let go of the idea that you have the "right" answer and to try out new positions.
7. An awareness and sensitivity to the group's conscience.

In summary, the use of circles and consensus decision making in group process provides a tool for equalizing power relationships. Not all community groups are set up this way, and many end up alienating the very people they set out to serve simply because their top-down structures are intimidating or inaccessible. In a world dominated by "power over" institutions, our biggest challenge is to find new ways to eradicate the structures of domination themselves. If we cannot, then those who have been victimized by the "system" will become oppressors in turn, perpetuating a replay of domination and violence among people. In Starhawk's words, "If we are to survive, the question becomes: how do we overthrow, not those presently in power, but the principle of power over?"

COMMUNITY POWER: LOST AND FOUND

If communities are to take over the ownership and management functions currently provided by professionals, bureaucrats and absentee owners, they will need to build their own power bases, drawing on broad neighbourhood support and citizen groups. Citizen participation thus becomes the focal point for achieving community power — but community power is not easy to resurrect. Social critic and theoretician Murray Bookchin notes that the rise of modern civilization with its hierarchical institutions has meant the *death of citizenship*. The development of cities as centres for mass production and consumption has gone hand in hand with the emergence of peoples dispossessed and alienated from work, from connections to the land and from meaningful social relationships.

The thrust of modern development has been toward increasing globalization and integration of world markets, with political power evolving along complementary lines. The result is a decline of local political involvement (only 30 per cent of Canadian citizens vote in municipal elections) and a loss of what it means to be an active citizen in a community. The impact of citizen withdrawal from local affairs and social responsibility has been the creation of a vacuum quickly filled by an expanding, powerful and de-personalized government bureaucracy charged with regulating our lives, from our activities in our homes and neighbourhoods to our care for our children.

To discover the roots of community power we need to go back to the medieval city, whose most outstanding feature was the exercise of local power, the rights to self-jurisdiction and self-administration. The medieval city itself was composed of various independent communities which co-existed in different areas radiating from a centre. The economy was operated by various collective enterprises — craft guilds, which were brotherhoods of artisans in the same trade. Production was the responsibility of the guild and considered a social duty. The individual artisan produced for his guild and was appreciated by people who knew the value of his work, as opposed to production for a mass market. In accord with the goal of self-reliance, goods could only be offered for export to allied communities *after* the local community was fully served.

The medieval city is an example of a noncentralist city-state, a city incorporated as a federation of small independent village communities. We can begin to imagine at this point what a noncentralist modern city might look like, with neighbourhood associations and community organizations empowered to maintain local control and self-management and at the same time belong to a greater alliance with other neighbourhoods which together make up the whole city. This was, in fact, the way cities operated in North America until the nineteenth century.

The history of North American settlement patterns shows that some of the earliest towns were settled, as in Europe, first as independent community villages by associations of family groups, religious communities and cultural groupings. These were incorporated as independent political units in the seventeenth century and evolved into neighbourhoods as cities expanded. It was in the nineteenth century, after the American Revolution, that villages lost their political autonomy and came under the control of central governments. In 1854, Philadelphia gained dominion over twenty-eight districts and townships; the same occurred for Boston, Detroit, and New York. Prior to that, independent communities held democratic town hall meetings to decide on local affairs, and they had political relations with one another. By consolidating neighbouring villages under one government, the central downtown soon became the focus for commercial development to the detriment of outlying neighbourhoods, which were impoverished by their loss of economic and political control. The annexation of neighbourhoods to a central government had the additional intended effect of stifling local citizen politics for many years to come.

The loss of neighbourhood control was further eroded by turning municipalities themselves into legal creatures of the province or state, thus distancing local communities further from the centre of power. Community concerns, two levels removed, could be easily disregarded by the people on high. A current example is the Manitoba government's restructuring of Winnipeg's municipal power base. With one stroke the province has reduced by one-half the number of city councillors representing people, and realigned municipal power to favor suburbs over inner city neighbourhoods. (The original proposal was to divide the city into pie-shaped wards radiating out from the centre. A number of communities threatened to break away from Winnipeg if their neighbourhoods were chopped up in this manner.)

Despite the past and present efforts of central governments to disempower communities, grassroot energies have continued to grow, motivated by the tensions of central and local interests. Community power began to resurface with noticeably renewed energy in the 1960s, which saw a revival of local politics in neighbourhoods across North America. Neighbourhood organizations formed to fight commercial developments which displaced housing and forced people out of their communities. They fought centrally planned urban renewal projects which tore apart neighbourhoods, separated families and placed poor people in high-rise ghettos which became dangerous places to live. They fought the imposition of freeways which split apart their neighbourhoods, forcing thousands out of their homes with no place to go. The political struggles of neighbourhoods in the 1960s stand as witness to the deep-seated conflict between the needs of local communities and the economic/ political interests of a centralized power structure.

One of the positive forces to emerge out of the conflicts of the 1960s was what might be seen as a new form of community government — the neighbourhood or community corporation — a democratic, grassroots organization set up to take over the management and control of local programs, including the provision of housing, social services, local planning and administration of community grants and loan funds. There are all types and sizes of community development corporations (CDCs) and neighbourhood associations, some more comprehensive and grassroots-based than others. In the 1980s and 1990s many of these corporations incorporated community economic development into their mandate as part of a sustainable community development strategy to improve conditions of poverty and unemployment. Today, we find a renewed interest in community power and tools for community control, especially the CDC.

CLAIMING POWER: MODELS FOR COMMUNITY CONTROL

Many organizations and community actions contribute toward developing community control. The list includes community development corporations, neighbourhood committees, nonprofit groups, land trusts, cooperatives, community banks, revolving loan funds, community run services, community-based businesses, government supports, umbrella organizations, self-help groups, sweat equity housing and volunteer organizations. The following sections look at four of these models — the community land trust, community loan fund, co-operative enterprise (in particular the worker co-op), and the neighbourhood/community development corporation — as examples of a growing experiment in establishing new, *decentralized,* and *grassroots* forms of ownership and decision making. The four models represent breakthroughs in terms of community control over land, capital, employment and delivery of services.

Control of land and housing — the community land trust

Private ownership of land plays a determining role in the development of communities and the provision of housing. More and more, however, the system is failing. In Toronto it is estimated there are at least 20,000 homeless people living on the streets in doorways, under bridges, next to luxury condominiums and a multimillion dollar domed stadium. This disparity is not surprising: it exists in every major urban centre and is a logical manifestation of the modern corporate city. The corporate city is a place where profits come first and people come last; where urban space is shaped, not by history or culture, but by the commercial dealings and transactions of developers out to make a profit. Land in the city is treated like any other market commodity, to be bought and sold to the highest bidder. Because land is a scarce resource, it commands increasingly high prices as urban populations grow.

Owning and selling property is big business for the speculator, the developer, the landlord — even the home-owner and tax department want a piece of the increased value. As a result, many lower income inner city residents and landlords have been pressured into selling their properties to developers to build commercial megaprojects or into selling to an upwardly mobile professional class which wants to buy into

110

a neighbourhood and convert existing dwellings into trendy houses and condominiums. In either case, the net effect is a loss of affordable housing in the inner city and the break up of long time, stable, lower income communities.

What happens to those left in the neighbourhood who can't afford to pay the increased taxes on their homes caused by escalating land prices, or who can't afford to pay the cost of increased rent? Many end up in social housing or on the street. If they don't voluntarily leave their communities, they will, in all likelihood, be forced out or locked out by the actions of newly formed property owner associations whose intent is to protect property values by "cleaning up" the neighbourhood — ridding it of poor people, social housing, hostels, prostitutes and homeless people — and seeing that no future social housing is built in the area. Examples of this NIMBY phenomenon (Not In My Back Yard) can be drawn from hundreds of neighbourhoods across North America, from Cabbagetown in Toronto to Kitsilano in Vancouver.

It might be argued that property owner associations are, themselves, a form of community control. We need then to ask, "Control for whose benefit?" It is certainly not for the people in the community most in need. Community control is especially needed for those who traditionally *do not* have access to political power, the ones who are shut out, shunted about and left without adequate and secure housing.

At the root of increasing land costs are private land ownership and profiteering from land as an exchange commodity. *The ideal solution is for a community to collectively own its own land.* In fact, we see this happening more and more with the growth of the land trust movement and, especially, *community land trusts.* In the U.S. today, new land trusts are forming every week; in 1987 three of these were given special merit awards by the United Nations. In early 1991, there were forty-two community land trusts in the U.S. which owned, managed and developed land in urban neighbourhoods, with another fifty-eight groups in the start up phase.[1]

A community land trust (CLT) is land held in common by a community for use by that community *in perpetuity.* How it works is that parcels of land, or, in some cases, whole neighbourhoods, are either donated or purchased by a community group and put into a land trust. The land is then leased out, typically for ninety-nine years, to members of the community who agree to *use* the land for neighbourhood housing (if the CLT is in an urban area) or perhaps farming (if the CLT is in a rural area) — depending on the goals of the land trust group. This chapter focuses on urban CLTs with specific reference to provision of affordable housing.

To begin the process, a CLT organization is created and a membership base in the community is established.[2] The next step for the CLT is to acquire land. In many cases, abandoned or run down properties in a neighbourhood are targeted for acquisition because they can be purchased cheaply (sometimes sold to the group for one dollar by the city) and because they need redevelopment. The CLT may act as developer, constructing new housing or rehabilitating existing homes in the trust, or it may work with nonprofit developers to do the same work. A CLT may also put together a financial package to allow prospective home-owners to do their own rehabilitation work. When the construction or rehabilitation of the houses is completed, homes are sold by the trust to first time homebuyers.

The house is sold but the land is not — *the land is kept as the property of the CLT*. By separating the value of the house from the value of its land (owned by the CLT), the market/purchase value of the house is substantially reduced, enabling families on low income to become *home*-owners, for the first time. At the same time, through community *land* ownership, the neighbourhood (or the portion owned by the CLT) is protected from speculators — outside business people who buy up properties and hold on to them, sometimes for years — allowing them to deteriorate until land values go up and then selling them for a profit. Speculators do nothing to improve the neighbourhood residents' living conditions. By contrast, CLT properties are committed to productive *use* by neighbourhood residents — buildings are upgraded, families are housed, and a neighbourhood is given new life.

The CLT is a unique model for balancing community interests with individual interests through a combination of community and private ownership. Because of the *shared* property interests (the individual owns the house; the community owns the land beneath it), the relationship between the individual and the CLT needs to be carefully spelled out in a *ground lease*. Generally the ground lease requires the person using the land to pay the CLT a single lease fee, based on the value of the land alone — a tax, as it were, separate from any improvements which may have been added by the leaseholder. The lease fee is usually a nominal amount, enough to cover taxes and minor administrative expenses. The leaseholder *owns* the house and improvements, but not the land. If a leaseholder/home-owner wants to sell the house, the CLT has the first option to purchase at the original purchase price (plus the value of improvements added by the home-owner) or at an agreed upon *limited*

112

rate of profit accruing to the home-owner. CLT houses thus revert back to the land trust and are sold at the same affordable price to other CLT members. (It should be noted that CLT membership is open to all community residents.)

One of the great benefits of the CLT model, winning it favor among social granting agencies, is that it can build *permanent affordable housing* in a neighbourhood. *Permanent* affordability is protected in two ways: (1) by restricting the amount of profit which can be gained from resale of houses in the trust and (2) by removing lands from the speculative market, placing them in a trust where they cannot be sold, but instead must be kept for use by the community in perpetuity. In other words, *community control* is built into the provision of housing. Other nonprofit development groups may be able to build affordable housing, but they haven't the means to control what happens to the buildings in five, ten or twenty years. As a result, many affordable housing units get lost in the market turnover when residents sell their properties. Chuck Collin's story is common.

Chuck Collins is a housing activist and a CLT advisor with the Institute for Community Economics. In 1983 he worked for a nonprofit organization in Springfield, Massachusetts, which purchased vacant homes from the city, rehabilitated them using donated labour, financial donations from individuals and churches, low interest loans, and government grants — whatever money, materials and labour the organization could get to reduce the cost of housing to low income people. In one case, the organization purchased a house for $20,000, and, after it added some $30,000 in direct and indirect community investment (grants, donations, volunteer labour, etc.), it sold the house to a first time home buyer for $30,000. One year later, that same property came onto the market for $129,000! After all the work and investment the community had put into making the house affordable, it was lost as an affordable house. Yet the story doesn't end here. After the initial boom, which saw neighbourhood housing prices skyrocket, there came a bust. The market took a downturn and people began to disinvest in the community. Today that same property has become a "crack" house used for illegal drug dealings.

By contrast, under a community land trust, land is removed from the cyclical boom-and-bust pressures of the real estate market, from control by outside developers, absentee landlords and speculators who push up the value of land beyond what people living in a community can afford. It also puts caring residents into the houses and gives them community support (classes on doing home repairs, on budgeting, etc.), to ensure that the community investment will be maintained over time. The CLT model thus helps to stabilize a neighbourhood and *gives a community control over the future development and planning of the land in the interest of the entire community.*

It should be mentioned that CLTs can work with different types of housing. Often they lease land to housing co-operatives (collectively owned housing), a set-up whereby residents, working together, manage a multiple unit housing complex. Many CLTs have policies that restrict housing in the trust to people of low and middle income. For example, the Good News Housing CLT in Providence, Maine is set up to help families with incomes of less than $25,000 buy up houses co-operatively. The Cedar Riverside land trust in Minneapolis, which covers an entire neighbourhood, leases land specifically to build housing for low and lower middle income people (with enough flexibility to allow residents whose incomes improve over time to stay in the area). With this type of control, choice areas, such as the Cedar Riverside neighbourhood near the University of Minneapolis, are protected from gentrification (the movement of middle class households into lower income neighbourhoods, displacing people and eroding affordable housing) as the community undergoes revitalization. Low income residents have a security of tenure that they would lack, if left to the open market.

While there are many types of land trusts being formed, from stewardship trusts (e.g., Turtle Island Earth Stewards in B. C.) to agricultural trusts (e.g., Marin Agricultural Land Trust), the neighbourhood/community land trust model is of special importance to people wanting to preserve and revitalize existing communities in the context of a changing city. A summary of the advantages include:

- protection from outside land speculation by removing land from the market.
- provision of affordable housing by selling houses separate from land.
- provision of *permanent* affordable housing through control over the resale of houses.
- strategic community control over the land use planning and future development in a neighbourhood.

The story of the United Hands Land Trust (*Manos Unidos* in Spanish) in the Kensington area of northeast Philadelphia is told at the end of this chapter, as an example of a CLT's work in turning around one of the most run down areas in the city. There are two other CLTs in particular — Milton Park community in Montreal and Cedar Riverside community in Minneapolis — which stand out as models for community control in the urban context. Their stories, also included at the end of this chapter, show the scope of community power and active citizen politics in claiming ownership and control over land and housing. Both have successfully saved their neighbourhoods from the wrecker's ball, restored homes in the area and kept the price of housing affordable for low income residents, while adjacent lands were gentrified over the last ten years.

Community loan funds — gaining access to capital

In our society, you need money to make money. While extended credits, not to mention government subsidies, are made available to large manufacturing companies, small scale producers and self-employed individuals often have a tough time securing even small amounts of credit for their businesses. And if you happen to be one of society's poor who does not own a car, a house or other material possessions deemed to be collateral, don't hold your breath waiting for a bank loan to start a business. Put simply, banks discriminate against poverty, which means that certain groups — women, minority groups, handicapped people, new immigrants — are restricted from equal access to capital.

In recent years, community-based revolving loan funds have emerged to fill the gap left by traditional lending institutions. The clients are community members who do not fit the mainstream and are considered too high risk by traditional lenders. In most community loan funds, finance capital is gathered from a variety of sources — foundations, corporations, labour unions, churches, government — and lent out, usually in small amounts (under $10,000) and often at below market rates, to finance initiatives which will benefit a community. As the loans are paid back, the incoming money is reinvested in new community-based enterprises.

There are hundreds of community loan funds operating around the world, each with a different scope and purpose. Each community loan fund will be set up differently, depending on circumstance, but despite differences in structure, their basic concept remains the same — to finance enterprises which are deemed beneficial to a community or neighbourhood, but which would otherwise be blocked from access to financing.

For example, the Women's Economic Development Corporation (WEDCO) operates a highly successful loan fund to help finance low income women starting in business in the Minneapolis area. These are women who, because of their "high risk" status, could never receive a conventional loan from a bank. Loans are under $5,000 and to be paid back in six months. The women applying for the loans all work with WEDCO in developing their business idea, so that WEDCO is familiar with both the client and the business plan. (See Appendix 1 for the story of WEDCO.)

The Women's World Bank (WWB) based in New York and its affiliate organizations around the world similarly operate a fund to help women set up businesses, but in this instance money is not loaned directly to women, but used as a *loan guarantee* to help women borrow money from conventional banks. Contributors to the WWB fund include foundations, women's organizations, banks, corporations and development agencies. The loan *risk* is shared among three different financial institutions, with the WWB of New York assuming 50 per cent of the risk, affiliate local organizations assuming 25 per cent, and the bank assuming the remaining 25 per cent. With 75 per cent of the loan covered by guarantees, traditional banks are generally willing to service "high risk" clients. One condition of the loan guarantee from the WWB is that the borrower attend a series of workshops on business management put on by the staff of the affiliate WWB.

Another type of community loan fund is the revolving loan fund operated by each local chapter of the international Habitat for Humanity nonprofit organization. The purpose of this fund is to construct houses at reduced cost for poor families who then become the new home-owners. As part of the package, the family receives a *no-interest mortgage* on its home, covering the basic cost of construction. The principal on the loan is paid back in monthly installments at an affordable rate and goes directly back into the revolving loan fund to build more houses. The loan fund is kept alive and growing by a continuing supply of donations by individuals and businesses; Habitat refuses government funding.

The Project for Pride in Living (PPL), a nonprofit corporation in Minneapolis, also operates its own revolving loan fund which is used to renovate substandard houses in the inner city and then sell them to community residents at no profit. Mortgage payments (with interest) revert back to the revolving fund. (Chapter Six looks more closely at the work of Habitat for Humanity and PPL.)

In another pioneering example, a Montreal Community Loan Association has been set up by a *coalition* of lenders, borrowers and technical assistance providers. The purpose of the loan fund is to mobilize capital for the poor and at the same time provide opportunities for marginalized people to learn capital management. The revolving loan fund which has raised several hundred thousand dollars from individuals, labour unions, service organizations and private business, lends to community groups and low income people to set up worker-owned and controlled businesses which are deemed to have long-term *social* (not just economic) benefits for individuals and the community. The loan association/fund is unique in bringing face-to-face investors, community members in need of capital, and the people who provide technical support to the initiative on an ongoing basis — a three way partnership which builds personal trust, fiscal responsibility and social awareness among *all* participants.

Banking institutions have viewed low income borrowers as high risk and expected higher rates of loss on their loans. Yet the institutions that specialize in community loan funds have found the opposite to be true — loan loss is *less* than average, perhaps because of the strong personal contact between borrowers and lenders, and the business training and follow-up which often accompany a loan. The Revolving Loan Fund of the Institute for Community Economics in Massachusetts is a good example. As of March 1991, the fund had made well over $18 million in loans to community groups — loans for low income housing projects, co-op businesses and some community services. The total loan loss has been only $11,003 — or 6/100 of 1 per cent of the total loans given out in twelve years! The Revolving Loan Fund has covered all its obligations; no lender has lost any funds.

"Peer lending" sometimes called "loan circles," is yet another innovative scheme with a proven track record in providing small capital loans (usually $2,000 or less) to microenterprises.[3] (Microenterprise development, e.g., home businesses like catering, handicrafts, computer processing, is being pursued by many communities as a CED strategy for employment of the unemployed or underemployed.) A block loan is made to a *group* of four to ten individuals — a loan circle — in which each member owns a business and receives a portion of the total loan. Every member guarantees all the other members' loans on condition that, should one individual default, no further loans will be made to the group until that loan is repaid. This structure creates an interdependence such that it becomes each person's interest to ensure that every other person in the group succeeds at business and pays back the loan. Peer interest, peer support and peer pressure make the peer lending program a success. Peer pressure provides banks with the security they require instead of personal collateral, allowing people on low income to qualify for a loan. In Canada, the Calmeadow Foundation, a private, nonprofit organization based in Toronto, has been active in promoting and initiating a number of loan circles, including one in Lockeport, N.S. and in various aboriginal communities. The Community Loan Fund in Montreal is also experimenting with this model.

Grassroots control of industry — small business to worker co-ops

Large corporations in the formal economy are operated on a hierarchical top-down management model where the owner stands as boss over managers and hired workers, deciding on their wages, hours and working conditions (within the confines of collective agreements and the law). All profits flow to the owner and are the sole reason the business exists. If technology can replace workers at less cost, then workers are out of a job. If an industry can increase profits by relocating elsewhere or by closing a branch plant, then workers are out of a job. In general, the bigger the corporation, the greater is the alienation between owners and management at the top and workers at the bottom. As often as not, owners and workers do not even live together in the same city or town.

At the other end of the continuum are small scale private businesses which are owner-managed and which put the owner (who is a worker in his own business) in face-to-face contact with employees on a daily basis. The owner lives in the community, has a personal stake in community events, knows the workers personally and therefore is more likely to take community and employee relationships into account in his or her business decisions. Locally owned restaurants, grocery stores, retail shops, small manufacturers and bakeries are examples of this kind of community-rooted business. The re-establishment of community-based businesses is the major emphasis of many CED organizations wanting to diversify and decentralize ownership and control of industry within a community.

There is a step further. Ownership and management of the *individual* business or industry itself can be decentralized and democratized under a model of collective or co-operative ownership. What is unique about the co-op is that it bridges the conventional splits among the worker, owner, manager and consumer by integrating all these various functions into a single body representing by the collective membership. For example, as a member of a food co-op I am not only a consumer but I have a say in how the business is managed, what is sold and at what prices. As a member of a producer co-op I not only have a job as a worker, but also as part owner I have a say in the conditions of my work, what I want to produce and how to reinvest profits. As a member of a housing co-op I am not just a tenant but a co-owner who is protected against rent increases by landlords wanting to make a profit.

In a co-op every member has one vote, giving each person an equal say in the running of the operation. Profits are distributed equally among the collective membership in the form of reduced prices (consumer co-ops), improved services (service co-ops), or else they are paid out in dividends, reinvestment capital or a raise in salaries (producer/worker co-ops).

The features of worker control, user participation and equalized distribution of surplus wealth among members make the co-op an especially attractive model for community development. Some communities have completely reclaimed control of their local economies through co-operative development, especially with worker/producer co-ops. On Fogo Island, Newfoundland, when the private fisheries all closed down in the mid-1960s, threatening to shut down the town itself, local people organized to create a workers' co-op to replace the abandoned fishing industry. As a result, the community survived and began to thrive as the co-op expanded. By 1985 the town's population had increased by 20 per cent.

In other cases communities have built up a complex network of co-ops whereby they support each other by buying products from each other and sharing technical and financial resources. Mondrigon, in Spain's Basque region is perhaps one of the most dramatic examples of a community built on an interdependent network of over 200 co-operatives; 100 of them are industrial co-ops employing some 20,000 people. The industrial co-ops are supported and serviced by other co-ops which include a technical college, a research centre, a university where students work half days in a manufacturing co-op on campus, a social securities co-op to provide employee benefits, a network of co-op grocery stores, co-op housing, co-op schools run by parents and funded by profits from the industrial co-ops, and finally a community credit union with $125 million in assets to help finance, plan, guide and monitor new co-op ventures started by any organized group in the community. Because of the pooling of the industrial co-ops' surplus wealth, no person in twenty-five years has lost a job because of economic recession.

Another success story on a smaller scale is the flourishing network of co-ops in the Evangeline region on P.E.I. Through worker co-ops, the community has turned a once dying economy dependent on fishing into a vibrant and diversified economy, thus creating a secure and sustainable future for generations to come. Worker co-ops in Evangeline employ nearly one-quarter of the area's population. Revitalization has been so dramatic that Canada's National Film Board in 1990 made the film *We're the Boss* about the community. (The Evangeline case is more fully described later in this chapter.)

Neighbourhood/community development corporations: the story of DERA, Vancouver

The CDC is an incorporated entity formed to represent a specific community, an umbrella organization which, because of its incorporated status, can receive and distribute government and private funds for community development projects. Very often it is involved in the initiation, co-ordination and delivery of a wide array of social, cultural and economic community programs. In many cases, the CDC began as a tenants' or neighbourhood association. It is important to note that the CDC mandate is the community itself, managed and controlled by residents to deal with a variety of local problems. In a way it is a form of community-based government.

CDCs vary in their approach. Some act as an intermediary or facilitator of community initiatives, funnelling money to the community from higher levels of government. In the U.S., many CDCs have been set up to receive and administer block funds from the federal government to revitalize deteriorated slum neighbourhoods which government efforts could not affect. The CDC as a form of community government is able to develop a broad and comprehensive revitalization strategy, which balances economic and social needs. The CDC is also a direct form of self-government, where community people themselves are the planners, decision makers and actors in shaping the community's future.

Some CDCs take on the role of community developer — building needed housing, forming partnerships with private developers, managing commercial properties and loan funds, and starting up new businesses and industries. In Canada, New Dawn in Sydney, Nova Scotia, is perhaps the best known and successful CDC of this type. In another example, in Minneapolis, the Cedar Riverside CDC has been instrumental in giving residents direct control over the planning and development of their neighbourhood. (The Cedar Riverside story is told later in this chapter.)

The Vancouver Downtown Eastside Residents' Association (DERA) provides yet another model for community control, through neighbourhood political action and community organizing.[4] The residents' association represents Vancouver's most down-and-out population and run down neighbourhood. Yet the people who live there *care* about their community, a fact that contradicts the dominant view of people in this area of town. DERA has over 4,500 members, out of some 12,000 to 15,000 residents in the whole neighbourhood. It holds open monthly meetings (nonmembers included) to discuss specific neighbourhood issues which are outlined in a newsletter distributed door-to-door before each meeting. About 100 to 200 people show up regularly to the meetings (often more than 300 will show), which always involve a translator to help communication between Chinese and English speakers. The issues are wide ranging, including treatment of the elderly, eviction of hotel residents, displacement of residents by downtown development, upgrading housing, building new housing, improving safety in the streets, and providing more green space.

One of the key gathering places for residents is the Carnegie Centre, which doubles as a library and community centre. This heritage building, donated to the city by Andrew Carnegie, sat vacant and boarded up while residents fought for seven years to have it allocated for their use as a library and community centre. According to DERA Executive Director Jim Green, the city just couldn't accept the idea that residents should have a library. Today, this library is the most populated in the Vancouver library system. When I visited on a weekday, the reading room was absolutely packed with people pouring over newspapers, magazines and books from all over the world. As a community centre, it is the most used in Canada, with meeting rooms, a chess area, an art gallery and a theatre. The building is a "living room" for the neighbourhood. When you walk in you see people congregating and talking on the stairs in a variety of languages — the area has the highest immigrant population in Vancouver. There are political meetings at Carnegie Centre as well as bingos and dances.

Among its many achievements, DERA has built over 500 units of resident and co-op housing costing over $35 million (making it Vancouver's biggest nonprofit housing developer). One of the buildings, the Four Sisters Co-op has received world acclaim. In 1991 DERA was one of five finalists for the World Habitat Award, given for the world's most innovative housing. DERA has also developed the popular Oppenheimer Park with baseball field, playground, and giant outdoor checker board square and was the main actor in getting the Crab Park water front park for the community.

DERA has also made major inroads in improving the area's safety. The downtown east side is where most of the city's murders happen and the area with the highest number of hotels with chronic heavy drinking. Through its persistent lobbying DERA was able to get the local liquor store and some of the worst hotels closed, with the result that community crime and murders have decreased. DERA was also able to get the back alleyways lighted so that the elderly, who make up the majority of the population, would feel safer when they take the short cut home down the back lane at night. DERA also kept pressure on city council until it enforced its own bylaws against hotels in the area. DERA joined with city inspectors to do an investigation of 23 hotels which were not providing adequate heat, water and cleaning according to the code — approximately 10,000 violations were found and charges were eventually laid. These are just some of DERA's many activities which have made a difference in the lives of community people.

Strong leadership has been one of the keys to DERA's success. Since its founding in 1973, three members from the association have been elected to city council. In 1991, DERA Executive Director Jim Green ran for mayor against incumbent Gordon Campbell and came close to winning. The theme of his campaign was the caring city. But most important to DERA's success has been the hard work of all its members and thirty-five staff, who nearly all live in the neighbourhood.

We can see from the DERA example that a neighbourhood association which is open, democratic and run by the community can be a powerful vehicle for local control over housing, safety, development and other community matters. The community development corporation is another vehicle offering flexibility, openness and grassroots opportunities, which allow a community to define its own needs and approaches to meeting them — instead of depending on government and social agencies which have their *own* agendas, often very different from the community's.

FOUR EXAMPLES OF COMMUNITY CONTROL

(1) Evangeline, P.E.I.: a co-operative community[5]

The Evangeline district is a small Acadian P.E.I. community made up of a cluster of villages. Of the 2,500 people in the community, over 400 are employed by a network of co-operatives. This has come about through the self-help efforts of community members who decided a number of years ago to work together to create a self-reliant, sustainable economy. The first co-op was established in the 1930s by poor fishermen who needed higher prices for their fish. After realizing that the man who marketed their fish was the same man who owned the local store and most other businesses in the region, they decided to create their own marketing co-op and, by volunteering their time and what money they had, they were able after a few years to double the price they received for their fish. Next, using their own physical labour, they went on to build a lobster factory.

Still the problem was that the fishing industry itself was unreliable because of factors beyond the community's control. In 1967 after a particularly bad fishing year, the community came together at a local parish hall to discuss what action to take — the result was a decision to start new co-operative businesses. A Pioneer Village was constructed that winter as a government make work project and later added a co-op restaurant and a dinner theatre. Suddenly, the unknown district of Evangeline blossomed into a tourist attraction. The popular dinner theatre still presents plays about the life, culture and history of the Acadian community — all acted, written and produced by local people.

Building on their success, a potato chip factory was started as a worker co-op, with each worker putting up $5,000 for equal shares. The employees are also the owners and directors of the company. As with many new businesses, the first few years were an investment by worker/owners to keep their jobs and stay in business. Today, the business pays for itself and provides steady, secure employment. Other worker co-ops have been started — a children's clothing factory started by women in the community, a co-op woodlot, a wood chip factory, a saw mill which sells lumber to a local, private boat builder, and a co-op funeral home. (Funeral services in other parts of the island are run by B.C. chain.) In another example, a person from Texas came around wanting to set up a cable company. The community refused and then proceeded to set up its own cable company.

Behind the co-operative success story is a network of community supports. A local credit union, owned and operated by the community, has established a venture capital fund to support new co-operative ventures. As well, a Co-operative Council and an Industrial Commission give assistance. Yet the greatest support of all is the people themselves and their commitment to the co-operative way. Co-op education is integrated into all aspects of daily life at home, at school or at work. Beginning in kindergarten, children pay five dollars to join a student co-op store which gives reduced prices for student supplies until Grade Twelve, when they get back their original investment.

Evangeline is a community which worked to turn a vision into a reality. Through self-help, co-operation and the interdependence of many parts, the community now owns and controls most of its local resources, thus providing a promising and sustainable future for its children.

(2) United Hands Community Land Trust, Philadelphia[6]

The United Hands (*Manos Unidos* in Spanish) Community Land Trust is in Philadelphia's Kensington section, northeast of the downtown. This area of several square miles is home to tens of thousands of Puerto Ricans and African Americans. This is a very poor community, a disinvested neighbourhood (i.e., where public and private investors have pulled out their money) with some 2,000 abandoned public housing sites here and there, along with other vacated homes and apartments. The crime rate is high — there were forty-five homicides in the neighbourhood in 1990 — as is drug and alcohol dependency. Only 25 per cent of students graduate from high school. In addition, there is a lack of city services and poor health care — most children don't get the necessary immunization shots. A walk through the neighbourhood is a chilling experience for someone from the outside — garbage piled in the streets, spray-painted graffiti everywhere, barred windows and iron-caged porches on the row houses, youths openly dealing in stolen goods and drugs on the street, and....murals — beautiful hand-painted murals on the sides of buildings every few blocks, dedicated to the memory of people in the neighbourhood who have died as victims of violence and drugs. The neighbourhood is the kind of place that governments and bureaucrats have written off as beyond help.

The families living there have not done the same. Kensington, despite the social problems, is a vibrant community. There are active community groups — antidrug groups, youth environmental groups, church groups, antiracism groups, housing groups — working hard to rebuild the physical and social structures of the community. United Hands Community Land Trust (CLT) is one of those groups, described by a resident as "one of the most vibrant community organizing projects in the entire city."

United Hands was incorporated in 1988. It has 182 members and a separate board made up of one-third home-owner/lessees, one-third general members from the neighbourhood (not yet lessees), and one-third from the broader community, representing funding organizations and community groups. Setting up the organization took many months of painstaking meetings. Participants had to learn how the city bureaucracy worked, who the group's allies and enemies were, and what resources were available. Out of the process developed a strong group of people with a vision. The vision is: (1) to provide low income people

124

with the opportunity to become home-owners; (2) to revitalize the community by bringing in and developing a new type of home-owner who would be *socially* responsible to the community; and (3) to act in coalition with other groups to further a broad social and political agenda for the neighbourhood.

United Hands acts as a housing developer as well as a land trust. It buys up abandoned houses from the city — buildings unfit for habitation, in need of extensive rehabilitation — and then redevelops them using low interest loans, government subsidies and sweat equity labour contributed by members of the land trust. (Sweat equity is a system which accepts a person's working hours on a project instead of money down. It allows people without capital to invest in home ownership through their own labour.) In just eighteen months, the organization rehabilitated and sold twenty-nine homes to low income families in the CLT and still retained ownership of the land and the right to purchase the property back at the original purchase price, if the home-owner wants to sell. Another fifty homes soon were in the rehabilitation process, and still another fifty had financing in place but were waiting to be turned over from the city to the CLT.

On the wall of the United Hands office is a neighbourhood map showing all the tax delinquent and condemned houses, and also the ones strategically targeted by the land trust for redevelopment. The organization expects to own approximately 25 per cent of area properties within a few years, giving it substantial influence and control over what happens to the neighbourhood. The community interest will be protected — houses kept from falling into the hands of drug dealers who are a constant threat to social stability, or into the hands of speculators who are a threat to housing affordability.

A typical house acquired through United Hands — completely rehabilitated inside and out — costs the average home-owner $110 to $130 per month in mortgage payments, amortized over fifteen years. This is *less than half* the amount that families are now paying in rent to slum landlords. It works by United Hands purchasing a condemned property for about $13,000. It then adds another $20,000 to $34,000 in materials and contracted labour to restore the structure to good condition. Most of these rehabilitation costs are covered by various government subsidies. The remaining amount — usually some $8,000 to $15,000 — is borrowed from the bank and becomes the mortgage responsibility of the new home-owner, with the land trust acting as intermediary.

Acquiring a home through the CLT is not a "give away" — it is a rigorous process that demands continuing participation in the CLT by prospective home-buyers/lessees. Anyone interested must first attend orientation sessions to learn about the concept of a land trust. Then they are assigned to sit on a standing committee which meets monthly. Members must also work on a sweat equity crew every Saturday for fours hours for about a year and a half, in order to accumulate work time in lieu of money as down payment on their future house. (An additional $500 must be saved up during this period for the down payment.) Sweat equity labour involves gutting houses, dry walling, painting, cleaning and finishing; any major structural repairs such as plumbing and wiring are contracted out.

The sweat equity component is a critical part of the program. It enables poor people to substitute hard work for real money, teaches new home-buyers (many women who are single parents) the basic skills of home repair, and builds personal community relationships, all at the same time. By working together every week on each other's houses, members get to know each other. "We feel like we're family," says United Hands president Madalyn Dillard. When a house is completed and title turned over to the new family, there is a *community* celebration on the street for everyone. The community-building aspect of the CLT organization cannot be overstated. One of United Hands' goals is to develop socially responsible individuals, not just to develop houses.

Heroilda Rodriquez is a new home-owner/lessee of the land trust. For thirty years she lived in a tiny apartment which cost $275 a month. Today, she owns a land trust house and the cost — including taxes, insurance and mortgage — is only $200 a month. "Its incredible....The only thing I wanted was to leave something to my children, so they won't have to go through what we did." Rodriquez says that the home-buyer's training program taught her how to take control of her life, helped her to find a job as a local community organizer, and got her off welfare. "I'm a believer."

United Hands has a commitment to a social agenda broader than just housing. It has joined with the antidrug coalition in the neighbourhood. Drugs and the violence that goes with them, are such pervasive problems that it would have been irresponsible to develop a block of houses where there were drug dealers and crack houses on the corner. As Pedro Rodriquez, CLT board member and community resident, said, "How do you explain to a family if their child gets shot because of a drug dealing dispute? You must address the underlying social problems concomitant to what you're doing." United Hands members have gone to where drugs were being dealt and stood vigil all night to disrupt business. They forced police to be accountable to the community by meeting with them, providing them with drug locations and following up the next week to find out what had been done with the information. Through their efforts, $5 million worth of drugs were confiscated in eighteen months. Today, certain areas which the land trust targeted for its drug clean-up operation, are basically *free of drugs* — a miraculous feat which must be credited to the community groups (where governments, police and other social agencies have failed). Many abandoned houses which were being used as "crack houses," are now being fixed up and sold at affordable prices to low income families. Streets are safer, and children can go out to play without fear for their lives.

After witnessing the achievements of the United Hands Community Land Trust, I concluded that miracles can happen. The park across the street from the United Hands office is the symbol of the neighbourhood's turning tide. It has been a notorious corner for cocaine dealings but today it is beautiful park (an award winner, in fact) built by the neighbourhood children, with flowers, benches, trees and pathways. It is surrounded by a chain link fence and has a padlock to prevent vandals from destroying it. There are many little transformations, such as the corner park, occurring in the neighbourhood, but to see them you have to consider the small things. Change is happening on a house-by-house, block-by-block basis. This is how the community is rebuilding, restoring and healing itself — not through large scale redevelopment or government planning from the top, but through the many thousands of small actions of community people, people who care about where they live. United Hands is living proof that, sparked by community spirit, *people can do the impossible.*

(3) Milton Park, Montreal: community ownership of land and housing

Milton Park is one of Montreal's most vibrant, culturally mixed and cohesive communities. It is situated in a six block, twenty-five acre area, just north of the city's downtown near McGill University. Its over 2,000 residents are a mix of French, anglophone and immigrant families; students, elderly people, handicapped people and ex-homeless singles. Architecturally, the neighbourhood has history and character. It is comprised of two and three story gray stone Victorian houses dating back to the 1860s. Adjacent to the area is Mount Royal, a myriad of small ethnic restaurants, bars and small stores. Milton Park is like a small village within a city. The only blights on the human scale landscape are concrete high-rises known as La Cité, which loom over the neighbourhood as a daily reminder of what almost became the fate of the entire community.

Milton Park has been able to maintain its vitality and diversity because the community owns, manages and controls the land and buildings it occupies, which it intentionally has kept affordable to low income people who are long time residents in the area. The neighbourhood is a community land trust where all housing units belong to fifteen different co-ops (600 units) plus six nonprofit corporations which provide for special needs groups — the handicapped, homeless and elderly. How it has gained this local control is an intriguing story of citizen struggle and community development going back to 1968.

In the 1960s, Milton Park was a rundown neighbourhood owned mainly by private landlords who rented out rooms and apartments to transient students, academics, immigrants, artists and drifters attracted by the area's colourful community, cultural life and affordable housing. During this time, a private development company, Concordia Estates, began quietly buying up properties until it had finally assembled a twenty-five acre package of land which it intended to redevelop as a "new city" — a massive complex of highrise towers which would contain a hotel, commercial mall, apartments, recreational facilities and offices. To accomplish this task, it would clear out the "slum" neighbourhood, as it was called, and of course the low income population along with it. City council was supportive of the idea, as was the provincial government.

What wasn't anticipated was the angry, political response by neighbourhood residents. A Milton Park Citizens Committee (MPCC) was formed in 1968, which held regular meetings, surveyed tenants, put out a newsletter and planned political actions. Over the following years there were protests, a march on city hall, an occupation of vacant houses to prevent their demolition (which resulted in fifty-nine arrests), and later a sit-in to stop bulldozers from destroying a site that the community wanted as a park. The citizen actions gained public attention but could not stop the 1972 demolition of 255 houses, nor the 1973 construction of the megaproject's first phase — a hotel, commercial mall, office and apartment tower.

After this first lost battle, a new political strategy and vision for the neighbourhood began to slowly emerge. What started out as a citizen fight to preserve low cost rental housing developed into a more comprehensive solution for the neighbourhood — a plan for a resident-controlled, co-op neighbourhood. To make this dream a reality, the community somehow needed to purchase the developer's land.

128

By the mid-1970s, the developer was in financial trouble and looking to sell what still remained of the original housing, about two-thirds of the initial six square blocks. Attitudes toward urban renewal and high density development were changing and beginning to favour preservation of older neighbourhoods. Individuals on the board of MPCC began to make connections with various individuals, groups and agencies who could help, notably Heritage Montreal and the Canada Mortgage and Housing Corporation. They undertook a feasibility study of what it would cost to renovate neighbourhood houses and turn them into co-ops for the existing residents. In 1979 Canadian Mortgage and Housing Corporation agreed to purchase the *entire* package of land from the developer and pay for renovating *all* the houses, which would afterwards be turned over to neighbourhood co-ops to manage on their own. No one in the neighbourhood would be displaced, and the monthly cost of paying off the mortage for the renovated co-ops would not be more than 7 per cent above what people currently were paying in rent.

The largest task was convincing and educating people in the community — lifetime renters — about the advantages of co-op ownership and then devising procedures for 2,000 residents to organize themselves into co-ops. Some residents wanted to own their houses privately. But it was an all co-op or nothing deal, with one exception — nonprofit organizations were allowed to deliver the housing for people with special needs — seniors, loners and handicapped people.

Today, after many conflicts inside and outside the community, all the lands have come under community ownership, including about thirty small commercial properties. This commercial component allows residents a say about the local services and businesses in the area. Co-ops and nonprofit corporations own the housing, which still provides some rented rooms and apartments at a slightly higher cost. The most recent addition to the neighbourhood is the Milton Park Community Centre in the newly restored Strathearn School built in 1912. The centre has offices for neighbourhood groups, classrooms for community education and programs, meeting spaces and a cafe.

Some people have argued that the public cost of $40,000 per unit for renovating the housing was excessive. It can also be argued that the cost was cheap, compared with the costs of building, administering and maintaining government social housing. Residents now have something they can call their own for which *they* are responsible, not the government. To top off the argument, it should be said that an entire neighbourhood has been revitalized and upgraded. The project has been so successful that there is a waiting list of hundreds to get into the co-ops.

By contrast, La Cité's expensive apartments, hotel and commercial mall have many vacancies and are losing money.

In 1989 the city attempted to raise the property taxes for Milton Park residents, reasoning that because adjacent areas were being gentrified and increasing in value, the same process applied to the land trust property. The community appealed, arguing that a land trust is exempt from increases in value because it is removed from the real estate market and cannot be sold. The community won its appeal, demonstrating the effectiveness of the land trust model in keeping housing affordable and land prices stable.

(4) Cedar Riverside Community, Minneapolis

Cedar Riverside is a stable community of about 6,500 people situated in central Minneapolis near the university. Its location and mixture of theatres, shops and restaurants make it one of the most desired neighbourhoods for gentrification. Yet today it remains as it always has been, a mixture of students and middle to low income people. The community's preservation has been possible because, after fifteen years of community organizing and battling with a developer and a federal housing agency, the community now manages and controls the development of its lands through a land trust (owned by the city and leased for use by community residents), a CDC, a community planning body and an agreement with the City of Minneapolis.

The story of Cedar Riverside is similar in many ways to Milton Park. In the 1960s a developer, Cedar Riverside Associates, began speculating and buying up all the owner-occupied houses in the neighbourhood with plans to level the entire area and construct in its place a "New Town in Town" urban renewal project — a massive complex of twenty high-rise apartment towers including 12,500 units. The plan, which would change the neighbourhood from low density single family homes to high density rental apartments, was approved by the federal department of Housing and Urban Development (HUD) and the city of Minneapolis, and was given federal funding.

The community responded by forming a Community Tenants Union and by setting up a local planning organization known as PAC (Project Area Committee) under the leadership of activist Jack Cann. In one of the early struggles, residents fought the university to save an old church in the neighbourhood, which was owned by the university and slated for demolition. Residents succeeded not just in saving the church but in taking it over for their own use. Today it belongs to the community and is known as the People's Centre — home to a variety of community services — legal, health, veterinary and family. Residents became well organized. They collectively established the Riverside Cafe, a meeting place and base for organizing, and they set up a co-op grocery for the community. Despite all their actions and loud protests against the planned "New Town in Town" redevelopment, the developers in 1972 succeeded in building the first stage of the complex — the double high-rise tower Cedar West Square, which looms over the community.

In 1973, the community took the developers and the city to court on the basis that an environmental assessment was not properly done for the area. In 1975 the Supreme Court ruled in the community's favor, describing the proposal as unsound from a planning viewpoint and granted the community the official right to plan its own neighbourhood. In the meantime, the developer's project was in financial trouble and ended in bankruptcy. The properties went into receivership and it took another five years in court to sort out the situation.

Three positive outcomes occurred as a result of the complicated court battle. First, the alternative institutions in the neighbourhood — the People's Centre, the worker-owned Riverside Co-op Cafe, the West Bank Co-op Grocery, the West Bank Community Development Corporation (CDC), and PAC — flourished and became stable elements of the community. This meant there were strong community organizations already in place when it came time for the neighbourhood to take over its own planning and development functions. Since 1975, all redevelopment and policy planning have been carried out by PAC, the West Bank CDC and the Community Tenants Union, in co-operation with the city.

Secondly, because of the community's "tax increment"[7] status, it was able to build up a large development fund to finance the construction of much needed low income co-op housing for the neighbourhood. In the last ten years, the neighbourhood has been almost totally redeveloped by and for the community.

The third positive outcome was that, in the end, the lands in receivership — about two-thirds of the neighbourhood (all except land owned by institutions, such as the hospital and university, and some commercial properties) — were purchased by the city of Minneapolis. These lands are held in trust for the community and leased to the West Bank Community Development Corporation to develop according to plans approved by PAC, the neighbourhood planning and policy committee. The West Bank CDC and PAC work closely together. In the land trust/ land lease arrangement, the lands are separated from the improvements to the land, so that buildings are owned by the CDC (usually in partnership with a limited equity or for profit developer), while land is owned by the city. The city's interest is to maintain long-term affordability for housing; removing land from the private market helps to keep homes affordable.

The different community institutions working together are the base and the expression of community power. The Project Area Committee, on contract with the city of Minneapolis, plans details for redevelopment of the neighbourhood, right down to designs for houses and commercial properties to be built. The committee is a group of elected residents from five neighbourhood districts, plus delegates from special interest groups (cultural, social service, business) and major institutions in the area (hospitals, the university). PAC, with the help of an architect, works directly *with* residents on a block-by-block basis to design the infill housing and other uses for vacant lots, with the result that each city block has its own unique character and design, which enhances the neighbourhood's personality. Volunteers, working with a contractor, determine which houses need rehabilitating. Where possible, sweat equity is used. The West Bank CDC puts together the financial package.

The West Bank CDC, the development arm for specific projects, was set up in 1975 to assemble an overall economic plan for the neighbourhood. The plan includes the organization, management and financial packaging of the housing units, co-op grocery store, co-op pharmacy, worker-owned Riverside Cafe, and other economic entities such as the CED revolving loan fund. Since the 1980s, it has developed 550 housing units, most of them co-ops leased from the land trust, and managed and controlled by the residents themselves. Three hundred units were new construction; the rest came from rehabilitating existing structures. Only fifty townhouses have been developed for home ownership.

There is a need for more single family, privately owned homes or for condominiums at this stage, because some family incomes in the neighbourhood have risen over the past ten years. To address this need, the CDC will develop single family homes, beginning in the spring of 1992. The idea is not to build for new high income families, but for local residents in order to keep them in the neighbourhood. A land lease stipulation limits the CDC to building homes for people with incomes no higher than 110 per cent of the median income, thus preserving the neighbourhood for the low to middle income range. If housing were developed for higher incomes, the CDC would have to pay the city for the land, making costs much higher.

The CDC has also stimulated small, local business development by assisting the start up and expansion of neighbourhood retail services through its loan fund. One of its first commercial strategies was to promote the area's cultural and historical identity as a theatre district. It has succeeded in doing this, and now there are six performing arts theatres in the neighbourhood, such as the Mixed Blood Theatre, an interracial acting company housed in a restored fire station. In more recent years, there has been a shift in business development aimed at helping neighbourhood *residents* start up small microbusinesses (e.g., publishing or telemarketing), often out of their homes — as a way of improving neighbourhood incomes. The CDC also offers classes on how to start up a business. A new CDC venture is commercial real estate development. Using its development and construction skills, the West Bank CDC is rehabilitating an old abandoned warehouse, the Bailey Building, as mixed retail and office space for community-oriented, neighbourhood-owned businesses, such as the community-based radio station.

Like all organizations, the West Bank CDC has suffered growing pains. In 1987, a large membership meeting was called to deal with increasing tension between the neighbourhood and the CDC — people were questioning what was getting done, who was benefiting, and who was in charge. The CDC at that time was being run by committees; roles were muddled and lacked clear accountability. Out of the membership meeting came a CDC reorganization and the decision to hire an executive director to answer to the community. People had social needs they wanted addressed, such as youth programs and daycare. Social services became incorporated into the CDC's mandate. To fill the need for daycare, the CDC built four new child care *homes*. A child care home is different from a daycare institution in that it is a neighbourhood home, architecturally designed to accommodate the daycare needs of about fifteen children. This unique concept addresses a number of community issues — it provides much needed daycare space, integrates daycare into the neighbourhood fabric, creates jobs and improved incomes for local residents, provides affordable housing and offers daycare at lower than normal rates because government housing grants were used in the construction.

In summary, Cedar Riverside is an example of how a small neighbourhood in a big city can retain its economic, cultural and political identity separate from its surrounding urban environment. When asked the secret of its success, Executive Director George Garnett answered, "persistence and clarity of vision. Cedar Riverside is a neighbourhood that wouldn't go away. The community outlasted the developers, the courts and the banks, and it has remained intact." Cedar Riverside is an example of how a community working together can protect itself against the capitalist and bureaucratic forces of urbanization which would otherwise transform the neighbourhood and displace the people. It is an example of a community taking control over the management of its own future through a network of community-based organizations and initiatives. It is an example of a community guided by the goal of sustainable development using democratic processes, building community self-reliance, and building pride in people and their neighbourhood.

CONCLUSION

While it is easy to be overwhelmed by the power and rhetoric of a global economy, I have tried to show in this chapter that there is another way — communities can establish models and structures which will give them authority and control over neighbourhood development to a large extent. Among the models considered were community loan funds, which provide communities access to capital to start local businesses, build housing or finance other projects *appropriate* for the neighbourhood. Also discussed were worker-owned industries and co-operatives as ways of giving working people a share in the benefits of industrial ownership and profit and therefore a greater stake in their community's economic development. I noted community land trusts as a model which can give a neighbourhood control over local land use and land prices and enable it to prevent land speculation by outside developers. The neighbourhood association and/or community development corporation was discussed as a forum giving local residents the power to define their community needs, decide on neighbourhood goals and priorities, and collectively work toward them. The neighbourhood corporation is a structure through which a community can become self-governing.

There are many examples which show that these models work — the text gives just a sampling of them. Yet it takes more than structures and models to empower a community. What makes a model work, what fuels the machine, is the community's *will*. Summoning a community's will is an elusive process, far more difficult than setting up an organizational model. It requires community organizing, motivating people to care about their community, and empowering people to act for themselves. At the start of the chapter I explored the concept of empowerment by defining different types of power — power-*over*-others (coercive, regulatory, authoritarian power); power-*within* (personal power to act, to create, a life spirit); lastly, power-*with*-others (sparked by joining and acting with like-minded people on an equal basis). The latter two types of power, power-within and power-with-others, are two of the necessary preconditions for establishing community will and a community power base which can challenge our top-down social powers and structures.

I looked also at group process and the use of "consensus" decision making as a tool for empowering individuals within a group. Because in consensus every person must agree, or at least *not disagree,* with the final group decision, each individual's opinion is valued much more than in a majority winner vote situation. Consensus teaches individuals to listen with respect to the words and feelings of others. Unlike the adversarial voting system, with consensus everyone is on the "same team;" people are motivated to work out their differences. This helps to develop a community will and a group consciousness which is especially sensitive to the individual.

In previous chapters I spoke about ecology and self-reliance as fundamental concepts in building a sustainable community. An ecological city is made of many small community units (cells), designed to be as self-sufficent and self-reliant as possible — communities which meet the full range of peoples' needs for work, culture, shopping and recreation; communities where people can walk and bicycle instead of having to depend on cars to transport them over wide expanses of concrete urban sprawl. Yet the creation of more dynamic, tighter and interactive neighbourhoods requires that residents be given the main say in *how* their neighbourhood is developed. We cannot expect the outsider, the intruding industry with owners and managers in another city or country, to care about the pollution or ugliness it leaves in a neighbourhood. The people who care about the quality of community air, water, safety and overall life are the people who live there. They are the people best suited to preserve and protect our neighbourhoods.

People in the environmental movement and advocates of sustainable development are sometimes misled into believing that we have global problems which require global solutions, when we really have only a multiplicity of local problems, and effective solutions can only come out of local actions. As author Wendell Berry puts it:

The question that *must* be addressed...is not how to care for the planet, but how to care for each of the planet's millions of human and natural neighbourhoods, each of its millions of small pieces and parcels of land, each one of which is in some precious way different from all the others. Our understandable wish to preserve the planet must somehow be reduced to the scale of our competence — that is, to the wish to preserve all of its humble households and neighbourhoods.[8]

I repeat: the people who *live* in the neighbourhood are the ones best suited to be its guardians and protectors.

ENDNOTES

[1] Statistics come from the Institute for Community Economics, Springfield, Massachusetts.

[2] The Institute for Community Economics (ICE) is an organization which gives technical advice on financing, organizing and managing land trusts. It also manages its own community loan fund (over $18 million loaned out to community groups to date). ICE holds regular workshops on starting community land trusts and keeping them going, keeps regular contact with organizations, offers continuing assistance, and publishes books and other resource materials on community land trusts. Anyone interested should contact Greg Ramm, Executive Director, Institute for Community Economics, 57 School St., Springfield, Massachusetts 01105, or call 413-746-8660.

[3] See "Peer Lending," in *City Magazine* (Vol. 13, no. 2, Spring 1992).

[4] For a more detailed account of DERA refer to the article "Success in Revitalizing the Inner City —The Story of DERA" by Kent Gerecke in *City Magazine* (Vol. 12, no. 4, Fall 1991).

[5] Information contained in the National Film Board video "We're the Boss," 1990.

[6] Information comes from a talk given by Pedro Rodriquez at the "Gaining Ground" conference on land trusts which was put on by the Institute for Community Economics in October 1991; a personal visit to United Hands; interviews with workers and residents; and various news clippings (*Philadelphia Inquirer, Community Focus, Phil-Lisc Developments*).

[7] Until 1987, the Minnesota state legislature offered a tax increment program designed to help cities establish development funds for neighbourhoods. If a neighbourhood was granted tax increment status, then any money generated by higher taxes due to new development went into a special development fund. In most neighbourhoods this development fund became a free pot for big developers. In the Cedar Riverside district, the tax increment money was used instead to build up a reserve fund which enabled the community to float its own bonds and

the community development corporations to finance the housing projects. From 1971 to 1987, the Cedar Riverside community accumulated some $800,000 to $1 million annually in tax increments, which were held by the Minneapolis Community Development Agency for the neighbourhood. Ironically, the tax increment money was mainly generated by the Cedar West highrise apartment buildings, the same ones residents had fought. According to Executive Director George Garnett, there is still a cash flow of about $2 million in a new arrangement with the city to finance projects. Yet for the most part, the entire neighbourhood has already achieved its goal of redevelopment and no longer requires the same amount of funding.

[8] Wendell Berry, "Work and Flesh," in *What are People For?* (San Francisco: North Point Press, 1990), p. 200.

Chapter Six

Meeting Individual Needs

...if we are going to reform the world, and make it a better place to live in, the way to do it is not to talk about relationships of a political nature, which are inevitably dualistic, full of subjects and objects and their relationship to one another; or with programs full of things for other people to do...The social values are right only if the individual values are right. The place to improve the world is first in one's heart and hands, and then work outward from there. Other people want to talk about how to expand the destiny of mankind. I just want to talk about how to fix a motorcycle. I think that what I have to say has more lasting value.

Robert M. Pirsig
Zen and the Art of Motorcyle Maintenance

6

Meeting Individual Needs

Development should be geared to the satisfaction of human needs, both material and non-material, rather than the mere accumulation of material wealth.

INTRODUCTION

In previous chapters I have looked at building sustainable communities from the perspective of generating local wealth, redesigning communities to be ecologically sustainable, and setting up new structures and processes to allow greater community ownership and control over resources. While these are necessary mechanisms to ensure the physical and economic security of communities, our discussion of sustainable communities would be incomplete without looking at *people themselves*, as the *greatest community resource and the whole reason for development in the first place*. The next two chapters focus on human development — the fullfilment of people's individual and collective cultural needs — as an essential element of sustainable community development.

This chapter focuses primarily on the *individual* and secondarily on the role of community in meeting the needs of individuals. A community, we must remind ourselves, is only as strong as its individual members. In a caring and lasting community, every person matters. There is a reciprocal social contract which operates between an individual and the community — individuals are expected to give something of themselves to the community through work, participation in community life and helping others; in exchange, a community provides the individual with security, protection, opportunities for work and self-fulfillment. In an ideal community every person's basic needs are met by the contract.

With the dissolution of community as part of modern development, the social contract has broken down — individual needs are *not* being met; increasing numbers of people are not being given protection, security or opportunities to improve their life. Neighbours have become strangers. Individuals are expected to fend for themselves in an increasingly impersonal, competitive and rootless society.

Institutional "systems" have replaced community as the provider of basic needs — the market system distributes jobs, housing, food and consumer goods to people; when that fails, government bureaucracy delivers social services and programs to compensate. People, instead of meeting their own needs (e.g., cooking dinner, growing food, repairing vehicles, caring for elderly parents) have become the receivers of consumer goods and public services, which they not only expect, but have come to require. Social relationships are depersonalized; individuals are devalued and reduced to a statistic. There is a general distrust and lack of respect all around — the system shows little regard for the special needs of the individual (as anyone trying to make their way through a bureaucracy well knows), and the individual shows little regard for the system. It is not surprising that so many people cheat on taxes, call in sick to work, milk the consumer or the government for what they can get, and applaud themselves for "beating the system" as though they were in a competition between the individual and society.

The social contract is dead. We live in a decaying society in which large segments of our population are allowed to suffer the debilitating effects of homelessness, hunger, alienation, stress, discrimination, low self-esteem, alcoholism, drug dependency and physical violence. The Canadian Association of Food Banks' preliminary counts for 1990 showed that nearly 500,000 people were lined up to get food from private charity handouts each month. One per cent of Canadians are homeless, while one in seven lives in substandard housing, yet the federal government has cut social housing programs by 15 per cent (1990). Two million Canadians, including 750,000 children, were on social assistance in 1990. What is our future?

We are left with damaged and broken communities which governments have simply written off because they are too big and costly a problem to handle. The Core Area Initiative Agreement in Winnipeg, which spent $198 million over ten years to revitalize the inner city, allocated no significant funds to the area of greatest need — Main Street. In Montreal, the badly neglected Grand Plateau community was shocked by a final refusal, after working for years to secure community development funds for the neighbourhood and gaining approvals from various levels of government all the way along. After prying into the federal cabinet, it was revealed that the neighbourhood had privately been written off by the government. In the United States, poverty has grown to such catastrophic proportions that there are TV ads appealing to the public to adopt an American inner city child, as there are for starving Third World children.

Recovering social health is not going to happen by simply throwing more money at the problem in the same old way — expanding government bureaucracy, creating more social programs and consultants' reports which pay out more in salaries to professional staff than they do to people in need. The Manitoba Northern Flood Agreement is a typical case. The ecological destruction to lakes and rivers in northern Manitoba caused by hydro dams has left at least six native communities destitute and struggling to survive in an environmental wasteland, while consultants and lawyers in Winnipeg and Ottawa have been paid millions of dollars to assess damages and negotiate a settlement with Manitoba Hydro. To the aboriginal communities, welfare cheques are no substitutes for people's lost capacities to feed themselves by hunting and fishing, and to live by their traditional culture.

A total restructuring of the social system is called for which will re-establish *community* as the focal point for meeting human needs. The current government model of top-down social service delivery has failed to meet people's needs on several counts. It has tended to reinforce the *status quo* — propping up the bureaucracy with consultants' reports, elaborate systems for delivering and monitoring government programs (all benefiting professionals), while keeping the people on the bottom trapped in poverty and dependent on the system. Worse, the structure has created a life style and culture of dependency for whole inner city communities which has lasting social and psychological ramifications far beyond the issue of income. Welfare dependency instills feelings of low self-worth and powerlessness to better one's life; powerlessness erupts into frustration and anger which finds social expression in violence against others and oneself — drug addiction, suicide, murder and assaults. The social costs are tremendous.

We seem to be caught in a double bind: withdrawal of public resources (as is occurring with government cutbacks today) only exacerbates the problem; but fighting a "war on poverty" from the offices of a centralist bureaucracy doesn't help either. Public resources need to be spent in a radically different manner — on weaning people off the system by building grassroots, community support networks which give individuals the skills and confidence they need to change their lives, and on supporting neighbourhood and self-help groups whose caring reflects back to individuals their essential worth and value as human beings.

As an example of how this might work let's look at the Core Area Initiatives program in Winnipeg. Of the $198 million spent, more than half went to bricks and mortar development — infrastructure, building a shopping mall and a festival market. Other money went to pay for consultants' fees, public relations, salaries to planners and high level administrators — what was left over went to fund community organizations for a temporary period. In 1991 the money ran out, and dozens of community groups running on shoe-string budgets with volunteer help were forced to close their doors. These child-parent centres, drop ins for youth, women's centres, street programs for prostitutes, and other groups had become a backbone of support for thousands of needy people.

I keep wondering what would have happened if that $198 million had been placed in a sustainable community trust fund to be held in perpetuity for the community, administered by an elected board of community residents and used to fund community groups, purchase community land trusts, provide loans to community businesses, and support other local initiatives aimed at empowering residents to become self-sufficient. The inner city would have in the order of $20 million interest annually to invest in its people and its future, without touching the original endowment. I am convinced this self-sustaining approach to social services and building community would effect lasting change in individual lives, which would be reflected in reduced costs to the rest of society.

In contrast to the institutional approach, which has failed to recognize the value of the individual, *community* is the key to meeting individual needs and to resurrecting the social contract between individuals and the whole collective. In this chapter, I provide examples of what some communities have done toward meeting community members' basic needs through grassroots supports and community processes.

Before we get to the examples, let us look more closely at the topic of human needs — what are they? — to understand better what it is we are working so hard for and driving our economies to satisfy.

WHAT DO PEOPLE NEED? — A MODEL OF HUMAN NEEDS

Human needs are most often discussed in terms of a hierarchy ranking in order from the lowest level — physiological needs — to the highest level — psychological and cultural needs. Within this model higher needs are only capable of being met once the lower ones are satisfied. Abraham Maslow, the psychologist who pioneered the hierarchy of needs theory, divides needs into five categories moving from the most immediate to the least immediate: (1) physical survival; (2) safety; (3) affection; (4) self-esteem; and, (5) self-actualization.

The question is: Can material and nonmaterial needs really be separated from each other? The answer is no. Deep down most of us know that life without quality or meaning is not really "life" at all. Yet Western society has put the emphasis on materialism, gearing human and technological development to meeting material over nonmaterial needs through rapid economic growth. The quality of life in the West is measured by our "standard of living" — how many cars or TVs we own and how much income we earn. Lest we think ours is the only way, we should know that non-Western societies, such as traditional tribal societies or Buddhist cultures, have geared human and technological development toward *balancing* individuals' spiritual and material needs. In E.F. Schumacher's words, a Buddhist sees "consumption...merely as a *means* to well being; the aim should be to obtain the maximum of well being with the minimum of consumption...with the smallest possible effort."[1]

We are traveling in quite the opposite direction. In the drive to spur our economies by expanding material consumption and production, we have been diverted from our primary aim: we have forgotten that development is about people, not about things. While we may be rich in material objects, *quality* of life is not something that can be measured by the number of cars we own, and basic human needs — which include spiritual, psychological and social needs, as well as physical needs — cannot be met solely by material gain.

In fact, "consumerism" and "quality of life" are increasingly coming into conflict with each other as pollution and waste from over-production wreak havoc on the quality of the air, water, soil, food, and natural environments we depend on for our physical and mental health. Furthermore, the level of stress caused by our work patterns and the pressure to maintain the standard of living demanded by consumer life styles take their toll on our psychological well being, physical health, and relationships with family and friends. If meeting human needs were truly the goal of development, we would begin looking for alternative arrangements to *reduce* the need for income.

The quality of our lives is further diminished when we realize that consumerism controls our lives like an addiction — hooking consumers by temporarily inflating them with an artificial sense of self-worth and importance, and then leaving them empty and dissatisfied when the novelty wears away. The consumer's "high" is maintained only by the constant stimulation of buying and discarding, a steady process of resource depletion which impinges on the security of future generations to meet their own needs and live in a healthy environment.

Consumerism infects not just the individual but the whole of society. Material objects are *symbols* vested with status and position. Those who cannot afford to pay for these symbols of status receive the opposite message, that they are unworthy and inferior. People end up murdered for their pairs of Pump running shoes or their Rolex watches. While these extreme acts are exceptions, this violence over *things* demonstrates how consumerism has become the focus of spreading hostilities between those who have and those who have not. In other words, consumerism is an obstruction to building authentic community.

Seeking to satisfy needs in the market place has obscured a deeper understanding of human needs, confusing "needs" with consumer "wants." We think we "need" a bigger house, a microwave oven, or a new computer, when probably what we really need are things money can't buy — peace of mind, meaningful work, a close relationship with someone who cares. A person who is poor, who has been abused as a child, who has no community support, no creative outlets and low self-esteem is unquestionably deprived. Yet can we call a person deprived who is income poor, but who has friends, creative activities, a strong self-image and who lives in a community which grows its own food, and shares its housing and child care? I am drawn to think the second person lives in abundance rather than poverty. The point is not that people should live without income, but simply that income is not the best measure of whether an individual's needs are being met.

Getting back to basic needs will require a total rethinking of what human needs are and how they can best be satisfied. The first step is to redress the imbalances in our system which promote mindless consumerism and neglect the very real, nonmaterial needs of people. The development of a balanced individual calls for an integrated *system* of human needs as opposed to a segregated hierarchy — a system which combines both the material "needs of having" and the nonmaterial "needs of being."

Such a system would consider needs as falling into three types: (1) *survival* needs; (2) needs of the self for wholeness or *autonomy;* and, (3) needs for *integration* as part of the community. *Survival* needs are straightforward: they include the needs for health, security and permanence, which tend to include material essentials like food, clean air and water, safety and protection of one's person, shelter, and a replenishing, sustainable environment to pass on to future generations. Nonmaterial needs or "needs of being" make up the other two need types — autonomy and integration. Each person has a basic need to develop as a unique and *autonomous* being, with a separate identity of one's own. The autonomous self doesn't develop in isolation: community plays an important role by providing opportunities for creativity and self-growth and by recognizing the value of each person's uniqueness, which, collectively, makes up a community's diversity. The community provides a context for social relationships and fulfills the individual's need to participate with others. The need to connect with community, nature, the cosmos — to be part of a greater reality outside the self — is the need for *integration*. There is a range of needs within the three broad types:

- **Needs of autonomy**: Includes: self-esteem; wholeness, meaning and identity; personal freedom; self-expression; creativity.
- **Needs of integration**: Includes: the need to belong, i.e., connect with something larger than oneself (community, nature, the cosmos); the need for affection and relationships; the need to participate with others.
- **Needs of survival**: Includes: the need for health; for security; for permanence.

Human needs are universal to all cultures and all historical periods. What varies are the methods by which needs are met by a particular community at a specific time. Geography, patterns of history, culture and availability of resources all play roles in determining how needs are satisfied. In speaking about needs, a distinction has to be made between "needs" and "*satisfiers*" of needs. Sometimes the two are confused, for instance, when we speak of the need for income, housing or medical care. These are *satisfiers* of the need for health and security, particular to our own Western industrial culture. For people who subsist off the land, income is not a necessity, and housing is only one kind of "home" or place of security. In some cultures "home" means family. For the Inuit, "home" is the warmth and security of the clothing they wrap around their bodies, not their igloos, as Farley Mowatt discovered.

The point is that people need the opportunity to define their own solutions rather than pressure to conform to designs imposed upon them by outside experts. By distinguishing between needs and *satisfiers* we can start to explore and validate alternative ways to satisfy needs. For example, the activities of the informal economy, self-help groups and community organizations can be acknowledged as critical supports for meeting certain basic needs such as participation, affection, identity and self-realization — needs largely ignored by our economic system. The following section explores how communities can meet the needs for autonomy, integration and survival.

NONMATERIAL NEEDS

Meeting the needs of autonomy

Each of us is a being with a unique identity, personality, "soul." There is a good side and a bad side to this human condition. On the one hand, our uniqueness makes us special, gives us a personal stamp, something no one else has — our own humour, personality, special talents — to attract friends and mates, and to contribute our gifts to the world. On the other hand, our individuality can make us feel separate, isolated, misunderstood and lonely. Anxiety and depression result, and we may become incapacitated. The remedy lies in building community — bonding with others, sharing our feelings, identifying what we have in common — because while we are all different, on another level we are also the same. We share many of the same feelings and experiences, and we depend on each other for survival.

According to psychologists, the goal of human development is to become *fully ourselves* — what Abraham Maslow called self-actualization, what Carl Jung called individuation. It is a goal that few of us reach, but still one that beckons us toward becoming "whole" beings. Psychiatrist M. Scott Peck, author of *The Different Drum* and *Road Less Travelled* explains that, as individuals "we are called to be unique and different....We are also...called to power...[and] must learn how to take responsibility for ourselves. We need to develop a sense of autonomy and self-determination....Furthermore, we are called to wholeness. We should use what gifts or talents we are given to develop ourselves as fully as possible."[2]

This is one half of the picture. The other half is that being mortal, we are incomplete and imperfect, and while we are called to wholeness, we are also called to accept our incompleteness. While we are called to power, we are also called to accept our weakness. And while we are called to autonomy, we are called to accept our interdependence — our need for community.

Self-esteem is one of the basic needs of the autonomous self, a prerequisite for coming into one's personal power. Yet millions of people function at just a fraction of their potential because of low self-esteem — a result of various factors such as childhood abuse, social discrimination, the shame associated with poverty, or the pressure of a physical, emotional or mental disorder.

One of the ways individuals can build self-esteem is to overcome barriers (mental, social, physical) which are keeping them incapacitated. The community has a major role to play here by providing community supports. Agnes Philbrow is an adult student in a community run literacy program in Winnipeg. By learning how to read she has gained new confidence in herself. "For years I struggled to fit in society," she says. "I had low self-esteem because people had to think for me so I could function. I knew...*I had to learn to read to gain my inner strength* [my italics]....Sure, it is a hard long road but when you can read an article the feeling is a key to your inner soul, that is self-esteem, the important part of you. Without self-esteem you are trapped and you keep hitting a wall....[F]or people who haven't started to try, I want them to know I was there...I want to someday help. I know I would feel like a queen."[3]

Agnes, through her own *self-development*, is beginning to realize her potential as a deserving, contributing member of society. It is especially noteworthy that, in coming into her own power, Agnes has discovered a new "social" self which wants to reach out to help others, and to volunteer her experience in the community. It is a story repeated again and again. People get help from helping others. It is estimated that today in the U.S. there are twelve million individuals who belong to some 500,000 assorted self-help groups. They give their time and effort not just to help themselves, but to help others like themselves.[4]

The mushrooming "self-help" movement of the last fifteen years thus needs to be appreciated from a different angle, as a "helping others" movement as well. Volunteerism, likewise, is a vehicle for self-development for many people, such as the one hundred volunteers who tutor two hundred adult students to read in the Beat the Street literacy program in Winnipeg's inner city. The productivity of volunteers and people helping others in self-help groups is exceptional, yet virtually unaccounted for by the GNP. Economist David Ross figures that Canadian volunteers working for formal organizations gave some $16 billion worth of unpaid labour in 1986-87.[5]

The biggest challenge to individual and community development is healing the wounds of a broken society characterized by violence, abuse and disempowerment of increasing numbers of individuals. To begin, we have to acknowledge the facts. For example, child abuse in our society is a rampant problem and a well-hidden secret. In Winnipeg, a major study revealed alarming statistics for the first time: out of the general adult population surveyed at random, "one in ten Winnipeggers has a multiple personality or amnesia triggered by severe childhood trauma." In most cases, that means abuse.[6] The implications of this dysfunction for the health of communities are enormous. As more and more incidents of abuse are brought forward — and the numbers are rising — we are beginning to recognize the alarming extent of the human destruction which occurs. Recent studies indicate that as many as forty million people in America have been sexually victimized as children (25-35 per cent of females; 10-16 per cent of males). Yet as late as 1975, one psychiatric text book, relying on 1930 statistics, taught that sexual abuse occurred in only one family per million! [7]

The broken personality and low self-esteem which result from abuse must find a way of mending itself, otherwise the compulsion to repeat what was done to us as children takes over and the cycle of violence is repeated — parents pass on to their children the sufferings from their own shattered pasts. One method of self-healing, which deals with "reclaiming the child within," has struck a responsive chord with so many victims of abuse that it has rapidly grown into a movement, with a proliferation of books, self-help groups, television series and workshops on the topic. There is an enormous need out there begging to be filled. At the risk of oversimplification, "reclaiming the child within" involves a process of remembering; of bringing to the surface and acknowledging the abuse one experienced as a child so that individuals can grieve for the hurt children they once were and forgive themselves, because children tend to blame themselves for the pain inflicted on them. As adults come to honor and respect the "child within," they grow to respect their own children and thus become more supportive parents in the end. In this way, the cycle of abuse between generations is broken.

The transformation that occurs with self-healing affects not just the individual, but all relationships the individual has with family members, friends, associates. A community starts to heal. We saw this outward healing process occur in the Alkalai Lake community (Chapter Four), where personal transformation, after individuals joined AA, became a force which transformed an entire community culturally, economically and spiritually.

The Alkalai Lake example demonstrates something eco-feminism has been saying — that *social change works from the inside-out* starting with self-healing, which in turn affects our relationships at home with children and spouses, and eventually transforms our social relationships and the institutions in society. In this sense, our social institutions are mirrors or reflections of our insides. We have to rid ourselves of the structures of domination and subordination that we carry *within* us, our feelings of inferiority or superiority and the roles we take on as a result of our socialization and upbringing — both as women and men — before we can rid society of its external structures of domination — its top-down organizations, its exploitation of workers, its discrimination against minorities, its domination of women. Eco-feminism believes that all forms of domination — be it violence against women or the domination of humans over nature — are interconnected.

Communities in many ways are like individuals. Just as the individual must dig into the past and bring to consciousness the painful events and anger buried there, so too must communities acknowledge and bring to light the horrors from their own pasts, including such things as the years of degradation and violence suffered by aboriginal children in residential schools and the victimization of native people by white society in general. In the words of Vern Morrissette of the Ma Mawi Wi Chi Itata native child care agency, "The thousands of native children attending Manitoba's thirteen residential schools between 1883 and 1969 have left generations crippled by abuse, substance abuse, neglect, suicide, family dysfunction, crime and violence....The effect of the residential schools is cyclical; it continues."[8] (These facts were confirmed by the 1991 Manitoba Aboriginal Justice Inquiry which found that 64 per cent of inmates in Winnipeg's youth detention centres were native; that eight out of ten aboriginal women had reported being abused.) A major step in the direction of healing was taken when Phil Fontaine, Grand Chief of the Assembly of Manitoba Chiefs, came out in 1990 to tell publicly about his own abuse in residential schools. Breaking silence is the first step. As more and more stories and allegations of abuse are revealed, perpetrators (the church, legal system, political system, schools) must resist the temptation to deny responsibility and instead offer support and affirmation to the wounded, be they aboriginals, women, children, or the handicapped.

While building self-worth and personal autonomy is an inner journey of the soul, a community can aid the process by its social attitudes, *by validating the worth of each person.* For example, white society could begin by acknowledging the value of aboriginal culture and learning from its traditions sustainable ways of relating to nature and to one another. Male society can acknowledge the value of female culture and learn from women's ways how to build trusting relationships through co-operation and care giving. From children we can learn spontaneity; from the handicapped how to live within limitations. *By listening to and learning from the experiences of others, especially those who have been so devalued in life, we demonstrate a respect for and a valuing of their unique beings.* This is a whole new attitude in sharp contrast with the current order which *devalues* individuals — women, children, visible minorities, the handicapped — who are positioned in the lower ranks of the social hierarchy.

A healthy community encourages individual self-expression in all spheres of community life — in art, politics, the family, schools, places of work. Unfortunately, many communities are restrictive and exclusive, not allowing members the freedom to be fully themselves without threat of moral or other sanction. Certainly a common complaint about many small communities is that they are stifling, parochial, intolerant of differences, and not conducive to self-growth. A balanced community, on the other hand, knows how to appreciate the differences among people rather than denying, changing or suppressing them.

Communities can also support individuals in their self-development by providing opportunities for creative and meaningful work. Instead of having to submit to the drudgery of a meaningless job, we should be able to work at activities that enhance the meaning and wholeness of our lives and communities — work that is challenging, thought provoking, self-fulfilling; work that helps to define our identity; work that has a social purpose.

The love of self and the needs for autonomy and wholeness are of equal, if not greater, importance than physical and social needs. The starting point for understanding and meeting human needs *is* the self, not the so-called basic needs of food and shelter. Prisons provide the latter, but they are the models farthest from our minds for meeting our needs. Of course lack of food and lodging makes us scream out for help or at least make our pain visible. Yet destruction of self-worth precedes material deprivation. Material supports cannot build a whole self, and this failure cannot be masked by more material provisions. In the end, prisons are not solutions.

Meeting the needs of integration

Everybody has a need to feel a part of something that is larger than themselves — to feel connected to others, to feel "at one" with nature or the world, or to feel a part of the continuation of history and of generations. The needs for affection (to give and to receive), the needs for participation with others, the needs for belonging, for meaning (making sense of the world around us) and for spirituality (belonging to a greater design, purpose or cosmos) — these all can be classified as needs of integration.

Alienation stands opposite to the needs of integration. Where integration has to do with wholeness in the world and the relationship of the individual to the greater whole, alienation is the human experience of being isolated and cut off from the whole. It is the outcome of living in a fragmented society where there is no comprehensible connection between the various parts and the whole, where consumers can buy products without any knowledge or understanding of the underlying destructive processes that produced the object, where someone can say (as someone once did to me): "Why should I care about farming? I get my food at the grocery store."

Our depersonalized bureaucracy and mass production/consumption processes are prime reinforcers of alienation in today's society. The "system" dehumanizes and desensitizes us and contributes to the meaninglessness associated with modern living. Marxists believe that social alienation is caused by the alienation of labour from the means of production, i.e., from the ownership of capital. Still, as ecologist Jonathon Porritt points out, "It is not alienation from the *means* of production or even from the *fruits* of production that really matters, but alienation from the *process* of production."[9]

As a step toward meeting human needs for integration we will have to rethink *how* we produce the things we need — what processes we use, what organization, what technology. Take work. Today, with technology replacing the work of people and doing it more efficiently, the message is that humans are of less value than machines. In contrast, there was a time before industrialism when production relied upon the creative skills of individual craftspeople. The quality of workmanship was a measure of status within a community. Craftspeople had a personal investment in what they produced. They were *creators*, not just producers. Furthermore, through the process of production the craftsperson was connected to nature which provided the materials — a lump of clay became a pot; a pile of bricks became a house; a lamb's wool became a sweater. The end product was something a person could participate in making and something that could be clearly comprehended as having meaning and purpose. With our highly specialized, compartmentalized production processes today, we can't even trace where our basic food comes from, what's in it, or what was the impact of its production on the environment or workers in some far away country.

Commodification — the process of turning people, places, and ideas into objects so that they can be exchanged for monetary gain and stripped of personal, nonmaterial value — is another expression of alienation. For example, a company transfers its employees from city to city as it transfers goods, without regard for family, friendships and community ties. More and more the things we once did for ourselves or gave freely to our families and friends are becoming commodities. Birthday parties at home are replaced by birthday parties at McDonald's, where for a price the company will manage the whole affair, including singing the birthday song. Commodification continues with public urban spaces becoming private shopping malls, where nonshoppers are unwanted loiterers.

Alienation is further reinforced by feelings of powerlessness to alter the course of events or to influence political decisions at the top. At the bottom, millions are denied the chance to work according to their real interests and abilities. Some of the most creative minds in the country are sitting idle or underemployed; others have limited access to work opportunities because of their low status in the social hierarchy.

In order to satisfy the needs for integration, we must focus on reconnecting individuals to their community in meaningful instead of alienating ways. The goal is to *humanize* development by providing opportunities for people to contribute to the whole community according to their abilities and aspirations, and by giving people an active, participating role in shaping their communities. Neighbourhood councils, community development corporations, community run services and planning groups all contribute to building a participatory democracy that has an underlying social ethic of co-operation and caring.

When we look at how communities can be designed to meet the needs of integration, one principle that stands out is mutual aid — a form of collective self-reliance by individuals within a community, based on the interdependencies of people who work together and support one another. In so doing, they contribute to the greater well-being and security of the whole. Co-operation, not competition, is the guiding ethic. The Local Exchange Trading System (LETS) described in Chapter Three works according to principles of mutual aid — individuals agree to barter goods and services among themselves on the understanding that this will mutually benefit all members by creating opportunities for work and meeting people's needs. We engage in mutual aid when, as community members, we help each other build houses, harvest crops, or prepare food for weddings and funerals. Self-help groups are based on mutual aid, an arrangement where people join together on the understanding that by giving to others they will also receive.

Yet another example is the Hutterite colony, which has survived and thrived as a community through the practice of mutual aid, expressed by common ownership of land and sharing of technology and labour among group members. Community relationships based on reciprocity are not only more caring but also more *efficient* than the institutional relationships of our modern world.

To illustrate the point, Hutterite businesses in Manitoba had the capacity to survive during the recession of the early 1990s, while other businesses of the same type failed, because the Hutterite businesses could do the job at less cost. (In one example, Hutterites bid $35,000 on a demolition contract, while the next lowest bid was $74,000.) A *Winnipeg Free Press* article reported that competing businesses were crying foul over Hutterites winning contracts, claiming it was unfair that Hutterites were exempt from paying minimum wages and workers' compensation premiums. In the language of the competitive global economy, the competitors wanted a "level playing field."

I could understand their argument, but I could also understand the Hutterite position: "Money is collective property....No Hutterite has personal wealth. As for workers' compensation, Hutterites have always taken care of their own sick, injured and elderly....We have nobody to pay, because everybody owns everything and everybody's a manager."[10] All the profits earned by the work are distributed toward meeting everybody's needs in the community. The point is that you can't compare two such different systems — one co-operative, the other competitive, one community-based, the other institutional. It is like comparing apples to oranges.

The debate highlights two contrasting models of social organization. It suggests that, contrary to popular belief, *co-operative* not competitive relationships are perhaps the most efficient means to achieving an end. The community of Mondrigon, Spain, described in Chapter Five illustrates this built-in efficiency — industrial co-ops there have the lowest rate of absenteeism in Spain; only once in twenty years has anyone been fired from a job; there are no foremen watching over workers; productivity is the highest in Spain.

It comes back to the social contract between the individual and the community. If businesses were worker-owned, if local communities were the prime care givers and providers of people's needs — in other words, if there were a social contract based on **personal trust**, as opposed to the contractual relationships enforced by an impersonal regulatory bureaucracy — the need for bureaucracy to mediate between competing interests (consumer/producer, labour/management, individual/society) would dissolve, and the benefits of integration could be gained.

MATERIAL NEEDS

Meeting the needs of survival

As a species, humans all have basic *physical* needs for survival — food, air, warmth, reproduction, health. These physical needs can be grouped under needs for *security* (protection, safety, shelter), needs for *health* (nutrition, clean air, sexuality) and needs for *permanence* (peace, sustainability, continuation of generations). As basic as these needs are, there are thousands within our own nation of abundance who find that meeting these physical needs is a daily struggle and an impossible feat.

That Regina has the second highest number of children depending on food banks in the country, while it sits in the middle of the world's breadbasket, is an ironic twist that can only be explained by an economic food system which views food not as nourishment or as life-replenishing material, but as a commodity to be processed, packaged and sold for profit. Yet food, like the air we breathe, is the stuff of life itself. You would think that a country that offers universal health care to its citizens would also offer universal access to basic nourishment. Let us pursue the matter of food further.

The "food system," from the tractor to the dinner table, is controlled by a handful of transnational corporations — Cargill, General Foods, Unilever and a few others — which produce everything, including chemical fertilizers, pesticides, seed patents, food processing, packaging, distribution. To give an idea of the size and power of these corporations let us look at Cargill Inc. Cargill, headquartered in Minneapolis, is the world's largest grain trader and largest private company in the United States. Its subsidiaries operate in fifty-five different countries at 800 locations. According to farm economist Brewster Kneen, the corporation is a major architect of Canadian agriculture and transportation policy. Its influence extends far beyond national borders, as shown by the fact that the corporation was represented on *both* sides of the Canada/U.S. free trade negotiations.

Quite opposite from providing nourishment, the takeover of food production from local farm producers by monolithic corporations and agribusiness has meant the *de-nourishment* of food in the interests of economic efficiency — through the use of chemical fertilizers, pesticides,

156

food additives, overprocessing and underripe picking in order to ship food over long distances. Furthermore, the unquestioning acceptance that food is a *commodity* for which we all must pay the corporation's price, and over which we have no control within our communities, means that access to nutrition is directly linked to what people can afford. Poor people are bound to suffer hunger and malnourishment, which in turn leads to greater incidence of ill health among the poor and diminished ability to concentrate in school.

Yet, *the need for food is so basic that the lack of it destroys not just our bodies but also our human dignity,* as though some of us do not deserve the right to food — the right to live — if we cannot afford it. Perhaps if food were seen and respected for being the source of life and spirit that it truly is, our politics of food would be different — in the current world of plenty, we would waste less, grow organically, eat healthily and share food equally among ourselves, as traditional native cultures have done. The problems of hunger and malnutrition do not happen because of scarcity in the world, but because distribution of food is left to global corporations and the global market. The same global market is forcing a loss of the family farm in North America to agribusiness, depleting the land's natural growing capacity, and turning Third World food crops into export crops to pay national debts with local people's hunger.

In a world of plenty, people should not have to suffer the indignity of begging for food or lining up at soup kitchens after days of not eating. Yet in our affluent country, the lines at food banks are getting longer by the day. There was a 30 per cent increase from 1989 to 1990, according to the Canadian Association of Food Banks.

FEEDING THE PEOPLE

The problem of food and nourishment is undoubtedly complex — rooted in our perceptions, values, economics, politics — and one hardly knows where to begin to address the crisis. One strategy is for communities and local regions to bring home the food system from the global market place, which sends the average food molecule travelling an average of 1,000 miles before it reaches our dinner table. Being caught up in a global economy certainly has not benefited Canadian grain farmers, who now depend on export markets to consume more than 90 per cent of their grain and who, because of an international trading war beyond their control, have seen prices drop to one dollar and fifty cents a bushel — less than it costs them to produce the grain. In Manitoba, the average net farm income for 1991 was $7,430. According to Statistics Canada, in 1990 seventy-five per cent off all farmers in Canada had average gross farm incomes of less than $24,000. (The remaining twenty-five per cent averaged gross incomes of more than $214,000, showing the widening income gap between the few large scale farmers and the majority of medium and small scale farmers.)

A whole new model of agriculture is needed, geared to self-reliance. Development should focus on *local production from local resources to meet local needs*. This means growing and processing food locally on a small scale and supplying local markets *first* before trading outward. It is the proximity principle — reducing the distance between production and consumption. In this way farmers will come to be supported by a local regional economy. There will be less energy expended and pollution created on travel, and food can be grown for its organically fresh and nutritious qualities rather than for its durability.

Many food analysts, such as Pat Mooney and Brewster Kneen, advocate repopulating the rural areas and decentralizing human settlement as part of a strategy to reconnect people with the agricultural land base from which they have been alienated by the forces of urbanization, industrialization and agribusiness. The challenge for rural areas is to create vital communities where people's *full* range of needs and aspirations can be met, including the needs for self-expression, creativity and feeling part of a wider culture. As it stands now, isolation and lack of opportunity are perceived as the major problems of living in the country and a reason why many young people are leaving for the cities. Some possibilities are: connection of the city to rural areas through good public transportation, computer networks where needed (possibly for rural doctors), or the creation of rural/urban exchanges where people could live part time in the city or part time in the country. Another idea is to build modern homestead communities, like Israel's kibbutzim, where people live and farm communally and where city people could participate in living and working for temporary or more permanent periods.

Still the most sustainable solution is to increase the population of the rural areas by reducing the size of farms. Wendell Berry, American poet and author of *Home Economics*, projects that if one square mile of reasonably good land were used for five family farms with an average of three children per family (instead of for one industrial farm), the population would increase from five to twenty-five persons per square mile. This fivefold increase in population would have a ripple impact on local towns and economies, which would have more businesses of every kind, more schools, more culture and more diversity. Studies have shown there is a direct correlation between farm size and rural poverty — poverty increases as farm sizes increase. The classic 1940s study by Walter Goldschmidt in California compared two communities — one small farm community and one industrial farm community — and found that in the small farm community there were nearly twice as many businesses, four times the number of elementary schools, and twice the newspapers and civic and cultural organizations.[11]

Small commercial farms *are* viable. Marty Strange, author of *Family Farming,* showed that in Iowa, from 1976 to 1983, small farms achieved more output per dollar invested than large farms. The reason why today's farmers are going bankrupt and being swallowed up by agribusiness is not poor farm management or low productivity — it is because farmers, in the 1970s and early 1980s, were encouraged by banks and farm "experts" to expand their farms by buying more land (as land prices were going up) and larger scale equipment, which could only be achieved by incurring huge debts. This was workable during the period from 1972 to 1981, when demand for agricultural exports was booming (U.S. exports in this period increased from $8 billion to $44 billion). But by 1984 the boom had turned to bust.

Exports fell but production continued at the same high rate, glutting the market so that commodity prices plummeted. Farmers had to go further in debt just to keep the farm operating. The value of land had risen during the boom to a point that it was worth more than what the farm could produce in income to pay for the interest on the mortgage. In other words, a farmer could no longer pay for land by farming it and high interest rates in the early 1980s compounded the problem of debt. In just fifteen years farms had moved from being self-sufficient to being owned by the banks.

The irony and tragedy is that, today, people with skills to farm — the farmers — can no longer afford to own farms, and people who can afford to own farms are no longer farmers but absentee corporations (75 per cent of U.S. farms are owned by nonfarmers).[12] The question is: how can we provide security of tenure to farmers and opportunities for them to practice their trade and pass it on to their children, given today's global economy?

One model which may provide a solution is the agricultural land trust, a growing new form of land ownership. The agricultural land trust, like the community land trust discussed in Chapter Five, holds farmland in perpetuity for a community of farmers who lease the land from the trust at a rate that reflects the land's agricultural "use" value, not its speculative market value. That means farmers can pay for the lease on the land by farming it. Often there is a set of principles built into the trust which must be accepted, such as maintaining and protecting the land by good stewardship. The land could be donated by farmers with no heirs or sold to the trust by individual farmers or banks which have foreclosed. It could be tied to a community economic development scheme through which a rural community sets up a land trust, using financial incentives from government programs like the Community Bond programs in Saskatchewan and the Grow Bonds program in Manitoba. Some examples of land trusts are the Wisconsin Conservancy, the Marin Agricultural Land Trust in California and the Ottauquechee Regional Land Trust in Vermont. In Manitoba, a group of farmers from Strathclaire have organized to establish an agricultural land trust in their community. There is also interest in the concept in Saskatchewan. The Department of Agricultural Economics at the University of Saskatchewan recently published a report, *Community-based Land Trust Models for Saskatchewan,* by W. Brown, R. Gray and P. Molder. The project was jointly sponsored by the Credit Union Central of Saskatchewan, Federated Cooperatives Ltd., the Interchurch Committee on Agriculture, and the Saskatchewan Wheat Pool.

So far we have looked at the food crisis from the perspective of the rural areas and the need for rural communities to reclaim ownership and control of the food supply system by growing, processing and consuming food (and disposing of food wastes) within their regions, within the closest distances possible. This action would be part of a community economic development strategy to revitalize rural regions, as well as a strategy for decentralizing food production and giving wider access to food.

In the urban context, the same principle of proximity applies — the distance of time and space between food production and consumption should be as short as possible. How can this happen? To begin, urban neighbourhoods need to look at their *own* resources and determine what opportunities exist within a neighbourhood or surrounding region to grow and produce food for local people. In Chapter Four, we looked at the Tall Grass Prairie Bread Co. in Winnipeg, to see how a small scale flour mill can enable local bakeries to buy grain directly from local farmers and mill the flour themselves, thereby reducing costs and keeping production local.

"Community supported agriculture" (CSA), is occurring in other places. City dwellers in Winnipeg, in Minneapolis and residents in various New England towns have developed a model whereby families collectively purchase shares in local farm production. The money pays for farmers to grow organic vegetables which are harvested and divided up among the community membership. Through CSA farmers can raise start up capital early in the season with community cash, and in exchange, the community is guaranteed a steady supply of organic vegetables during growing season. Producers and consumers *share* directly in the real costs of production. In Kimberton, Pennsylvania, 100 families became shareholders for $320 each, which provided them with seven months of home fresh vegetables twice a week and gave the growers $32,000 to finance their greenhouse. Families were allowed to contribute what they could afford within a $100 range, so that everyone would have access to affordable vegetables.[13] In Winnipeg, for $140 consumers can receive a $14 basket of fresh, chemical free produce once a week for ten weeks starting in 1992. According to organic farmer Dan Wiens, the project, known as Shared Farmer, hopes to bring farmers and consumers closer together while eliminating food chain intermediaries like banks and retailers. Prices will be kept to supermarket rates — 20 per cent less than the going rate for organic produce. At the time of writing, two weeks after the announcement of the Shared Farmer project, 140 families had already enrolled.

Urban farming, greenhouses and community gardens can play a significant part in giving people access, control and a chance to participate in producing their own food at nominal cost. This is not a new idea — during the 1930s depression, the grounds of the Manitoba legislature were used to grow food for the poor. Today, with poverty on the rise, once again we see vacant lots in run-down areas being converted into garden plots in all the major cities, from Chicago to Toronto to Vancouver. Cities can promote this process by donating city land and by requiring speculators holding on to vacant land to allow communities to *use* it for gardening and farming. As well as giving people greater access to food, it would help revitalize neighbourhoods by turning empty dead spaces into growing, living places. In Vancouver, a community garden has magically turned a rubble filled piece of vacant land on Francis Street into a place where children and adults get together to socialize and plant flowers and vegetables. (On this same property just six months earlier, there was a battle between developers and community in which developers demolished six houses and forcibly ejected scores of squatters.)

In New York City, a Green Guerrillas nonprofit organization works with 200 community groups each year to help them establish community gardens in their neighbourhoods. Drawing on 300 volunteers from all walks of life, they offer technical assistance, workshops, lessons on urban horticulture, and give away over $100,000 of recycled plant material. We can imagine greenhouses becoming a regular part of our local community centres, which would treat gardening as a form of community recreation where people can get together and participate in food growing, as one of other community activities.

Another example of community self-help is the restaurant co-op planned in Winnipeg to address the need for inner city residents to have access to adequate nutrition. People will pay five dollars for a lifetime membership and then pay twenty dollars a month in exchange for twenty nutritious meals. In addition, members donate two hours a week of their labour toward food preparation and clean up. The restaurant co-op is a small but important alternative to food banks, giving people a sense of dignity, ownership and a place to go to each day and be part of a community. Participants can build social relationships at the same time as they provide food for themselves.

MAKING A SAFE PLACE TO LIVE

Food is just one of our survival needs. The needs for security — i.e., safety, shelter and protection — are also critical to survival, as are the needs for permanence — i.e., peace, sustainability and continuity of generations. Each of these can be understood in terms of the community.

For example, the needs for safety and protection are best achieved in small scale communities where people know and trust one another. Crime and violence are the products of social alienation; the antidote is building communities where people feel a sense of belonging and identity. It has been demonstrated that when people feel ownership of their neighbourhood, when they bond together as a community, then incidents of crime decrease. A good example is the closely knit Logan Community in Winnipeg's inner city (one of the "roughest" areas in town) — a community run, self-sustaining housing development of about 250 people (forty-three rental units, thirty-five owner-occupied homes) — which has seen the rate of crime drop dramatically in the neighbourhood since the community association was formed ten years ago. The Logan community, in fact, has a crime rate that is one-thirtieth the crime rate of the surrounding area (1989 police statistics by zones)! "The community is like a small town," says Lori Smith, manager of the Logan Community Development Corp. "Maintenance costs for the forty-two rental units are cheaper per unit than other public residential complexes in Winnipeg." The association hires people from the community to do repairs and maintenance — people who care about where they live. A neighbour-hood park is watched closely by residents across the street to protect it from vandalism and to prevent their children from being hurt. In addition, the small but caring community boasts that "all except one kid from Logan was a perfect attender at the local school," in an area of the city where consistent school attendance is drastically low and where school transfer rates are over 50 per cent.

The safety of women in the city is another important community issue. One in four women can expect to be a victim of a sexual assault and, according to the 1982 Canadian Urban Victimization Survey, 68 per cent of sexual assaults occur in public spaces. Because of the vulnerability which so many women feel on secluded streets, in parking lots, in public entrances to buildings, in parks — and also because of the many restrictions they live with to ensure their personal safety, such as not going out at night — there has been a growing movement by women's groups to work with communities, the city and police to make the urban environment a safer place.

In Toronto, studies carried out by groups such as Women Plan Toronto and the Metro Action Committee on Public Violence Against Women and Children (Metrac) — the latter did a safety audit of subway stations — led to the city's adoption of the *Safe City Report* in 1988. The *Safe City Report* included thirty-seven recommendations covering urban design and planning, community participation, public transit and policing; the recommendations are aimed specifically at preventing acts of public violence against women. Staying at home behind locked doors as a way of protection seriously limits women's opportunity to participate in social and cultural life. At the same time it isolates women from the support of others who could help them in situations of violence. In contrast, the goal of a safe city as stated in the report, is to "achieve solutions based on enhanced community, not fortified privacy....A safe city is a participatory city." A primary focus of the Safe City Committee, set up in 1989 to implement the report's recommendations and develop further policy, has been outreach to communities, where it has given out safety audit kits, offered free courses on Wen Do (self-defence), and asked women their ideas for changing the design of outdoor spaces to improve safety.

Several urban design initiatives have been undertaken as a result, including the set up of designated safe zones in subway stations which are under surveillance and have emergency call buttons and the de-velopment of a set of design guidelines for the planning department, dealing with things such as improved lighting in public spaces, landscaping guides (high shrubberies or fences restrict visibility), internal security in parking garages and common areas of apartments. The *Safe City Report* notes, as did Jane Jacobs, that the safest streets are streets filled with people walking on them. To this end, the report recommends a mixed residential/workplace land use approach, with corner stores and businesses serving local populations (rather than drawing in strangers from around the city), and so promoting familiarity among neighbours.

HOUSING THE PEOPLE

As with food, shelter needs are not being adequately met by our economic and political systems. The facts that 130,000 to 250,000 Canadians are homeless and that 20,000 people in Toronto are living on the streets without adequate shelter testify to the inequities and imbalances of our current market system for distributing housing. As with food, access to shelter depends on income. *Dropping incomes* for the majority of people because of rising unemployment, the replacement of permanent jobs by low paying, part time service work, and loss in purchasing power relative to the rising costs of living, even while *land costs keep going up* because of population pressures and global corporate investment in land. (One Japanese company has set aside $150 billion — 12 per cent of its investment portfolio — to invest in real estate as a pure commodity abstracted from any concept of geography or community.) These are all factors making it impossible for thousands of people to pay shelter costs for themselves and their children. The welfare cheque doesn't stretch far enough.

While the housing crisis is too complex to be solved by any single local action, there are various steps a community can take toward gaining greater control over the supply and access to local housing. Some of these — community land trusts, co-operative ownership of housing — were discussed in Chapter Five. There are other models too, such as *urban homesteading*, a growing phenomenon in the U.S., in which abandoned homes and apartments are given to squatters and homeless people on condition that they agree to do painting, restoration and other improvements, in the same way that homesteads were given to early pioneers on condition that they improve the land. In this case, the urban poor are the new pioneers.

THREE HOUSING STORIES

This section presents the stories of three different community-based housing initiatives — Street City in Toronto, Habitat for Humanity worldwide and Project for Pride in Living in Minneapolis — aimed at providing shelter for the homeless and poorest people who always seem to fall through the system's cracks. What is remarkable about all three projects is the care and attention paid to human dignity and self-worth as part of the project. Building community is as much a part of their process as building homes.

(1) The story of Street City, Toronto

How do you describe a place that is *so different* — a city made up of homeless people, a community made up of society's dropouts, a small town complete with houses, streets and trees *inside* a warehouse, a place where society's indigents — the alcoholics and schizophrenics of the street — meet with their own mayor for a town hall gathering and decide to invite the "other" mayor of the big city of Toronto to a dinner they will prepare in his honor?

Perhaps the graffiti scribbled on the wall when you walk into Street City says it all — "This is no ordinary city."

Street City was an idea born in 1988 by a group of half a dozen men known as the Balcony Bunch, who lived on and off the streets and were working in the hostels. The idea was to provide a new type of shelter for homeless people — permanent housing (permanent for a few years, anyway) which would belong to a *community*. The community would provide the social support to residents to help them gradually reconnect with the mainstream by eventually finding steady work, permanent housing and a relatively stable life.

The Balcony Bunch presented their ideas to the mayor of Toronto and after gaining his personal support, secured funding for Homes First Society (a nonprofit developer staffed by former street people) to begin work on the project. A site at 393 Front Street was chosen: a two-and-a-half story vacant Canada Post warehouse in an abandoned industrial district at the edge of Toronto's downtown. The doors opened in December 1988. For over a year, forty homeless men slept in the building on mats on the floor, head to toe, while they met with architects and development staff to plan the physical design and social set-up of the future housing.

While working and living together for a year, the men formed close bonds and a mutual support network which became a kind of social foundation for the housing project's future community. When the time came for construction to begin, several of the men were hired on the construction crew, the first jobs they had held in a long time.

What is so amazing is that Street City was initiated, designed and built for the most part, by street people — men and women who know homelessness first hand, who have slept under bridges at night and walked the streets by day, people most of us have written off as hopeless and helpless. What has happened at Street City is no small miracle. The project has won an award. There is currently a feature length movie being made about it, with residents working on production. Street City is something to stop and notice.

The innovative design is one aspect of the project; the other more important aspects are self-development and community development. The design chosen was six houses (three for men, three for women) inside a very large open warehouse. Each house has twelve or thirteen private rooms (each room has a window), a large open kitchen, large bathrooms and an open common space. Since they were built inside an existing structure, the housing units turned out to be the cheapest to build per room in Canada.

Yet this description doesn't nearly get at the feeling of the place. When you walk in, you are struck by the many large, growing trees and plants (donated by the Parks Department); the streetscape and courtyards between the houses; the bright sun shining through a full length skylight on the ceiling, bringing a feel of the outdoors into the interior space; the hustle and bustle of people coming and going, talking, shouting, joking with each other. On the doors and walls you see drawings and wall hangings, and there are messages on the message board. All this gives you the distinct feeling that people at Street City like where they live. Just the fact of having an address makes a world of difference because people can start to receive social assistance and have a certain steady income. The seventy-two men and women who live in Street City now have a place they call home where they can bring friends and cook meals; they also have a community to turn to for emotional support.

Self-determination is the guiding philosophy of Street City. Personal and community development is the primary goal. One of the first things that happens to people struggling to survive in back alleys and on park benches is they lose their hopes and dreams for a better future and their belief in their own capacity to change their lives. Self-dignity and self-esteem have been snuffed out along the way. Apart from providing shelter, meeting the needs of the homeless means giving them back their *dignity* and *power* to act for themselves. Privacy is very important for people coming from the public street. Individuals all have their own sets of keys for their private rooms.

Instead of having to submit to the rules and curfews imposed by hostels, residents at Street City have developed their own set of rules designed to fit their special needs. As one man put it, "You know what's different about living here?....You feel like a human being, like a grown-up, a man. Other places, like the hostels, they treat us like children. So many rules and curfews."

The process of developing rules has been difficult. At first, I was told, the place was like a zoo — no rules, loud parties, fights, drunkenness — until residents finally got together and said enough is enough. They set up a conflict mediation committee made up of six residents, a staff person and a Homes First board member. The committee at first met twice a week for several hours at a time. Some 80 per cent of residents participated. Conduct rules were developed, which balanced with much delicacy and tolerance the need for individual freedom and the need for individual and community security. The collective process of problem solving, decision making and working out conflicts has been a binding force in the community, and also a force for self-determination and self-development. In addition to the mediation committees, residents hold "town hall meetings" every three weeks to discuss goals, future projects and immediate concerns. They also operate an intake committee to decide who to admit when a Street City spot becomes available.

All of this social interaction and work together has developed a strong mutual support network of people helping each other. For example, to encourage one man to get alcohol treatment, his neighbours promised to keep and protect his space for three months. In another example, at the start of the project some residents set up a night bicycle patrol during the winter to give out blankets and hot drinks to homeless people living out of doors. Tolerance and generosity is a noticeable characteristic of street people.

The day I visited Street City there was a town hall meeting. Sandwiches and drinks were served. "Frankly Bob," one of the two mayors of Street City (one male, one female) was facilitating. I was amazed at how people were able to work things out. The issue of cats was raised. The occupancy agreement allowed people to keep cats in their room, but it seemed there were now *too* many cats everywhere. It was agreed that since you really can't keep cats locked up, there had to be some control over the numbers. After much discussion, it was decided to put a freeze on new pets unless they have town council's approval. Another issue was strangers coming in off the street to use bathrooms or to hang around. Guests, naturally, were welcome (unless on the "barred" list) and people who signed in at the door could use bathrooms, but uninvited strangers were seen to be a violation of privacy and security at Street City. It was my impression that safety and security were high priorities; someone was always on duty at the entrance.

During the meeting there was a loud banging and yelling at the side door — someone wanted admission. It was Lenny, a former resident who had been barred from the place — a victim, apparently, of his own undoing. When he was called to mediation twice for drunken violence, he, out of desire to quit drinking, asked that the next time he drank he be evicted. Now Lenny was on the outside, banging at the door, wanting to come back in to the place that had been a home.

One of the Street City goals is community economic development to provide people with skills and opportunities for work. A main difficulty in employing the homeless is that, for one reason or another, many are not able to work steadily. Flexible work arrangements are being tried at Street City. A resident maintenance crew is paid to do the cleaning and odd jobs around the premises. In addition, residents operate and run a Tuck Shop with some staff help. The Tuck Shop is a nonprofit store that sells low cost food and encourages people to cook for themselves rather than go to soup kitchens. A number of residents have organized community dinners every Sunday, and charge one dollar and twenty-five cents a meal prepared by themselves. Residents also run their own bank and thus eliminate the need for money marts, which charge to cash welfare cheques.

Despite its imperfections, Street City has been an astonishing success as a model for housing the homeless yet the building will one day be demolished to make way for a new commercial housing development in the area. This plan was known from the start, when the city leased out the abandoned property. Still the life skills people have gained from taking part in the community will probably last a lifetime. The homes were never intended to be permanent, but to be only a stepping stone — a place of safety, privacy and community support, where people could wean themselves from an isolated existence and learn the necessary community skills to re-establish themselves in society. Many of the residents will find permanent housing in the new development planned for the area. A number of homeless people who came to live at Street City have since gotten jobs; some have gone back to school for upgrading. As one resident said, "I'm learning how to do things for myself and by myself. I like that feeling." When Street City goes it won't be the end but the beginning of a new future for many.

One might ask, will Street City disappear like a dream, an experiment which came and went and was forgotten? I think not. It appears that a second Street City is in the offing and if it goes ahead, current residents could find jobs as staff members of the new project. While Street City will one day have to dismantle its physical structure, its *process* will stand as a model for other projects elsewhere.

(2) Habitat for Humanity

Habitat for Humanity is a nonprofit, nondenominational Christian organization dedicated to building decent and affordable housing for the poor worldwide. Jimmy Carter, former U.S. president, is one of Habitat's strong supporters and committed volunteer workers. He regularly joins with hammer and nail in the work camps to build houses for poor people in the dilapidated U.S. inner cities.

Habitat was founded on the principle of "justice for all people," a biblical ideal that sets the almost inspirational tone of the organization. Habitat's approach to the provision of housing is unique, based on a deep spiritual commitment which incorporates a belief in partnership, community, self-help and the right of each person to a decent home. The idea for Habitat grew out of the vision of two Georgia men who, realizing the enormous need for housing among poor blacks, organized a work project where volunteers joined with their poor neighbours to raise money and build houses up from the ground. Established as a nonprofit organization in 1976, Habitat has since mushroomed into a network across North America with more than 330 affiliate organizations.

While each local Habitat group concentrates its efforts on meeting specific local needs, 10 per cent of its donated funds are set aside to support Third World housing projects. In this way, local and global perspectives are linked together.

One of Habitat's basic principles is that people need *co-workers, not caseworkers* — the idea is that by *working together* with others, the poor will learn new life and employment skills to help them improve their lives. Families who are accepted into the Habitat program agree to give 500 hours of their labour as sweat-equity in lieu of a down payment on a house. Labour is equated as real value which allows families without money to buy their own homes. The families pay off their houses by building their own, and other, Habitat houses. But to keep building costs down, many more hours of volunteer labour are needed. What makes Habitat unique are the *thousands* of volunteers who donate their time and skills to literally build houses together with prospective home-owners.

Plans for design and construction are made a year in advance; all the donated and bought materials are collected. Then it is time for the work camp — a short intense period in which volunteers from all walks of life and backgrounds come out by the hundreds to pick up hammers and nails and begin to raise the houses. Everyone is invited to join the building party; food is served under tents. Plumbing, electrical systems, studding, walls, windows, wallboard, paint and grass — all appear like magic in a matter of a few days. In Winnipeg in 1987, the year Habitat started there, 450 volunteers came out to build two houses and renovate seven. Within a day, the two houses were framed; within five days the families were occupying them. It was like a barn raising. There was a great feeling of accomplishment and inspiration in seeing one's creation rising from the dirt so fast.

What makes Habitat such an attractive model for volunteers is that, in meeting the poors' needs for housing, it also provides a way to satisfy the deep and often neglected needs people have for integration — for meaningful participation in a greater community, for work at something with a social purpose, for involvement in a process bigger than themselves. Habitat draws on people's needs to create, to give and to affect the world. As part of a worldwide network engaging hundreds of thousands of people, Habitat gives individuals a sense that there is something tangible they can do locally, here and now, to make a difference. The feelings of instant community, of friendship, of receiving by giving, are hard to convey in words but they are the essence of Habitat and what makes it work.

Another basic principle of Habitat is that *people living in inadequate housing need capital, not charity.* Charity and welfare are handouts from the top which keep people trapped on the bottom in a state of minimal subsistence. Charity does not offer the opportunity to improve one's position in life, to gain skills or the self-respect and confidence which come from being self-sufficient. Charity is a one way, patronizing model that downgrades the worth of the individual as if she or he had nothing of value to give in return. In contrast, Habitat values the worth of what an individual can give in time and effort in exchange for what he or she receives.

It is Habitat's belief that people are kept poor because they have no access to capital to invest in property. Habitat provides access to capital by offering *interest free mortgages* on their homes, amortized over 12 to 15 years. Habitat doesn't believe in interest. In the words of Jake Pauls, president of Winnipeg Habitat, "Interest is a way for people who have, to make more and those that don't, to pay double." New homes are financed through a revolving loan fund. The fund gets its money from a variety of sources — donations; interest free loans from churches, individuals, businesses; the monthly payments by home-owners toward the principal on their new house. Land is usually given to Habitat at no or low cost by the government (Habitat accepts no government money). Costs of construction are kept to a minimum with volunteer labour and donated construction materials — $50,000 and less for a house in Winnipeg, as compared to $350,000 that government pays per rental unit of social housing over fifteen years! Thus, through a combination of donations, loans, volunteer labour, sweat equity and interest free mortgages, families on low incomes are enabled to become home-owners. Habitat in some cities also restores and builds co-op apartments as well.

Winnipeg Habitat in May 1991 opened up a first-of-its-kind "Habitat Re-Store" which sells, at greatly reduced prices, recycled building materials which have been donated from all over the city — a country club being remodeled, a government housing project undergoing renovations, private businesses, home-owners wanting to give away sinks and windows sitting in their basements and salvage from building sites. Revenues from the store, after expenses, go to finance new house construction by the local Habitat. The depot offers all types of materials from plumbing, to drywall, to screws, to doors, and has struck a popular chord with home-owners who want to renovate at affordable prices. In the first few months of operation, revenues exceeded all expectations (the first two months brought in $28,000). The Re-Store is also conceived as a conservation project to divert waste which would otherwise end up in landfill sites. One unique aspect of the depot is that it allows people on low incomes to trade their skills and time in exchange for building materials, a system consistent with Habitat's underlying philosophy of "work versus welfare."

In summary, Habitat for Humanity is a model of development which draws on principles of self-help, mutual aid, spiritual caring and community spirit to build houses for people in need. While the numbers of houses being built are miniscule within the whole picture of housing needs, the model is important as a concept for how development can be done differently — how a wide community can be attracted into becoming part of the solution for meeting low income people's housing needs. As a highly organized, worldwide co-ordinated effort which is growing each year, Habitat has tremendous potential. For example, in

June 1991, to celebrate its fifteenth anniversary, Habitat International launched a fifteen week building campaign, an effort which brought together over 2,000 volunteers from fifteen different locations, who then travelled in work camps across North America, building homes (1,500 of them) and raising public awareness of people's need for shelter.

By bringing people from all walks of life together, Habitat is a vehicle to bridge the gulf between those who have and those who have not. Bridging and making connections is a first step toward ridding society of its fear of differences and raising consciousness about how the other half lives. For this alone Habitat needs to be credited as one of the new pioneers, breaking new territory of the mind, as it were. Habitat is a step in the right direction.

(3) Project for Pride in Living, Minneapolis

The Project for Pride in Living is a nonprofit corporation in the Phillips inner city neighbourhood of Minneapolis, founded in 1972 by Joe Selvaggio, a former Catholic priest and community activist of the late 1960s. Minneapolis is a sprawling, automobile dependent city with two-thirds of its population living in the suburbs while inner city neighbourhoods have been left to decay, as in so many other cities. Housing is substandard. A line from the Bible — "The temple stands unfinished *until all are housed in dignity*" — expresses the organization's major goal of providing decent, affordable housing to poor people. What became Project for Pride in Living (PPL) started out as a group of advocates helping residents to deal with landlords and the bureaucracy, but shifted its focus in 1972 to become a rehabilitator and developer of low income housing.

Over its twenty year history, PPL has operated with donations from corporations, foundations and individuals; with government co-operation; with volunteer assistance in everything from stuffing envelopes to professional consultation in complex legal and financial transactions. PPL has grown into a multimillion dollar nonprofit enterprise which has built and renovated over 700 housing units and established 162 co-op or leasehold co-units. It manages 333 units of rental housing co-ops, runs a tool lending library, a neighbourhood general store, and a home and office surplus store that trains and employs "hard-to-employ" neighbourhood residents and then helps place them in mainstream jobs. Since its inception, PPL has increased the construction/tax base for the city by $21.7 million and is working to reverse the outflow of population from the inner city neighbourhood — a monumental accomplishment for a nonprofit community organization which functions with the good will and commitment of churches, business people, volunteers and neighbourhood groups, as well as with the good management of its programs.

Despite its having become a $5 million dollar business (its annual operating budget), PPL has managed to maintain its grassroots, human need-oriented, one-on-one approach which grows out of a belief in self-help as the way to improve people's lives. The PPL motto is: *"Give me a fish and I eat for the day; teach me to fish and I eat for a lifetime."* Employing people of colour, giving people tools to fix their own homes, providing families with good quality homes they can be proud of, training residents in life and work skills to ease them off of welfare and chemical dependencies: these are some of the ways PPL has helped to instill pride in people's lives.

PPL began when Joe Selvaggio arranged with the University of Minnesota's Housing Design Department that students, as part of a course, would work with inner city families to repair deteriorating homes. The home-owner was to enlist family and friends to share the labour. Some skilled tradespeople donated their time and some businesses agreed to donate materials. By the end of 1972, forty-five projects had been completed. The next year, using student volunteers, more donated materials (which businesses could write off as tax deductions), and a $20,000 grant from the government, PPL bought a house for $11,500 and refurbished it for rent to a low income family. In 1974, PPL persuaded Midwest Savings and Loan Association to finance a $1 million revolving loan fund from which PPL could borrow to renovate abandoned houses and then retire that loan with a final mortgage which Midwest Federal would issue to the new home-owners from the same $1 million pool. With the revolving loan fund, PPL was able to raise further donations from churches, businesses and other organizations. By the end of 1974, the group had bought and sold five more houses; was operating a volunteer maintenance program on fifty-two homes for repairs; had completed design projects on twenty-five houses through the university class; had distributed labour and material worth $200,000. In 1975, PPL renovated and sold eighteen more homes. The formula was to buy abandoned houses from HUD (federal department of Housing and Urban Development) at a minimal price, restore them and then turn them over at the lowest possible price to low and moderate income families.

In 1975, PPL began contracting its construction work to a company called Stonehammer, a group of native people subsidized by a government training program through the local American Indian Centre. In 1976, a community Tool Lending Library was started for $5,000, in a garage attached to the PPL headquarters. This allowed residents to borrow tools to fix their own homes. The library proved to be an enormous success with 1,800 transactions in the first year alone. By 1978, PPL topped $1 million in business, mostly construction, and had established a substantial reserve fund. Slowly but surely, the neighbourhood was turning around. Available and affordable housing was bringing people back into the neighbourhood. In 1982, PPL began to renovate and develop multifamily housing. It has since built or rehabilitated 668 homes.

Aside from housing, PPL in 1982 set up a separate business, PPL Industries. The idea was to receive contracts from local companies to do particular, labour intensive tasks for them, such as stuffing envelopes, sorting, making crates and recovering metals. The goal for PPL Industries was to provide temporary jobs for unskilled and unemployed minorities in an environment which would serve as a stepping stone toward permanent employment. The racially mixed board included business and social service people. By 1991, PPL Industries was taking in revenues over $1.1 million and was employing 75 full-time and 20 part time workers. Many of the people who come through the doors have come from halfway houses, are dependent on alcohol and may never have held steady jobs in their lives. PPL Industries has an alcohol treatment counselor who organizes support groups among the workers and gives one-on-one attention to people who want help. Although much of the work is routine, there is an easy going, spirited and supportive atmosphere in the workplace. Over the past ten years PPL Industries (now operating as People Unlimited) have seen ninety workers graduate into mainstream jobs.

PPL also started a much needed discount surplus store in the neighbourhood, called the General Store, with a $50,000 foundation grant. At first the Store struggled to keep afloat. Today the Store sells $600 a day worth of new, low cost merchandise donated by local retailers and employs five to eight minority trainees from the community. Another self-supporting business, SHOP, was started by PPL in 1988. It is a recycling enterprise which sells office equipment and surplus merchandise donated by various companies and individuals. Its main goal is to provide jobs and job training to people who are the hardest-to-employ. Trainees put the products into saleable condition, and the store sells them at affordable prices, with about $600 a day in sales.

PPL's work in the inner city does not end with the provision of housing, employment and job training. Its Self-Sufficiency Program, set

174

up in 1988, offers a support program to individuals and families who want to improve their lives through personal development. The program is open to all PPL residents and offers counselling for career, education and parenting skills; programs for children; links to community services for residents and trainees; financial help for clients in transition from welfare to employment.

Project for Pride in Living is an example of an urban-based community corporation which has succeeded in strengthening the social and economic base of an inner city neighbourhood through an integrated approach to meeting people's needs for security and self-worth. It owes its success to the group's unrelenting effort to bring together and co-ordinate the community's untapped and underused resources, namely, its local businesses, churches, volunteers, government programs and the university. What makes PPL a particularly outstanding example is its success at community building, which has established an extensive network of supports. These supports are the community's real strength and long-term security.

In summary, the three housing stories presented above illustrate an important point — that there *are* alternatives for meeting peoples' shelter needs which are independent of both the market system and government housing system. The alternatives involve people meeting their own needs as individuals and as a community. The approach is radically different because human development — not profits, not maintaining a system — is the focus.

A central theme common to all three housing models is respect for human dignity. The philosophy is plain and simple — *people matter.* From this starting point, *how* we organize to meet people's needs for shelter, or for food, safety or whatever, is more vital than the end product — do the processes allow for self-development and self-determination? Do they add to the quality of life, and do they integrate individuals into a community?

CONCLUSION

This chapter has offered a perspective slightly different from previous chapters. The "individual" has been the primary focus, with community examined secondarily for how it can support individuals in meeting their needs and aspirations. Human needs have been presented as an integrated *system* which includes both material and nonmaterial needs.

After all is said and done, it is people's *total* well-being, not the creation of objects, which must become the focus of development. While humans require food and shelter, they equally require identity, self-worth, personal freedom to act, and they need to feel part of a larger culture and community which they can rely on for support. It is these latter nonmaterial needs that give life meaning. If quality of human life, not quantity of goods, were the aim of development, we would begin to see a different world where art, personal expression, human spirit and community were valued over the endless stream of disposable gadgets and name brand consumer items. In any case, since this wasteful consumer life style cannot be sustained by future generations, we had best begin planning for the alternative.

This chapter has outlined a model of human needs based on the concepts of autonomy, integration and survival and presented many illustrations of the model. It is an alternative to the "consumer" model of human needs which is currently dominant, an alternative which looks at individuals and their *self-development* as the essential first ingredient of human needs. This is then extended to the needs of belonging, integration, and finally the material needs of food, safety and housing are discussed. The model quite intentionally has an "inside-out" orientation which relies on the inner strengths and psychological well-being of individuals as the foundation for a healthy community.

This discussion primarily focuses on the positive alternative, rather than on criticism of the failing consumer/welfare model for "meeting" human needs. This consumer/welfare model expands needs into wants and tries to satisfy them through increasing consumption. Not only is this an impossibility, but it also further exaggerates the inequalities, adds frustration through the false promise of trickle-down (hand-me-downs from the rich), and depends more and more on the welfare state to pick up the pieces.

The current model, which looks upward and elsewhere for solutions to personal and local problems, only serves to render individuals powerless over their lives and alienates people from one another. Professionals define what it is we need; mass culture determines what it is we want; the global economy delivers the goods and jobs on which we depend. Soon we stop asking ourselves the essential questions _ what is life about; what do we need; are we truly happy, or is there another alternative? Rather than more analysis of this failing model, we need reminders about the rising permanent underclass and the loss of community to a meaningless consumer culture. We need to get on with the task of developing the alternative.

Central to the model of human needs I have presented (autonomy, integration, survival) is a strong reciprocal relationship between individual human needs and the community. While individual needs are the starting point, the *sine qua non* so to speak, they cannot be treated in total isolation. Community has an important part to play in meeting human needs.

It is hoped that this discussion will lead to a new way of seeing needs, defining them, and getting a sense of our true self-interest. The first step is to shake ourselves out of this bad dream of "happy" consumerism and rediscover our worth and potential as individuals and as communities in meeting our *authentic* material and nonmaterial needs.

ENDNOTES

1   Schumacher, Small *is Beautiful,* p. 48.

2   M. Scott Peck, *The Different Drum* (N.Y.: Simon and Schuster, 1987), p. 54.

3   *Inner City Voice* (May 1991), p. 9.

4   "Getting Help from Helping," in *Psychology 90/91* (Connecticut: Dushkin Publishing Group, 1990), p. 184.

5   Canadian Council on Social Development, *Perception* (Vol. 14, no. 4, 1990).

6   Findings came from a two-year study conducted by a University of Manitoba medical student, as reported in the *Winnipeg Free Press*, 18 September 1990, p. 1.

7   Alfie Kohn, "Shattered Innocence," in *Psychology Today* (February 1987, pp. 54–58). Author refers to a Gallup Poll in 210 Canadian communities; a 1985 national telephone poll of 2,627 randomly selected adults; personal interviews by Diana Russel in San Fransisco, indicating 38 per cent of women report being sexually abused as children.

8   "Schools legacy haunts natives," in *Winnipeg Free Press*, 3 July 1991, p. 8.

9   Jonathon Porritt, *Seeing Green: The Politics of Ecology Explained* (Oxford: Basil and Blackwell, 1984), p. 81.

10   *Winnipeg Free Press*, 22 July 1991, p. 3.

11   The relationship between social conditions and size of farms is further discussed by Marty Strange in *Family Farming: A New Economic Vision* (Lincoln and London: University of Nebraska Press, 1988), pp. 84–103.

12   Ibid. p. 41.

[13] Pat Stone, "Community Supported Agriculture," in *Mother Earth News* (November/December 1988).

Chapter Seven

Building a Community Culture

We must create in every region people who will...know in detail where they live and how they live: they will be united by a common feeling for their landscape, their literature and language, their local ways, and out of their own self-respect they will have a sympathetic understanding with other regions and different local peculiarities. They will be actively interested in the form and culture of their locality, which means their community and their own personalities. Such people will contribute to our land planning, our industry planning, our community planning, the authority of their own understanding, and the pressure of their own desires.

Lewis Mumford
The Culture of Cities

7

Building a Community Culture

Development should emerge as an expression of a particular culture and history of a community as opposed to uniform development based on a set of corporate standards or externally defined "norms." In place of a universal model there will be a pluralistic pattern to development arising from the unique traditions and values of each community, stemming from its own history and the meaning of place.

The fifth and last ingredient for development of sustainable communities is the discovery and revival of a community-based culture. Not everything that happens in a community revolves around economics, power, the environment or the individual needs discussed in previous chapters — how we dance together, talk to each other on the street, think about the world and interact socially also determine the quality of our lives and the type of communities where we live. Just as an individual has an identity, so too does a community. This identity grows out of a *community culture* which is sometimes hard to pin down but nonetheless exists and defines what is special and unique about a group of people or a place.

The reason why *community culture* is important in sustaining communities is that culture is the *glue* that holds communities together and makes them last over generations, even more than economic or political power. **Culture is the soul and life force of a community** — the collective expression of values, perceptions, language, technology, history, spirituality, art and social organization in a community. I am referring here to culture as a *way of life*, distinct from culture as the "high brow" arts.

In the final analysis, communities are able to sustain themselves over generations, not just on the basis of material wealth or power, but on the basis of something deeper and much more intangible — a common identity, purpose and *culture* which bind people together and guide them toward a common destiny. If you destroy a community's culture, its soul, then you also destroy a community. The two are interlinked. As one aboriginal chief from Belize said to an environmental gathering: "Without our culture we will not survive."

So long as culture is kept alive communities will persist, even under threat of extinction by war, economic depression, natural disasters and persecution. Ironically, often the struggle for survival itself helps to strengthen community as people bond together for mutual aid and come to realize their *unity of purpose* and *common identity*. For example, people in Winnipeg remember back to the days of the 1950 Winnipeg Flood as a time of heightened community spirit when people joined together to pile sandbags day and night and help out those who needed relief. Temporary as this occasion for "community" was, it does help us understand part of what creates a sense of community — the mutual sharing and co-operation toward a common purpose and common fate. Other exemplary struggles have resulted in more lasting communities, such as those that formed out of fights to save neighbourhoods from destruction by large developments.

A true community has a heart, a source of feeling and spirit. Its life blood is its culture — the local ways people do things together, their common feelings and values, the way they express themselves in art, their identification with a landscape, their shared experiences of the past and shared dreams and hopes for a future. Obviously these are not items which can be manufactured, bought or ordered: they are life patterns which evolve over time.

What I am speaking about here is *authentic* culture of communities as opposed to mass culture of the Global Village. Where a community culture grows out of the history and unique experiences of a particular people or place, mass culture is an image projected onto our communities (and into our private living rooms) from outside — a manufactured product represented by a Rambo doll, a pair of Jordache jeans, a three bedroom house in the suburbs. Mass culture produces mass *uniformity*. Uniqueness and differences of people, of communities, instead of being nurtured and developed, are rejected for the "single look," be it the World Class City or personal life style culture from California. "McLuhan, for all his glib brilliance," writes Canadian author, Brian Fawcett, "didn't understand that the Global Village was going to be Los Angeles, where the majority of television programming originates."[1]

In the Global Village, conformity replaces diversity. Making culture into a commodity and leveling it to a single common denominator are dangerous and *unsustainable* trends, not only because the "culture" we are buying into is an artificial throw away one, packaged and designed for waste, but also because this "culture" destroys the authenticity and unique character of our communities along with our feelings of community pride in where we live and our histories. In the end, mass culture offers us only meaninglessness, uniformity, and more of the same.

By preserving and rediscovering the particularities of where we live, and by cultivating a local culture tied to our own experience, we can begin to bring back diversity to this world and discover our own identities associated with place. Diversity is one of the keys to building a sustainable world, both in nature, as we saw in Chapter Four, and in human society, because by appreciating and celebrating diversity, we come to respect our differences as people and as distinct communities.

We stand today at a turning point, where the forces of sameness and the need for authenticity are wrestling in a game which can have only one winner. One can see and feel the change — the loss of identity, the victory of the laugh track. What can one do?

The many stories in this book and, hopefully the identification of the five sustainable community themes, show that the future is ours to make. Regarding community culture, I suggest two starting steps for saving and building it. First we must be aware of where to find the culture of communities. I have outlined where to look in the next three sections under the titles (1) *social history;* (2) *natural history;* and (3) *cultural groups*. Second, we must have some direction for our action to rebuild local culture. My findings suggest that *community building* is our essential focus for retaining culture, identity and meaning. The last part of this chapter looks at community as the target of our work to ensure vital cultures.

DISCOVERING THE CULTURE OF COMMUNITY

Reclaiming our social history

Authentic culture evolves from the collective memory of social experiences over time. It is a process of unfolding, of continuity — a process that grows out of *history*. The problem is that in North America history is continuously being eroded in favor of some new fad, instead of being celebrated as a part of who we are today. Buildings and places from the past are not only disregarded, but also discarded to make way for the newest faceless high-rise development.

Russell Jacoby calls this forgetting of our historical roots "social amnesia." Others have named it the "culture of estrangement" and the "culture of narcissism."[2] Whatever its name, we are speaking about the same thing — fragmentation, discontinuity and alienation, where people no longer understand themselves as part of a continuous pattern of generations stretching from the past into the future.

Sustainable community development, on the other hand, is founded on a commitment to the *continuance* of communities, with history an essential ingredient in that continuity. History links a community to its past and in so doing gives it an identity which is more than just passing, more than just superficial. One way to keep the past alive is through story telling about how our communities came to be, where our ancestors came from, what hardships they suffered and how they survived. Telling stories is also a way of getting to know one another. In Wendell Berry's words, "If [people] do not know one another's stories, how can they know whether or not to trust one another? People who do not trust one another do not help one another, and moreover they fear one another. And this is our predicament now."[3]

History can also be kept alive in our physical surroundings. *Heritage conservation* for example can make the past a living part of a community's identity, a source of community pride, and an economic tool to revitalize a neighbourhood at the same time. Heritage does not have to be limited to artifacts in a museum, monuments or designated buildings. Heritage can also mean maintaining and reviving the character of old neighbourhoods — houses, streets, parks, flea markets, shops. As one early heritage conservationist, Carl Westmoreland put it, "People mistakenly view heritage preservation as an elitist activity, not as a tool to revitalize inner city, low-to-moderate income neighbourhoods."[4] Westmoreland is a black activist who helped establish the St. Auburn Good Housing Foundation in Cincinnati which in 1967, with a private grant of $7,000, began buying up absentee-owned houses in a badly deteriorated neighbourhood, renovating them and turning them into affordable housing co-ops or houses for sale on a one by one basis, starting with the worst slum housing. In less than ten years the nonprofit housing group had used its leverage to become a $9 million business, restored hundreds of housing units, several commercial properties, employed and trained hundreds of local people, got the city to upgrade services, and rekindled pride in the neighbourhood by saving its heritage Victorian row houses and mansions for decent housing.

Similarly, in Pittsburgh in the early 1970s, a citizens' group, the Pittsburgh Historic Landmarks Foundation (PHLF), successfully fought and stopped the city from bulldozing all of its history away. The PHLF was instrumental in setting up a city wide preservation effort to save buildings and neighbourhoods with architectural character, using a revolving loan fund as a tool for renovating neighbourhoods on a house by house basis. The efforts were combined with government assistance programs designed to allow the approximately 75,000 poor people living in the historic areas to continue to live there after restoration. The method developed by the PHLF for historic restoration was a pluralistic, community approach which worked with neighbourhood groups to analyze the unique character of each neighbourhood — its history, demography, cultural life and architecture — and come up with a neighbourhood plan for how to proceed. Arthur Ziegler, one of the founders and key actors in PHLF, said, "We emphasized the uniqueness and goodness of neighbourhoods — not the deterioration — and the need to save buildings as a significant resource for the city." This was in contrast to the message given by the Urban Redevelopment Authority that people's communities were bad places that needed redevelopment.[5]

In Chapter Five we looked at the Milton Park community, another example of a heritage neighbourhood which used restoration, in conjunction with a community land trust, as the way to maintain the neighbourhood's historic social and cultural character. What is now being seen is that heritage is more than buildings: it is what goes on, in and around the buildings as well. Heritage can mean *preserving a way of life* for a community. Preserving a way of life is preserving a community culture. In Toronto, the Kensington market is an old European style market filled with a diversity of smells, crowds of people and stalls which stretch over several city blocks. There you can find everything from clothing, to kitchen wares, freshly killed chickens, vegetables and spices which you couldn't find in a regular supermarket. This is not a market plunked down as part of a redevelopment scheme, like the festival markets being promoted in water front redevelopment packages across the country, but is an organically evolved and integrated part of the community's multiethnic identity.

Kensington market has become a *cultural heritage resource* for the city, an expression of Toronto's rich multiculturalism attracting people and visitors from all over each weekend. Still the market is mainly a support to the people in the neighbourhood, mostly poor new immigrants for whom the market is a place to buy, sell and bargain for fresh foods and other items of daily use at affordable prices. We are fortunate to still have this market. In the 1970s, city planners, showing wanton disregard for the meaning of place and community, had plans to demolish the area until they were stopped by a general halt put on all urban redevelopment in Canada.[6]

A similar story can be told of the Strathcona Chinatown district in Vancouver, which was also to be torn down and redeveloped. A long citizen struggle eventually saved the area, which today is not only one of the most vibrant parts of Vancouver's downtown, but has helped to revive adjacent areas as well. In both these cases, the preservation of neighbourhood culture and local ways of life have had spinoff benefits for the rest of the city, while securing the future of the local communities.

In Minneapolis over the past ten years, the Cedar Riverside community has restored several local theatres as a step toward revitalizing the unique cultural history of that community, once Minneapolis' major theatre district. The neighbourhood community development corporation worked with theatres, businesses and community organizations to upgrade the theatres and create new commercial activity around them.

In downtown Winnipeg, the old Walker Theatre, once famous for drawing big crowds to hear speakers and live theatre from the 1920s to the 1940s, has recently been restored after years of operation as a chain cinema. Not only has the historic three story domed structure been restored to its original design, but the building has been restored to its original *use*. I was intrigued when recently I attended a double bill lecture at the theatre — one hour on Winnipeg's urban climatology by a local geographer and one hour on the plight of chimpanzees by Jane Goodall — to discover hundreds of people lined up around the block, waiting to get into a full house. This tells me there is a deep desire for this type of community gathering place.

Heritage gives *symbolic* meaning to a place. As I write this book there is a raging debate going on in Winnipeg over whether to take down the barricades at the historic corner of Portage Avenue and Main Street, which were put up in 1976 to prevent pedestrians from crossing the street and to divert people instead through an underground shopping mall as the passage to the other side. Portage and Main has been the most important Winnipeg intersection and a vital part of Winnipeg's history for over a century, as early photographs from the 1870s attest. The famous 1919 general strike was staged on this corner. Over the years the corner evolved as a symbol of the city's identity and a source of local pride; hearty Winnipeggers boast it is the coldest and windiest corner in Canada. The decision to divert pedestrians into the mall was a behind-closed-doors deal struck between the city and developers at the intersection's four corners, who wanted to increase commercial trade with an underground mall. At the same time, the barring of people from the historic corner was supported by traffic engineers whose vision of

186

the street (and city) is limited to traffic flow and does not include people, meaning or history. Despite citizen protest, the barricades were erected.

Here is a sorry example of what can happen when a community's history, instead of being nurtured and integrated into its future development, is disregarded in favor of short-term commercial gain and "efficiency" planning. As *Winnipeg Free Press* editor Christopher Dafoe says, "The barriers at Portage and Main constitute a grave insult to the people of Winnipeg. They honor the automobile over the mere human being: they serve notice that those set in authority regard the rest of us as little more than a herd of sheep to be penned in, directed and controlled."[7] Yet the fight for the historic intersection is not over, and there has been a recent call for it to be re-opened.

Reclaiming our natural history

In 1957, twelve women chained themselves to a 100 year old elm tree, which sat right in the centre of Wolsely Avenue in the old Wolsely neighbourhood of Winnipeg, to prevent the tree from being cut down by the city works department (which had decided in the name of planning efficiency that the tree had to be removed to allow increased traffic flow through the neighbourhood). It was one of those magnificent old elms whose size and splendor had given it a special place and meaning in the history of the old neighbourhood. The original road had been built *around* the tree, leaving the elm as a landmark in the centre of the street. The elm tree became a hot political issue, with local residents and the parks department trying to save the tree while traffic engineers tried to destroy it. The tree met a tragic end when it was dynamited in the middle of the night by an unknown assailant, but the memory of the Wolsely Elm still lives on in the community through the continuing stories about it.

What often isn't realized by planners and developers is that people are very attached to the natural features of their communities — the particular trees, birds, flowers, rivers and unique climate. (What else could inspire someone to boast about living in forty below weather?) Thus a place's *natural history*, along with its social history, is an important factor in shaping a community's identity. Where we live includes the local streams, indigenous plants and animals, and special geographical features such as woodlands, moraines, hills and gorges. To our detriment, many of these natural features have been lost in our modern experience, particularly in the cities where landscapes have been levelled and paved over for development, streams diverted underground into sewers, and buildings erected which block off sunlight and visual and physical access to the rivers.

I grew up in Winnipeg, built at the junction of two major rivers, yet I never experienced those rivers except to see them occasionally from a car window as I crossed a bridge. The recent reclaiming of the rivers' junction from the Canadian National Railway for public use has been a major step toward integrating Winnipeg's natural and social history into its present and future self-image. In Montreal, the unique natural feature that identifies the city is its historic Mount Royal, where McGill University is situated. McGill College Avenue opens up to the mountain with a view that is quite spectacular. In 1984, the developer Cadillac Fairview, backed by Mayor Drapeau, came up with a redevelopment plan for the street — a combined concert hall, office towers and commercial mall — which would block off the view of the mountain. Citizen groups, heritage groups and others fought together to save their mountain view which had been a part of the history of the city since 1850, and they won. Toronto's downtown lake front has been cut off from the rest of the city by the giant Gardiner expressway which runs directly along the lake. Recent recommendations from the Commission on Toronto's Harbourfront have called for the expressway to be dismantled in order to integrate the lake and the city.

The Kitchener-Waterloo region of Ontario, on the other hand, has been active in preserving the natural history of its local region before the damage is done. The region's official plan has mapped out and designated what are called Environmentally Sensitive Policy Areas (ESPA) for preservation and protection. These are "areas characterized by species and ecological conditions that are unique and/or rare at the local or regional level and...are highly sensitive to human land use impacts." They include woodlots, bogs and swamps, marshes and lakes, flood plain areas, rivers and streams which are regionally unique in terms of the flora and fauna they produce. Many of the ESPAs "provide a linking system of undisturbed forests or other natural refuge for the movement of wildlife over considerable distance." In the City of Waterloo there are 548.5 hectares of woodlands, remnants of the Northern Hardwood Forest which the city is developing legislation and programs to protect. Over 90 per cent of these woodlands are owned privately, and guidelines for development and human intervention need to be carefully evolved. Since the mid-1980s the city has required that a predevelopment plan be submitted to maximize tree preservation in both subdivisions and individual lots. The projects are monitored during construction by an environmental inspector.

A natural restoration project is going on in San Francisco with the historic Mission Creek off Mission Bay. Some 150 years ago the area was a salt marsh, teeming with wildlife and marine life. The Coast Indian nation lived off the marsh at Mission Bay for 5,000 years. Then the new immigrants arrived, and over the next century the bay was filled in, parceled out for sale, paved, and turned into railway yards. Today, the lands are undergoing a redevelopment once again, only this time to be restored to their original state. The Mission Creek Conservancy, a public benefit organization supported by the Southern Pacific Co. (the major property owner), has developed a plan to restore the narrow creek — a remnant of an original wide-spreading tidal marsh — into a tidal park consisting of forty-four acres of land and about forty-nine acres of water with islands, marshes, mud flats and wildlife. Woven into the park will be a new residential community built adjacent to the mud flats. The Mission Creek Conservancy in 1986 published the book *Vanished Waters,* which tells the detailed social, biological and geological history of Mission Bay and so re-acquaints San Franciscans with their lost waters.

This brings me to a project which is unfolding in Winnipeg — the redevelopment of 100 acres of historic lands at the junction of the Red and Assiniboine Rivers, known as The Forks.

THE FORKS: DISCOVERING THE MEANING OF PLACE

The Forks is a very special and unique place, not just to Winnipeggers but to all of Canada and North America. What makes it unique is that the Red and Assiniboine Rivers come together here and nowhere else, right in the heart of the continent. Because of the confluence of these two rivers, the Forks became a natural meeting place for humans as far back as the receding of the glaciers. In fact, this site is the birthplace of all western North American exploration and settlement and the crossroads of native North American and European cultures in the region. Archeological finds date its use back 6,000 years. This site was the centre of native tribal politics and struggles in the West; the location of five fur trading forts; a settlers' village; the first experimental agricultural farm in western Canada; the original railway terminus for the Northern Pacific Railway; the transfer point for new immigrants to Canada moving West. Because of the regular flooding which created even layers of sedimentary rock, artifacts have been neatly filed in the soil like a time chart, making it an extremely rich and valuable archeological site. Archeologists have said that these lands should be classified as a World Heritage Site.

Despite the natural beauty and the rich heritage of the Forks site, Winnipeggers have had it hidden from them for over a hundred years since the CNR built its rail yards on the land in 1886, barring people from the site. For one hundred years it was as if the lands had never existed. Then in 1989, after much negotiation, the lands were liberated from the railroad with a public purchase that resulted in a small national park and walk-way being developed in a strip along the river bank; the rest of the lands were turned over to the Forks Renewal Corporation (FRC) for development. (The FRC has the three levels of government as its board members but is constituted as a private, arm's length corporation.) Upon experiencing the site, people have become attached and re-aqcuainted with the lands as part of their own history. In just a few years it has become the location of numerous outdoor festivals and gatherings — Canada Games, International First Peoples Gathering, Children's Festival, Festival du Voyageur, Environment Days.

That is the good part. The bad part is that the historic lands are under serious threat of being paved over and developed for commercial purposes. When the FRC was set up it was given a mandate requiring it to become financially self-sufficient through management and development of the lands. As a result, the Forks Renewal Corporation has courted revenue-generating projects — a hotel, a commercial leisure centre, a market, a tourist centre with spaceship simulator ride, and, at one time, a hockey arena. None of these developments speak to the unique natural and cultural history embedded in the place. The bricks and mortar type of development does not blend with the open, already existing parklands nor the kinds of outdoor activities which people seem to want.

At the same time, the closed structure of the private corporation does not allow the public to know what plans are being negotiated behind closed doors. As a result of a lack of public accountability, certain fiascos have arisen, such as a proposal to build a multimillion dollar German Cultural Centre on the site, subsidized with more than $2 million of public money. Winnipeg's multicultural community protested because it seemed that one ethnic group would be represented at the Forks while others were not. The general public opinion was that only a *multi*cultural centre would be appropriate for the site, except for a separate Aboriginal Centre, in respect for the aboriginal people's long history on the site.

From letters to the newspapers, editorials and local talk shows, it seems that people in Winnipeg want a historical and cultural park, not concrete buildings and parking lots. The citizens' group eening the Forks (of which I am a core member), has called for a new structure to manage the historical lands. *Preservation,* not development, is to be the guiding principle. The structure proposed is a Heritage Land Trust which would have an open membership and be operated by a citizen board consisting of representatives from interested community groups (heritage, ecology, neighbourhood, downtown business) and elected persons from the membership at large. The guiding principles for development would be heritage principles: preservation, restoration, maintenance, reconstruction and adaptation to *compatible* uses. Projects that fit under these guidelines would include such things as cultural gatherings, community festivals, restoration of indigenous prairie grasslands, archeological digs, a Hudson's Bay museum in the existing buildings on the site, or a newly constructed aboriginal or multicultural centre. A public structure to manage the lands would allow citizen input, and the adoption of heritage principles to guide land use would insure that the unique meaning of place would be respected.

Winnipeg is a city of diverse ethnic cultures. It is also home to the largest urban native community in this country. If the Forks were to live up to its historic meaning as a meeting place, the lands would be maintained as a heritage park and continue to be used for such things as public gatherings, cultural events, festivals and other uses which bring people of all types together. Winnipeg does not have a major park in its core area. The Forks has the potential to become an urban sanctuary in the heart of a busy city, filled with spirits of the past and the healing spirits of nature. It could be a place where different cultures meet, as it was in the past. The reclaiming of the Forks lands is a step toward the bonding of the city's cultures. It could help people to appreciate in a new way the continuity and historical connection between our ancestors of European and native descent. This is especially important today when white and aboriginal communities are facing each other over many painful issues such as historic land claims and the abuse of native children in residential schools.

In conclusion, the Forks is an example of how development could evolve out of the *meaning of place and history* and give to a community a sense of cohesion and cultural identity. To take a piece of land (or street corner or building) and say, "What is the most *appropriate* use for this land given its social and natural history and its meaning to a community?" — this is an altogether different approach from letting the market decide on use depending on "what the market will bear." In every community there are special places which hold symbolic meaning for people. Were "community" a first consideration, these places would be developed with the goal of preserving the meaning of place.

Cities and nature are often thought of as opposites. Is that to say that human habitat, as it grows to a certain size and complexity, cannot co-exist with nature? This is a real and serious question we will have to answer for our future. The Gitskan and Wet'suwet'en nation's history points to the existence of a large city-state in the Pacific Northwest some 6,000 years ago, called Dimlahamid by the Gitskan and Dzilke by the Wet'suwet'en. Anthropologists credit the ancient civilization as being the most elaborate and sophisticated material culture ever produced by a hunter-gatherer society. According to oral tradition, the ancient city, which spread for miles along the confluence of the Bulky and Skeen rivers, suffered a series of internal wars and ecological upheavals (accounts backed by archeological finds). The people eventually decided to abandon the city-state and disperse in all directions because they could see that their society had lost its social and ecological balance. The Gitskan and Wet'suwet'en still carry the lessons of Dimlahamid today, in their local traditions and stories passed down through generations for thousands of years. These traditions tell of the need to respect the delicate relationship which people have to the earth and each other.[8]

Dimlahamid could perhaps be a lesson for us today. If we are going to continue living in large populated areas, it is our challenge to develop an ecological sensibility which respects the natural and social histories contained in our cities and to make this heritage part of our *community* development. The community is the best place to start because it is there, at the neighbourhood level, that people truly know each other and also love their creeks, birds, river banks and trees as a part of themselves.

CULTURAL GROUPS: THE MULTICULTURAL WEAVE

As the 1991 Citizens' Forum on Canada's Future pointed out, Canada is both a nation of diverse *regions* and diverse *cultural groups*. Cultural diversity is a cornerstone of Canadian society and Canadian identity. Any discussion of the culture of communities would be incomplete, therefore, without considering the diverse cultures which make up our society. The Citizens' Forum tells us that from the time of its founding in 1867, Canada chose to preserve the "diversity of Canadians....The acceptance of diversity as a source of pride and richness was to be the cornerstone of the new state." It asks, "Will the Canada of 1992 continue to be founded on respect for all of its diverse peoples?" Then it answers, "Yes, based on a conviction that all Canadians...will benefit socially, culturally, economically, from a revitalized federation that will recognize the diversity and different needs of its many peoples."[9]

Canada's future hinges on whether, as a society, we can discover our "unity in diversity," to borrow a term from ecology. To achieve "unity in diversity" we must do two things: (1) accept and respect our *differences* as cultures, as distinct communities, as people; and (2) find ways to get to know each other and work co-operatively together, as a *community-of-communities*, linked by a common vision and unity of purpose.

Cultural diversity is one of the cornerstones of Canadian society. But, for there to be diversity, there have to be distinct cultures, *distinct communities* which are recognized and appreciated for their uniqueness. I would like now to examine two distinct cultural groups — the women's community and the aboriginal community — to see how their cultural traditions and ways of life are influencing and guiding the social/economic/political development of their communities. Both groups have been trapped on the bottom rung of the social hierarchy, facing low incomes, discrimination in the workplace, low self-esteem and limited access to mainstream economic activity. Having been shut out of the system, both groups are now turning inward and discovering their strengths within their unique cultures.

In recent years, women in North America have become aware that there is, in fact, a distinct women's culture based on a shared set of values, ways of relating to the world, specific needs and common historical experiences. Out of a commitment to their shared culture, women have formed an active and evolving "women's community" comprised of women from all walks of life and from diverse groups, who are all concerned with women's health, family violence, safety in the streets, women's spirituality, improving women's economic conditions, even urban planning as it relates to women.

I would like to make special mention of one group in Minneapolis — the Women's Economic Development Corporation (WEDCO). WEDCO is an outstanding example of a community economic development organization in which women help other women to become financially self-sufficient through business ownership. The success of this small organization has defied all odds. It helped set up 564 new businesses in the first three years, of which only five have failed. Most amazing is the fact that the majority of women who WEDCO helped start businesses have been poor immigrants on welfare, with incomes below $10,000. What is the secret to WEDCO's success? It is that the organization (which consults one-on-one with clients, facilitates workshops, operates a loan fund) *respects the special needs and ways of women,* and tailors its programs to fit with these. For example, WEDCO recognizes that women prefer to take less risk in business than men and start smaller. Also, helping clients build confidence in their own capabilities and business judgement is an essential part of the WEDCO process, which is more than just creating a business plan. The women's approach to development exemplified by WEDCO is an important model. There is a more detailed account of its work in Appendix One.

The aboriginal community is the other cultural group I want to briefly mention here. Spurred on by the events of Meech Lake (Elijah Harper's famous "No") and the Oka blockade, the aboriginal community has been gaining confidence and assertiveness in all areas. This is evident through a whole range of activities including pressure for aboriginal self-government, an aboriginal justice system (supported by the landmark 1991 Manitoba Aboriginal Justice Inquiry) and settlement of native land claims. There are also strong court challenges to provincial hydro megaprojects such as James Bay and Conawapa. The 1991 convention to choose a new Assembly of First Nations' chief captured the interest and respect of the Canadian public. Polls taken that year showed that Canadians have more trust and regard for native leaders than for their own elected politicians.

In Winnipeg the aboriginal community is in the process of purchasing the 150,000 square foot Canadian Pacific Railway (CPR) station for conversion to an Aboriginal Centre, which will provide space for aboriginal businesses, agencies, conferences, an aboriginal newspaper and is big enough to hold indoor powwows for 2,000 people. The centre will be a focal point for aboriginal people in the city. It is part of a holistic revival of aboriginal culture which is instilling community pride and providing a direction for the future. Traditional culture is the healing agent — a spiritual power to transform family relationships, instill feelings of self-worth, bring about community empowerment, create respect for nature (the aboriginal community held an International Environmental Gathering in Winnipeg in 1991), and even heal criminals (a camp has been set up in northern Ontario to teach aboriginal offenders about their culture, using sweat lodges and other cultural traditions.) Because the future of the aboriginal community is important to all Canadians, I have included a more detailed discussion of this topic in Appendix Two.

194

In order to attain "unity in diversity" in our local communities and in our larger multicultural society, we must respect the different ways of people and their unique cultures. It is not easy, as the Canadian constitutional debate has demonstrated. Differences scare people. As a result there is racism and discrimination. Much of the racism and discrimination in our society stem from simply not knowing one another.

An incident highlights this point. A native woman in Winnipeg was standing at a suburban bus stop with her twelve year old daughter. Three teen-age boys arrived and began laughing and making Indian war whoops. The taunting continued on the bus with racist insults and throwing pennies at the woman and her daughter. Hurt and angry, the woman decided to go to the boys' school and speak with their principal. The teens were hauled down to the office. After much consideration, the woman decided that what she wanted more than anything else was for the boys to see that she was as human as they were. So, swallowing her rage, she arranged for the boys to spend time with her, to come with her to work and other activities. As it turned out, the woman was an associate producer for CBC radio and had been trying to put together a series on racism in the city. The boys came with her to work, went to speak to a newspaper columnist and visited a core area native family services agency. What occurred was something of a miracle. The boys and the woman got to know each other well, and out of that grew a deep respect and friendship. The boys were so transformed by the experience that they told their story on local and national radio, along with the woman. The incident has become a kind of parable and is now being filmed by the National Film Board of Canada.

The moral of the story is that if we are going to live in a culturally diverse society we must come to *know* each other, both our differences and our commonalities. In this regard, a friend of mine has come up with a scheme in which all Canadians, when they turned eighteen, would be given the opportunity to live and work in other communities across the country for a period of two years as part of their service to the nation. Aside from being a broadening personal experience, it could help to forge bonds and linkages among the many separate and distinct communities and be a step toward creating a *community of communities*.

In Canada's pluralistic society most people identify with a number of different communities with distinctive boundaries. For example, I belong to a women's community, an ethnic community, a neighbourhood community, an activist community and an arts community. Other people have different but similarly mixed lists. Identification and interaction with these various "communities" (with some I have stronger bonds than with others) has *enriched* my life, rather than causing me conflict. At the same time, as I cross over boundaries I bring to each community a piece of myself from all the different groups to which I belong. The extent to which I am able to cross over is mutually reinforcing both for myself and for the various communities. If we take this single case and multiply it a million times over to include all the people in our country, we will see a very dense and complex network of overlapping and crisscrossing relationships. The crisscrossings are what creates sharing and communication *among* communities and gives reinforcement to our social fabric.

In short, the "community of communities" calls for a balance between *unique cultural expression* and *cross-cultural sharing*. The culture of specific groups can be a source of strength and knowledge which help to empower these groups and at the same time contribute to the richness and knowledge base of the broad society.

Our brief examination of social history, natural history and cultural groups shows the texture and strength of local culture. One of the things we have discovered which will be useful in building sustainable communities is that a community's culture evolves out of a bonding of people to *each other* and to the *special places* where they live. A culture rooted in a local community promotes ecological land stewardship because "a culture contains, and conveys to succeeding generations, the history of the use of the place and the knowledge of how a place may be lived in and used."[10] The second thing we have discovered is that history finds its safe home in a *living* community, not in museums but in the memories and daily activities of people who live there. To create living communities we have to restore the moral basis of relationships, which evolves from our community history.

BUILDING A NEIGHBOURHOOD CULTURE

Culture is an evolutionary, organic process — it can't be manufactured. Yet we *can* do things to nurture and stimulate the process of cultural growth from within our communities. What we can do is build dynamic communities which have a life and integrity of their own — authentic communities.

Community has to do with a *bonding* which occurs among people. Committee groups are not communities. Empty places on a map are not communities. Suburbs which people leave during the day to go to work and come back to at night in cars are not communities. To begin with, there has to be continuing, *meaningful* human interaction in order to create the social bonding which is a prerequisite to building community culture.

One of the first things we need to do to build neighbourhood communities is to create the social conditions for bonding to occur. Many of our geographical neighbourhoods are not communities because people do not rub shoulders with each other or share experiences together. Building neighbourhood communities means creating human interaction where we live.

At one time people walked to markets, sat and gathered in squares, and interacted in public meeting spaces, which were the community living rooms. Today, people have become much more isolated and atomized. In fact, community has been unraveling since the end of the Second World War, when the automobile began to take precedence over people, and people began to move further and further away from the centres into segregated, sprawling suburbs connected by thoroughfares, freeways and bridges. New census data shows that suburbanites will soon make up the majority of people in North America.

As people moved out of the centres, inner city communities became places for people left behind, mostly the poor and indigent. Inner city neighbourhoods were seen by planners and politicians as eyesores, cancer spots to be removed. In many instances, whole inner city neighbourhoods were bulldozed to make a way for cars speeding from the suburbs to some other destination. People were uprooted, separated from their friends and relatives and herded into government projects which had no history, no community, no neighbourhoods, no informal mutual support networks. Cut off and alienated, many people turned to violence, drugs and self-destruction. There are forces at work today in a number of inner city communities to turn this situtation around. An outstanding example is the Downtown Eastside Residents' Association (DERA) in Vancouver which, in the traditional "skid row" area of the city, has improved safety, added parks, upgraded and built housing, established a community centre and reclaimed the neighbourhood spirit to the extent that it has elected several people to City Council.

It has not been just core areas which suffered from the loss of community — the suburbs *never* managed to gain community. Many studies[11] have revealed how alienating the suburbs are as places to live, lacking in social supports and culture, and demanding a life style chained to the automobile. Suburbs abound with shopping malls, seas of parking lots, giant food and hardware stores you have to drive to, fast food restaurants, strip malls, and housing subdivisions plunked down like islands in the middle of nowhere. What has been lost are local neighbourhood businesses, corner stores, streets which invite people to walk along them, places for people to congregate informally, and most of all, a feeling of community. (Most suburbs even lack sidewalks.)

A move is now underway to avoid these maladies. An architect/planning team from Miami, Andres Duany and Elizabeth Plater-Zybeck, from their extensive research of old towns over the past ten years, have developed design guidelines for recreating new old-fashioned communities in the suburbs, based on traditional designs of eighteenth and nineteenth century towns. The new old town communities are people-oriented places designed for walking and social interaction.

In 1991 the architects completed construction of their first town in Maryland. The principles of design require that the town centre be no more than a five minute walk from any house; that houses be built close together or side-by-side and close to the street to foster a tighter feeling of community; that streets are narrow and built in comprehensible patterns which encourage walking to meaningful destinations (as opposed to meandering cul-du-sacs); that architectural style be based on the specific history, traditions and particularities of a region, with buildings contracted out to many different architects and builders to ensure a diverse patchwork as opposed to a formula design; that civic buildings and parks be located as focal points. In addition, the team has developed an ordinance that can be adopted by local councils (200 planning departments have ordered copies of the ordinance) which lays out codes which specify details such as the *requirement* that there be corner stores.

As promising as this sounds, the physical environment can provide only a shell within which interaction can occur, when the time comes to actually build community. Communities need people and activities and *reasons* for getting together. The "reasons" are everywhere, when we have "community" as our goal. We need only look around us and use a bit of imagination to uncover a multitude of projects in our neighbourhoods which would be suited to building community pride and identity. For example, we might:

- establish a community newspaper.
- develop a community hub — a centre for people to gather.
- start a popular theatre group.
- encourage the formation of many kinds of community groups.
- set up neighbourhood councils.

198

- pick an issue that matters to people and fight a battle together.
- organize collective work activities around improving the community.
- put on community festivals featuring local musicians, crafts and foods.
- start a neighbourhood recycling project.
- write a book about the neighbourhood and its history.
- hold visioning sessions about the future of the community.
- plant a community garden.
- run community education courses.
- compile a community inventory.

This is just a partial list of some of the diverse activities which bring people together, instill community pride and start to build a community culture. Other examples in previous chapters, such as land trusts and community economic activity, also contribute towards the goal of creating an interactive, dynamic community where social bonds can form.

A neighbourhood newspaper can be an important vehicle for organizing a community and people getting to know each other by providing information on community issues, sharing community views, telling the stories and history of the neighbourhood and encouraging people to become active in the community. The *Inner City Voice*, a monthly newspaper in inner Winnipeg, is a good example. Its purpose is to unite and empower the people who live in the core area of the city. News stories are almost all written by residents themselves about their lives, their feelings and everyday issues that affect them. Covered are topics such as people's experiences with overcoming illiteracy, questions and answers from the Community Unemployed Help Centre, local school events, political issues such as public transit fare hikes or social program cuts, racism, what it's like being a teen mother, and poems and short stories by local people. Its honesty and directness make it one of the most readable and stimulating newspapers I've read.

The paper has an outreach worker who goes to community meetings and inner city schools, where she gets children and teens involved in writing. In some cases people have discovered a hidden talent and have gone on to do more writing. The newspaper also organizes regular forums on community issues and invites everybody to come and express their views. Financially, the paper is supported by local advertising, a government grant and subscriptions from across the city, but it is provided free of charge to the community. Anyone who knows the city would have to agree that the *Inner City Voice* has been a major force in building inner city confidence, pride and identity.

A community hub is also important for bringing people together, since it is a place where people can gather informally and interact with each other. In Vancouver the Carnegie Library, a restored heritage building on the corner of Main and Hastings, acts as a hub for the community where people come to read, meet, talk, play chess and take part in a multitude of community activities. This building, donated to the city by steel magnate Andrew Carnegie, had been sitting vacant for years. DERA, the local residents' association, fought for seven years to have it turned over for the community's use. Today, it stands as the *most* used library in all of Canada. But it is also a community centre used for political meetings, dances and bingos. The Carnegie Library is a kind of community "home" which provides people with a place to go to and a community to join, whose only other "home" is likely to be a 10' by 10' room in a residential hotel.

Other neighbourhoods have similar hubs. A converted church known as the People's Centre in the Cedar Riverside neighbourhood of Minneapolis is the centre for community planning, health, education and other activities. This building, originally owned by the university and slated for demolition, was fought for by the local residents' association. The fight itself helped to focus and organize the community in the area. Apart from the People's Centre, there is another community hub — the local Riverside Cafe, intentionally set up in the late 1960s as a meeting place to organize residents in their fight to save the neighbourhood. (This fight is described in Chapter Five.) In Milton Park in Montreal, the old Strathearn School, a heritage building, has been restored and converted into a centre which has offices for community groups, a theatre, a cafeteria, and space for community workshops, lectures and meetings. In Winnipeg's core, a converted old railway station has become the community centre for the area. This building is more than a city block long and houses meeting rooms, decentralized government services, a daycare, a gymnasium and more. On a smaller scale, the Logan community in Winnipeg has as its hub, Logan House, which is the location of the *Inner City Voice* office, the housing office, an aboriginal school and a gym for Logan residents. Down the street, Rossbrook House, a converted old church, is now a drop in centre for youth run by nuns and a meeting place for the community. What is significant about all of these places is that they have become the "living rooms" for the neighbourhood, places where people feel welcome outside their homes.

Another way to foster community interaction and social bonding is through community work projects which are really fun projects with a social purpose. In one example, the residents of Sudbury, Ontario undertook an ambitious land reclamation project to restore the damage done to the natural environment caused by years of pollution from the Inco nickel smelters. The whole community got involved in replanting trees and restoring the landscape to its original state. One man, who was a youth when the reclamation began, remembers the occasions as outdoor picnics and festivals with his family and friends. As a result of the community-spirited effort, Sudbury has been transformed from an acid-bleached, barren landscape to a green, living landscape.

Working on a short-term, concrete project together with a large group of people who share the same community purpose can be an awe-inspiring event, much like the experience of building houses for Habitat for Humanity. Cleaning up local rivers is another type of short-term, concrete work project which gives people a common, community-minded purpose and feeling of accomplishment. In Waterloo, local politicians and citizens worked side by side for three days in their grubbiest clothing, picking up garbage and silt from the bottom of the shallow river stream running through their community, which was blocking the water flow and damaging the habitat for fish and other wildlife. A videotape was made of this river restoration project to show other communities what can be achieved when there is a collective will and spirit.

Though highly interesting, examples are not theories, nor do they offer easy points for summary. The Waterloo story is just another way of seeing that neighbourhood communities can become the action ground for building a community-based culture. Similarly, it uses an appreciation of natural history to focus community building and action. While none of the examples I have cited could be considered a grand scheme to fix everything at once, each one is a small piece of the picture and a move in the right direction. As should now be clear, the answers lie within us, our homes and communities, in the many small but direct actions we can take with other people to improve our communities.

CONCLUSION

Culture, as I said at the start, is the soul and life force of a community. It is the glue which holds people together with history, tradition and values passed on to new generations. Authentic culture cannot be manufactured. It grows and evolves over time and emerges as an expression of our *uniqueness* as communities and particularities associated with place. Mass culture, on the other hand, is a manufactured product, a "way of life" sold to us by mass media, pressuring us to conform to the right brand name of clothes, car or personal image. Mass culture, as a commercial product, is the antithesis of a home grown community culture.

With the full weight of the global economy behind it, mass culture is wiping out diversity and pluralism as it insinuates itself into the farthest reaches of our communities and personal lives, and obliterates what is special and unique about ourselves and our communities. Mass culture is the denial of local expression, history, experience and community identity.

This chapter has tried to show how we can take action to restore cultural diversity and rebuild local culture from the grassroots, from within our communities. Building a community-based culture means first, creating authentic communities — places where people live and interact with each other in meaningful, continuing ways and where people also have a *common social purpose.* It may mean discovering what that common social purpose is. It entails creating avenues and vehicles for people to get together and get to know each other — community newspapers, festivals, local activities and events.

At the same time, we need to be learning about and rediscovering the *meaning of the places where we live.* We need to familiarize ourselves with the *social* history of our communities and the *natural* history as well; we need to preserve, maintain and integrate this rich heritage into our present development and future visions of our communities. Lastly, we need to celebrate the diversity of cultures within our communities as a way of enriching all of our lives and reinforcing the alternatives to mass culture.

A last word: with mass culture rendering the very idea of community obsolete, it is ever more crucial that we take action to reclaim our communities. It will take a conscious effort and hard work to preserve and build upon what little remains. Where history has been lost or cultures erased, we may have to use our imaginations to envision what our communities might become. As a wise woman once said about the loss of women's history, "If you can't remember, then make it up."

In the end, community must become the source and producer of culture.

ENDNOTES

1   Brian Fawcett, *Cambodia* (Vancouver: Talon Books, 1986), p. 56.
2   Starhawk writes about the "culture of estrangement" in *Dreaming the Dark* (Boston: Beacon Press, 1982) and Christopher Lasch writes about the "culture of narcissism" in *Culture of Narcissism* (New York: W.W. Norton and Co., 1979).
3   Wendell Berry, "Work of Local Culture," in *What are People For?* (San Francisco: North Point Press, 1990), p. 157.
4   Roberta Gratz, *The Living City* (N.Y.: Touchstone, 1989), p. 73.
5   Pittsburgh, Cincinnati and other community historic preservation efforts are discussed by Roberta Gratz in *The Living City*.
6   In 1968 Paul Hellyer, federal minister in charge of housing, headed a task force to investigate urban renewal and planning. The task force came to the conclusion that massive urban redevelopment was inappropriate because it destroyed habitable houses and viable communities. This effected curtailment of urban renewal in Canada. In the words of David Bettison, "The minister froze urban renewal and public housing because the task force came to the opinion that many programs were wrongly conceived or were being abused." Urban renewal funds, said Hellyer, "were going primarily into commercial development." David Bettison, *Politics of Canadian Urban Development* (University of Alberta Press, 1975), pp. 204–220.
7   *Winnipeg Free Press*, 23 June 1991, p. 6.
8   For the complete story of the ancient civilization, its living oral history and its relationship to the Gitskan land claims, read *A Death Feast in Dimlahamid* by Terry Glavin, (Vancouver: New Star Books, 1990).
9   *Winnipeg Free Press*, 29 June 1991, p. 11.
10 Wendell Berry, "The Work of Local Culture," in *What are People For?* (San Francisco: North Point Press, 1990), p. 166.
11 The bell weather studies on the subject of suburban alienation and sterility are: *The Organization Man*, by William Whyte (Garden City: Doubleday, 1956); *Crestwood Heights: A Study of the Cutlure of Suburban Life*, by John Seeley et al. (Toronto: University of Toronto Press, 1956); more recent references in *The Power of Geography*, by Jennifer Wolch and Michael Dear (Boston: Unwin Hyman, 1989).

Conclusion

The Way Back Home

Conclusion

The Way Back Home

This book has attempted to map out a new ethics of development which centres on five major themes: (1) an economics of self-reliance; (2) an ecological sensibility; (3) community empowerment; (4) meeting individual needs; and (5) developing a community culture. In addition to embodying an ethic, the goal of this alternative development is to revitalize and reclaim *community* as the nucleus for human interaction and as the catalyst to integrate and focus development according to the five themes. The five themes explored in this book together form a framework for a holistic approach to development oriented toward cooperative, community and ecological values. The themes are laid out as guideposts, in no particular hierarchical order. They are not a blueprint or a prescription for success: rather they are meant to stimulate discussion and help map out a new *direction* — sustainable community development.

All of the themes are interrelated: an economics that relies on local markets will respond to the basic needs and demands of people in a community. At the same time, localized production and consumption reduces long distance transport of goods — i.e., local activity is more ecologically efficient. Local production also creates greater accountability to the community for the quality of goods produced and the ecological impacts of industry. Likewise, when a community has control — either through political power, organizational authority or planning rights — over what is developed and how, the interests and needs of the community will be foremost. (We saw that when the West Bank CDC in the Cedar Riverside community of Minneapolis, grew in size and began losing touch with the community, its membership, that same community, voted to restructure the organization to make it more accountable to the neighbourhood and the social/income needs of residents.) As people in neighbourhoods get drawn into daily dealings and interactions with each other — organizing neighbourhood projects, working/deciding together in employee-owned enterprises, joining in community politics, helping each other out in times of trouble, bumping into each other on the street — they come to know and trust each other and build long standing relationships, a factor which adds to both the safety and security of a neighbourhood and the development of a community culture. A community culture, as opposed to a consumer-based culture, grows out of the particularities of a place and has ties to the land and its history. Culture, thus, is a safeguard and guardian over the local environment.

In short, all of the five principles or themes are intertwined. They are the sketchings of a new vision or SCENE — S (self-reliance), C (community culture), E (empowerment), N (needs of individuals), E (ecological sustainability).

The five-pronged model of development, in many respects, turns the current model upside-down and inside-out. It proposes a shift in orientation away from the global to the local, from self-interest to community interest, from top-down control to self-determination, from large scale development to human or "appropriate scale" development, from centralized to decentralized power, from mass uniformity to cultural diversity, from impersonal bureaucracy to face-to-face relations, from corporate management to personal responsibility, from competitive to co-operative values, from an economics of "more" to an economics of "enough," from dependency to self-reliance, from producing quantity to enhancing quality, and from reactive to proactive planning.

Ecology may be the strongest interpretive word which defines the alternative. There is a pattern to the discussion on self-reliance, personal autonomy, self-determination of groups, uniqueness of cultures and so on. Each refers to a quality of cell-like containment, be it of the self, a community or a particular culture. But self-containment, from an ecological perspective, is only half the picture — the other half, and *both* are needed, is co-operation and interdependence. The *paradox* of "autonomy and interdependence" is what ecology is all about — the *relationship* of parts to wholes, in which each "part" is autonomous, yet integrated into a larger whole — a difficult concept to grasp, particularly in a world of either/or and segregated hierarchies. The ecological idea of *unity in diversity* as an ideal, as the strength of our society, as the essence of an ecological society, is paramount in my vision.

Ecology is not as abstract as it seems. Freeways, taxes, TV and civic elections all relate to ecology. The exportation of wealth, the worship of the automobile, the World Class City, the Global Village, the loss of local democracy — these have diverted attention, resources and care away from neighbourhoods, undermined the integrity of communities, destroyed neighbourliness and attachment to "place," and blurred the lines of responsibility about who are the stewards and guardians of the land base. Are the stewards industry, federal or provincial governments, bureaucrats, or the people who live in an affected community? While people who *live* in a community may have the greatest knowledge and concern about what is happening to their local environment, they seldom have the power or the right to decide how land is used — a matter generally left to market forces, professional planners, and piecemeal private development by people from outside the community. Ecology, the study of relationships, is a powerful tool to raise awareness and bring about change. It brings us to the core of our daily experiences, making us think about the connections among what we eat, what we do with our waste, the things we buy, the way they were produced and how we relate to our built and natural environments. In so doing, ecology always poses confirmation or *change* as our choices.

Nowhere is the power of ecology more demonstrated than in the desire of large scale institutions to take over its language and concepts. The most obvious example is the word "sustainable" which, as I mentioned at the start of the book, has been co-opted by nearly every type of organization from global corporations, to conservative governments, to institutions of resource management. Their definition of sustainability, however, bears no relation to the grassroots, alternative development I have presented in this book: rather it seeks to retain top-down control of the environment. By contrast, *real* change must encompass a shift from a global to a *home economy*, from production to create wealth to production to *satisfy needs*, from centralized to *decentralized power*, from larger to *smaller organizations and industries*, from mass culture to a *culture of place and community*, from mediated, bureaucratic relationships to *direct dealings with each other*.

Not everyone will agree with this direction. There are still those who hold that we can have our cake and eat it too, that we can have "sustainable development" *and* unlimited economic growth. They say that we can continue to build freeway cities and mass consume as long as we become "green" consumers and use sustainable technologies like electric cars, while we work very hard at becoming more competitive on the global market. This is far too simplistic a solution. Even if we could learn to "manage" the world from on high, using new "sustainable" technologies, is this the world we would want to inhabit?

The way back is so simple that it seems to have eluded our mental grasp. The road to our salvation is the road that leads back home. "Home" is more than just a house. In the words of poet Robert Frost,

"Home is the place where, when you have to go there, they have to take you in....Something you somehow haven't to deserve." Home is *community*; it is a place of security, acceptance, a place that gives us identity and the knowledge of where we fit in the world. It is time to wake up and recognize that the answers to our problems do *not* lie with governments, professionals or global corporations — they lie within ourselves and our communities.

I and others in the ecology and bioregional movements believe that the rediscovery of the meaning of home and community is essential for re-establishing a human grounding to the earth, a connection with history and a rootedness that is missing in our social relationships. If reclaiming home and community became a general concern in social consciousness, it could emerge as a force to challenge and reverse the tide of globalization, rootlessness, alienation in the world, and the treatment of people and things as commodities.

POINTS FOR FURTHER DISCUSSION

This book has proposed a direction which challenges many of the basic assumptions about the way we organize as a society. No challenge can go unchallenged. Even the most sympathetic reader will have questions about how we get from "here" to "there." For example, how do we deal with issues of "equity" and "universality" in a decentralized society in which community self-reliance is a goal? Are these concepts even relevant? Is there a role for higher governments or regional and national administrative bodies to redistribute wealth, or to oversee and monitor the activities in local jusrsdictions for the good of the whole? What mechanisms would allow communities to co-ordinate among each other while respecting their rights to self-determination? These are critical questions for which there are no black and white answers, and which call for further discussion and debate in the context of building sustainable communities.

As a vision to work towards, we might consider a system of elected community councils made up of local residents who answer directly to people in their neighbourhoods. Community councils could join together in confederated assemblies to decide and co-ordinate among themselves on municipal and bioregional matters they hold in common. This cellular type of political network would give people greater access, power and say over how their communities develop.

Today, however, we must work with what exists. In this regard, there *is* a role for governments to play in assisting communities to become self-sufficient without taking ownership of the process (e.g., setting up community trust funds to be administered by community boards, providing seed grants, sharing information and power). The role of government must always be to *support,* not to control.

Some critics might point out the contradiction of community groups accepting funding from outside sources while promoting the aims of community self-reliance. To this I would only say that contradictions are unavoidable in the transition from a globally controlled to a community-directed society. Working toward self-reliance is a weaning process which occurs in steps as a community builds its internal capacity to meet its needs.

In thinking about social change, the question of politics frequently comes up. What is the role of traditional politics today? Should we be lobbying our politicians at the provincial, federal or civic level to give political and economic power to communities? Because traditional political parties — both right and left — all too often have interests, policies and structures which conflict with the self-determination of communities, it seems we may make better use of our time by working separate from government in the community, defining issues and organizing projects.

The impersonal, mediated quality of relationships in a state bureaucracy promoted by the "left," and the bureaucracy's formal rules and red tape hamper individual freedom, reduce spontaneity and opportunities for *direct* relationships to occur and to evolve as a basis for building community. On the other hand, the "new right" worships individualism, but in the form of dog-eat-dog *competitive* individualism (may the best man win), pitting person against person. This type of individualism lacks the social, co-operative ethic needed to build sustainable communities and instead, evolves into a model for all relationships, pitting business against business, community against community, region against region.

As both sides, left and right, attempt to grapple with the social and ecological problems in the world, it is interesting to note the increasing confusion and crossovers in ideology. The blurring of political lines, for example, is evident with the Manitoba Conservative government setting up a first-of-its-kind loan fund to aid workers in buying out industries threatening to close or leave town. Where worker-owned industries have been considered a type of collective socialism, today they are coming to be seen as a way for communities to participate in their economic future, a type of collective entrepreneurship, as it were, combining elements of both traditional left and right wing ideologies.

I do hope that we don't get stuck in obsolete contexts for change, where left and right politics often lead us. What we can do today is simple and within our own powers.

WHAT CAN WE DO?

What we can do is a three-step process — self-awareness, community action, and linking with others outside the community.

As a start, we can take up the challenge of **seeing the alternative**. This book has attempted to provide an outline for exploring the alternative of a sustainable community. Much more work needs to be done, and more examples added to make this vision an everyday natural perception and ethic. As our awareness of the world changes, we will be motivated to become more ecological, support local industry and local culture, and find ways to promote the alternatives in our work places.

Next, we can act in our community — seek out areas to make changes in our homes and neighbourhoods. What these may be will be unique to each of us, but with eyes wide open we will find endless ways to **take action**. This book offers many examples of community projects — possibilities of what we could do right now, if we choose. No one project is *the* solution — most are small efforts directed at a few hundred or a few thousand people in the context of millions. Their value is as *experiments* in an approach to development which starts with people — their needs, history, strengths — and uses these as pillars upon which to build sustainable communities.

Finally, we can connect with people in other communities. Local action invariably leads to hearing about actions in other places, allowing us to **make linkages** with others on a similar mission. The examples in this book are about places where we can visit, exchange ideas and have continued correspondence. By linking with other communities we gain outside support for our local actions; at the same time sharing our experience can help other communities in their pursuits — the principle of mutual aid. News of success spreads quickly through the network and soon people in other places are taking up similar actions.

The year 1992 marks the 500th anniversary of Columbus's "discovery" of North America. Celebrations have been planned. Counter-celebrations by aboriginal and ecology groups have also been planned to protest the 500 years of colonization of North America and the exploitation of native people and the land's resources. I would suggest yet another kind of celebration. In a new pioneering spirit — not the spirit of conquering nature or other people — we could begin rediscovering and resettling the lands around us — our cities, farms, towns and neighbourhoods — according to a *new* set of relationships based on co-operative values, self-reliance, human dignity and balance with nature. My hope is that we all catch this pioneering spirit and use it to build ecological, sustainable communities as a legacy for our children and the future. Good luck and keep in touch.

Appendices

Appendix 1

WOMEN'S ECONOMIC DEVELOPMENT CORPORATION, ST. PAUL

The following is the story of how one women's organization — Women's Economic Development Corporation (WEDCO) in St. Paul — has, using the unique experiences, culture and specific needs of women, created a consulting business which has successfully assisted hundreds of women to start up businesses of their own. WEDCO is the first program in North America to provide small loans to low income women.

The Women's Economic Development Corporation (WEDCO) was founded in the fall of 1983 by Kathy Keeley, an energetic, creative and practical-minded woman, and former director of Chrysalis, a Minneapolis women's centre. Keeley holds a social work and community development degree. Working with women who were victims of family violence or victims of a degrading social welfare system which kept them dependent on government, it became apparent to her that women needed the freedom and means to choose a different life for themselves. Without an independent income, women were too often trapped in destructive and dangerous home situations. Economic self-sufficiency for women as a process of empowerment thus became the guiding mission of WEDCO. With 57 per cent of women in the St. Paul/Minneapolis area living below the poverty line, Keeley decided to turn her counseling, business and administrative skills toward assisting women achieve economic self-sufficiency through self-employment and business ownership.

In the few years it has been operating, WEDCO has stunned the business world with its unpredicted and unexpected success, covered by national magazines such as *Venture* and *Ms*. In the first three years it helped set up 564 new businesses of which only five failed, as well as expansions of 300 existing businesses — all owned by women. To date, it has helped start up over 1,000 new businesses in Minnesota. As well, it has made more than $900,000 in business loans to clients with a loss rate of only four per cent as compared to the fifty per cent loss rate WEDCO was told to expect when it started. "What that tells us," says Jan Morlock, former vice-president of WEDCO, "is our borrowers are not only much better credit risks than anybody thought they would be, but they're better than the population at large."[1] Most of these women are single parents who are struggling to support a family, they are on government welfare, are immigrants, are not well-educated or have no previous experience in business. Some 75 per cent of WEDCO's clients have annual incomes below $15,000, with 52 per cent below $7,000.

Banks classify WEDCO clients as the highest risk type of borrower. Their requirements for collateral exclude most women from access to loans. So WEDCO operates its own loan fund of last resort to help out clients who cannot otherwise receive bank loans. WEDCO has also worked out an arrangement with one of the local banks to wave standard collateral requirements in special cases and grant loans on the strength of the business plan itself. The types of businesses WEDCO has helped start include a diabetic and health food candy company started by a woman making candy for her own diabetic child; a fishing lure business; a flower business which started with a small five-day loan over Valentine's Day and from there grew into a business grossing $60,000 a year; a design sweat shirt company employing six women; a snowploughing service; a hat maker; an upholstery business.

How does WEDCO work? WEDCO is set up as a nonprofit consulting business operated by ten women, all of whom have expert business training and experience. They do everything, including private consulting, holding seminars and workshops, lobbying government for changes in law, packaging loan funds and giving speaking tours.[2] Its doors are open to women of all ages, backgrounds or incomes, resulting in a wide diversity of clients from the highly educated corporate drop out to the uneducated mother on government welfare. Consulting is done for a sliding fee, according to income.

What is important is that there is no screening process. Self-evaluation is the guiding rule. "Individuals must assess their own business ideas, skills, and abilities to market and finance a business."[3] In other words, the role of WEDCO staff is not to judge, but to support clients by giving them the tools and skills they need to market, finance and plan their business. The relationship between staff and clients is close and flexible, and continues even after a business is set up — whatever is needed to make it work. The complicated tasks of working out a business plan with its cash flow and market analysis and completing loan applications are made less intimidating and more achievable using a step-by-step process whereby clients work their way through a series of attainable goals. The whole process takes an average forty-two hours of training and individual consultations spread over a year or more.

To fully understand WEDCO, one needs to be familiar with four basic premises of its operation:

(1) *It is geared to women's needs.* In contrast to men, women prefer to start out small in business, to incur less debt, less risk and grow steadily, but not too fast. Business development loans offered through government are aimed at subsidizing large capital costs of buildings and machinery. For the size of businesses most women want to start, large scale business development misses the boat. What is needed instead is short term financing to cover operating expenses — cash flow supports. WEDCO fills this gap with its own short term loan fund which has proven to be the catalyst for starting many businesses and a pivotal factor in keeping many businesses afloat during temporary lapses.

(2) *Interpretation and communication.* Many women are unfamiliar with and often intimidated by the language and operational styles of the business world. WEDCO staff act as interpreters for people who have not had access to the economic system. They are translators between the neighbourhood and bank. WEDCO staff are also sounding boards for clients; they provide a safe medium in which to experiment with ideas before introducing them to the world of bankers and businesspeople, where it is often feared they might not be taken seriously. According to Keeley, women who are accustomed to being victims of failure need special counseling along the way to prevent them from sabotaging their own success in business.

(3) *Networking.* WEDCO is a place where women can build the networks they need in business. In our society, women have been excluded from the various business and athletic clubs where men make their business connections. WEDCO helps women find alternative networks. It also provides women with access to attorneys, corporations and accountants who are either on WEDCO's board of directors or sympathetic to WEDCO.

(4) *Expertise and tough expectations.* In addition to their high level of professional expertise, all staff members including the secretary have had first-hand experience owning a business. WEDCO does not judge the market place for a client, but instead, makes sure every client receives the marketing, financial and business planning skills needed to assess her own business ideas. All the research and financial projections are done by the client herself so that she has a thorough

understanding of and confidence in her own product, along with the blessings of WEDCO, when it is time to go to the bank for a loan. For WEDCO, **success is defined by the process**, not the end result. It is not the number of jobs created that counts, but whether a client is able to come to some decision about her own future, whether that means starting a business or deciding that business is not for her.

WEDCO serves not just individuals, but responds to **social goals** as well. It has worked hard to set up a pilot program in conjunction with the government for women on welfare, whereby payments would continue for one year while clients attain the skills needed to set themselves up in business. To get around laws that won't allow welfare recipients to own capital, WEDCO has set up its own holding company to lease the capital equipment needed for their businesses to women on social assistance. When the business is established and the person is off social assistance, the equipment becomes her own property.

WEDCO is an example of how development can grow out of the special needs and culture of women — one of the secrets of its success. Among the "female" characteristics that distinguishes *this* economic development from more mainstream economic development corporations are:

- A personal **caring** for clients which acknowledges that each woman is coming from a different place and needs a different kind of attention and development program, with continued counseling after businesses are started.
- Success is measured by the **process** of self-learning, not simply by how many businesses get started.
- Businesses are encouraged to start small and incur less risk in the interest of **security**, which is preferred to making big profits quickly.
- **Self-evaluation** of the business plan demonstrates a respect for the woman's judgement and builds her self-confidence.
- **Non-hierarchical** partnership structure, where the women who work at WEDCO share in all the different tasks.
- Services made **open and accessible to all women** through a sliding fee scale.

These WEDCO practices make it distinct from most other economic development corporations or business support groups in which clients are usually screened; loans are large (in the range of $25,000) and for capital, not operating costs; programs are standardized, not personalized according to needs; clients are left on their own afterwards, without an ongoing support base.

WomenVenture

WEDCO's growing success, reputation and skills in the field of community economic development (CED), led the organization to broaden its outreach and economic focus beyond business development and into career training, consultations with national women's groups and other CED organizations, work with women in low income housing communities and other initiatives. WomenVenture was established in 1989 as the vehicle to carry out this broader agenda with a wide array of programs (WEDCO is now a part of WomenVenture). New initiatives include a pre-apprenticeship program to recruit women into the building trades; a program to help women move from food service jobs to higher skilled, better paying jobs within the same bargaining unit; a career planning program for women in high school; the development of an Enterprise Development Institute to train women in economic development practices; leadership of a National Women's Enterprise Development Project which has established development programs based on the WEDCO model in ten cities in the U.S.

In 1990, WomenVenture served some 2,300 women through its career and business programs, providing them with financial, technical and moral support. In eight years, it has helped to improve the social and economic situation of thousands of families in Minnesota by empowering women to discover their business/career potential and giving them the skills and encouragement they needed to pursue new economic opportunities.

ENDNOTES

1   Statement from a public lecture reported in the *Winnipeg Free Press*, 8 March 1987.
2   WEDCO started with an $80,000 operating grant and a $50,000 loan fund from a private foundation. Today, 65 per cent of its budget still relies on private and corporate foundation grants, with the remainder from clients' fees and speaking tours.
3   WEDCO Newsletter, Winter 1986.

Appendix 2

ABORIGINAL DEVELOPMENT IN WINNIPEG[1]

After years of having their lives dictated by a nonnative economic and social system which has kept them isolated and down, the aboriginal community is demanding self-government with a strong and unified voice. The "No to Meech Lake" incident, in which Elijah Harper put a stop to the unpopular Meech Lake accord with his single vote, has helped to highlight aboriginal issues for all of Canada and brought respect and a new credibility to the leaders of the aboriginal community. In fact a 1991 poll indicates that where only seven per cent of Canadians found their own leaders credible, 80 per cent found aboriginal leaders to be credible. In the Citizens' Forum headed by Keith Spicer, Canadians expressed strong support for aboriginal self-government and for a fair deal in settling Indian land claims. There was also admiration and incredulity at the fact that aboriginal people could speak with such a unified voice.

The forces unifying aboriginal peoples are their common historical experiences and traditional culture, which are both unique to region and tribe and yet the same in terms of fundamentals — there is a deep respect for nature as an integral part of human life, respect for the wisdom of elders and a belief in a collective conscience to guide decisions. These perspectives are clearly different from the white culture's perspectives, originating in Europe. At an international gathering of aboriginal people from around the world, including representatives from New Guinea, the Caribbean, South America and all regions of North America, the message was that indigenous people everywhere have suffered the same debilitating impact of colonization. It has left them poor, on the margins of society and incapable of sustaining themselves from lands which were either taken from them or destroyed environmentally by development (dams in particular). The answers about how to become empowered as a community and as a community-of-communities, how to get rights recognized by governments, how to improve material and social conditions — all the answers lie in the teachings of their traditional culture. Therefore rediscovering, reclaiming and restoring traditional culture to fit today's context is key to developing a strong, self-sustaining aboriginal community.

In Winnipeg, the Aboriginal Cultural Society was created in 1990 "to draw upon the principles of Aboriginal traditional culture in helping to improve the quality of our lives *today* and to promote the well-being of all people and the natural environment." Its statement continues, "Our goals are to organize activities aimed at *celebrating our culture, addressing our concerns, protecting the natural world, and helping to heal the divisions between us and the larger multi-racial and multi-ethnic society.* We believe that it is only through a *holistic* approach, in itself a *traditional value,* that genuine *personal* and *social* health and healing is possible." Traditional culture — powwows, pipe ceremonies, sweat lodges, pot lucks — thus becomes a transformative spiritual power to reconnect aboriginal people to a whole way of being and thinking; a new "old way" which could reshape all aspects of aboriginal life — family relationships, feelings of self-worth, community empowerment, political process, economic development, basic respect for nature.

For three weeks in June 1991 in Winnipeg, the aboriginal community was the focus of international political, cultural and environmental gatherings which included the election convention of the Assembly of First Nations, the largest international powwow competition, a week long International Mother Earth's People Environmental Gathering, an International Artisans' Festival and an International First People's Gathering to discuss issues and unified strategies for the next 500 years. What was most noticeable to me was the holistic perspective. For example, at the environmental gathering, one day was devoted to workshops on traditional teachings on the environment (e.g., pipe, sweat lodge, medicine wheel), another to honoring women and Mother Earth (women's issues), another to defending the earth (alliance building, hearing from James Bay Crees about their fight to stop the hydro project), and the last day was devoted to healing (sharing circles, traditional drumming, singing, friendship dances and feast).

While traditional culture is providing a direction for aboriginal development and building community pride, there is still a long way to go before the health of aboriginal people is restored. The aboriginal people still suffer from the highest rates of poverty, suicide and infant mortality, the lowest formal education and the worst social conditions.

In Winnipeg, there are many different aboriginal organizations working on different fronts toward the same goal — to help aboriginal people become self-reliant, self-determining and feel a sense of pride in themselves and a sense of belonging to the community. Some of these organizations are support groups, service groups and community economic development groups. The groups provide mutual support for each other.

The Winnipeg Native Families Economic Development Corporation (WNFED) is an umbrella organization created to bring together a number of different projects within the aboriginal community, in order to provide linkage and a support network. The organization was formed after a number of people from the aboriginal community went through a Métis Economic Development Program during which a community profile was completed and community meetings held to identify key areas of need. Three areas were targeted — adequate housing, affordable food and employment. Four projects were then identified to deal with these areas: a housing co-op, a food store, a commercial daycare and a craft shop. Each development trainee took on one project and, together with a working group, developed business plans. The craft project was dropped after a decision that it wouldn't be viable. The other three projects have all come into being.

One of the projects is Payuk Housing Co-op, with five duplex units and a new forty-two unit apartment block (120 residents). Payuk has a policy of providing a secure, nonviolent, drug free environment for women and children, including many who have previously experienced various forms of abuse. The co-op members have a commitment to these and other social goals, with membership aimed at "people who want to become actively involved in developing a co-op housing community which goes beyond 'housing'." All members belong to one of seven committees that run the co-op: (1) Social and physical environment; (2) Children's activities; (3) Education and skill development; (4) Health and recreation; (5) Special events; (6) Membership and staff; and (7) Finance. The main floor has a meeting space and a daycare set up for 30 children. Payuk is much more than a nonprofit housing development. It is a mutual support community which nurtures and protects women (and the men who live there too). With basic needs for safety, housing and child care met, women are able to take the next step toward self-sufficiency by going back to school or work.

Another project of the WNFED network is the Neechi Foods Community Store, run co-operatively by its Indian and Métis workers as a worker co-op. The store sells a full range of groceries including fresh produce, meats and housewares, and also sells traditional native foods like bannock, wild rice and home-cooked pies produced by members. What makes Neechi distinct from other grocery stores is its commitment and involvement in the social and economic needs of the local community, primarily an aboriginal community. For example, it provides personal money management services to help customers budget their food dollars. Neechi takes an active role in promoting good nutrition by working with schools and presenting workshops on food issues. The store does not sell cigarettes, but it sells fruit to children from a separate bin at reduced prices. Neechi Foods also provides a delivery service to those who cannot get out to shop (the elderly and sick) and co-ordinates car pools for people without cars who want to shop at the store.

Another member of WNFED is the Ma Mawi Wi Chi Itata Centre, Canada's first major urban native child and family support program. Ma Mawi has an all native staff of about 55. It operates a youth program which started its own cleaning business called the One Earth Collective, a small but self-sufficient enterprise which has provided part time work for inner city youth. The Aboriginal Women's Economic Development Corporation is another member of WNFED. Its mandate is to promote self-reliance among aboriginal women and to help with basic needs of food, shelter and employment. One of its members is the Original Women's Network (OWN), a resource centre and a communications network for women (operating primarily with volunteer help). It has its own radio program called "Not Vanishing" and puts on workshops for self-development and business development geared to aboriginal women. The Native Women's Transition Centre provides support programs and transitional housing for women who have grown up as victims of a welfare system, including many who have found themselves in trouble with the law. Besides life skills and family violence workshops, the centre provides a cultural program where every two weeks the women go to the Roseau River first nation to meet with Elder Mary Roberts. The idea is to try to reverse the negative stereotypes people are carrying inside themselves about being aboriginal and to instill a sense of cultural pride.

The aboriginal community has its own self-owned-and-run printing company, Mikisiw, which was started up in February 1990 with three employees, 1,800 square feet of space and one small press. In one and a half years its floor space has tripled; it now employs eighteen people of whom sixteen are aboriginal, and it has monthly sales of about $40,000. Among other things, Mikisiw publishes a Manitoba aboriginal newspaper, *Weetemah,* which it started in July 1990. In less than a year, the newspaper has grown from a monthly to a biweekly paper because of increased demand. In May 1991, Canada's first monthly business magazine for aboriginal people started in Winnipeg, *The Aboriginal Circuit.* It is a self-supporting venture as well. There are many other aboriginal enterprises beginning to succeed. One is the dry night club

Club Morocco High and Dry, open from 8:00 P.M. to 4:00 A.M. on weekends. The man who started the club used to work at a detox centre on Main Street and understands the need, after a person stops drinking, for a place to hang out where there isn't the temptation of alcohol. After one year, this club is doing better than projected, and there are now plans to buy the building and open four more clubs in the form of a medicine wheel in the north, south, east and west ends of the city.

Perhaps the most exciting and promising project of all for the aboriginal community is the Aboriginal Centre which is planned to go into the Canadian Pacific Railway (CPR) station — a national historic site.[2] The centre will become a spotlight for aboriginal culture and a symbol to aboriginal people and the rest of the city of a positive aboriginal presence. The station, which is 146,000 square feet, will be completely owned by the native community and self-managed. Revenues from rent could exceed $700,000 annually, making it a capital-generating economic development vehicle, much needed in this poor community. Its location is ideal, on Main Street and Higgins, right at the centre of the largest concentration of aboriginal people in the city.

Currently, there are 51 aboriginal organizations in the city and a great need to bring many of these together under one roof. Offices will be rented out to at least 16 organizations which provide a range of services including banking, entrepreneurial support, child and family social programs, adult literacy, employment assessment, pre-employment development, medical and dental services. In addition, there will be space for starting new businesses with opportunities for resource sharing (incubator facility), a full scale printing outlet, a cafeteria and the Manitoba aboriginal newspaper. Larger spaces will be leased out for the many aboriginal conferences and workshops which are now paying rent elsewhere. As the aboriginal people begin to use the centre regularly, it will spark new commercial enterprises. In Winnipeg there are more than 12,000 aboriginal people whom the centre would serve. The jewel of the project is the 20,000 sqare foot rotunda on the main level which extends upwards for three floors, creating a special space which lends itself to large gatherings such as powwows and conventions. The rotunda has already been used twice this year for powwows.

In conclusion, the Aboriginal Centre, in the historical CPR station will give a high profile presence to aboriginal people in the city. It will be a symbol of self-affirmation in the community and help to build aboriginal pride, purpose and unity among the people. As a revenue-generating business it could be a source of capital to stimulate further economic activity and the goal of aboriginal self-reliance. Over time it could be instrumental in moving the aboriginal community from a state of dependency to independent action in the city. As the prospectus states "the presence and ownership of a facility in this location enables the Aboriginal community to become a stake holder in the issues and opportunities facing the Main Street area."

In all of the above examples (which are just small samples of what's happening in the aboriginal community) we can trace a common thread — the guiding force for change and the framework for how to do it is being discovered in the traditional teachings, values and ways of life, whether it is social, spiritual, political or economic conditions which are being affected. Culture is the binding force.

ENDNOTES

[1] Information was collected from a variety of sources: personal interviews, organization reports, *Inner City Voice Newpaper, Winnipeg Free Press, The Aboriginal Circuit Magazine* (May and June 1991).

[2] At the time of writing, an offer of $1.1 million has been accepted by Canadian Pacific. Financing was still up in the air, however, awaiting final approval of government funding.

Select Bibliography

ON THE GLOBAL ECONOMY

Adams, Patricia, and Lawrence Solomon. *In the Name of Progress: The Underside of Foreign Aid.* Toronto: Energy Probe Research Foundation, 1985.

Barlow, Maude. *Parcel of Rogues.* Toronto: Key Porter, 1990.

Drache, D., and Meric Gertler, eds. *The New Era of Global Competition: State Policy and Market Power.* Quebec: McGill-Queens University Press, 1991.

Hurtig, Mel. *The Betrayal of Canada.* Toronto: Stoddart, 1991.

Kolko, Joyce. *Restructuring the World Economy.* New York: Pantheon, 1988.

Nelson, Joyce. *Sultans of Sleaze.* Toronto: Between the Lines, 1989.

Roger and Me. Feature length film about the decline of Flint, Michigan. Written and directed by Roger Moore, 1990.

Toffler, Alvin. *The Third Wave.* Toronto: Bantam Books, 1981.

ON ALTERNATIVE ECONOMICS AND SELF-RELIANCE

Berry, Wendell. *Home Economics.* San Francisco: North Point Press, 1987.

Dag Hammarskjold Project, *What Now? Another Development.* Report presented to the Seventh Special Session of the United Nations Assembly on Development and International Cooperation. Sweden: Dag Hammarskjold Foundation, 1975.

Daly, Herman, and John Cobb. *For the Common Good.* Boston: Beacon Press, 1989.

———. *Steady-State Economics.* San Franciso: W.H. Freeman and Co., 1977.

Ekins, Paul, ed. *The Living Economy.* London: Routledge & Kegan Paul, 1986.

Hawken, Paul. *The Next Economy.* New York: Ballantine Books, 1984.

Inglis, Mary, and Sandra Kramer. *The New Economic Agenda.* Scotland: Findhorn Press, 1984.

Jacobs, Jane. *The Economy of Cities.* New York: Vintage Books, 1970.

———. *Cities and the Wealth of Nations: Principles of Economic Life.* New York: Vintage, 1985.

Morris, David. *Self-Reliant Cities.* San Francisco: Sierra Club Books, 1982.

———. *The New City-States.* Washington, D.C.: Institute for Local Self-Reliance, 1982.

Nerfin, Marc, ed. *Another Development: Approaches and Strategies.* Sweden: Dag Hammarskjold Foundation, 1977.

Nicholls, W.M., and W.A. Dyson. *The Informal Economy.* Ottawa: Vanier Institute of the Family, 1983.

Plant, Christopher, and Judith Plant, eds. *Green Business: Hope or Hoax?* Gabriola Island, B.C.: New Society Publishers, 1991.

Schumacher, E.F. *Small is Beautiful: A Study of Economics as if People Mattered.* London: Abacus, 1974.

ON COMMUNITY ECONOMIC DEVELOPMENT

Blakely, Edward. *Planning Local Economic Development.* Newbury Park: Sage Publications, 1989.

Campfens, Huber, ed. *Rethinking Community Development in a Changing Society — Issues, Concepts and Cases.* Selected papers and proceedings from a conference held at Geneva Park, Lake Couchiching, Ontario, November 1982. Guelph, Ontario: Ontario Community Development Society, 1983.

Clarke, Roger. *Our Own Resources: Cooperatives and Community Economic Development in Rural Canada.* Langholm, Scotland: The Arkleton Trust, 1981.

Dorsey, Candas, and Ellen Ticoll. *The Nuts and Bolts of Community-based Economic Development.* Selected papers and proceedings from a conference held in Edmonton, Alberta, November 1982. Alberta: Edmonton Social Planning Council, 1984.

Dykeman, Floyd, ed. *Entrepreneurial and Sustainable Rural Communities.* New Brunswick: Mt. Allison University, 1990.

MacLeod, Greg. *New Age Business: Community Corporations that Work.* Ottawa: Canadian Council on Social Development, 1986.

Mungall, Constance. *More Than Just a Job: Worker Cooperatives in Canada.* Ottawa: Steel Rail Publishing, 1986.

Ross, David, and Peter Usher. *From the Roots Up: Economic Development as if Community Mattered.* Ottawa: Canadian Council on Social Development, 1986.

Wismar, Susan, and David Pell. *Community Profit: Community-based Economic Development in Canada.* Toronto: Is Five Press, 1980.

ON ECOLOGY AND DEVELOPMENT

Andruss, Van, Christopher Plant, Judith Plant and Eleanor Wright, eds. *Home! A Bioregional Reader.* Gabriola Island, B.C.: New Society Publishers, 1990.

Berg, Peter, Beryl Magilavy and Seth Zuckerman. *A Green City Program for San Francisco Bay Area Cities and Towns.* San Francisco: Planet Drum Books, 1989.

Bookchin, Murray. *The Ecology of Freedom.* Palo Alto, California: Cheshire Books, 1982.

———. *The Modern Crisis.* Montreal: Black Rose Books, 1987.

Brundtland, Gro Harlem, Chairperson. *Our Common Future: The World Commission on Environment and Development,* 1987.

Capra, Fritjof, and Charlene Spretnak. *Green Politics: The Global Promise.* New York: E.P. Dutton, 1982.

Crombie, David, Commissioner. *Watershed: Royal Commission on the Future of the Toronto Waterfront,* 1990.

Gerecke, Kent, ed. *The Canadian City.* Montreal: Black Rose Books, 1991.

Gordon, David, ed. *Green Cities.* Montreal: Black Rose Books, 1990.

Gortz, Andre. translated by P. Vigderman and J. Cloud. *Ecology as Politics.* Boston: South End Press, 1980.

Porritt, Jonathon. *Seeing Green: The Politics of Ecology Explained.* Oxford: Basil Blackwell, 1984.

Register, Richard. *Ecocity Berkeley: Building Cities for a Healthy Future.* Berkeley: North Atlantic Books, 1987.

Shiva, Vandana. *Staying Alive: Women, Ecology and Development.* London: Zed Books, 1988.

Todd, Nancy and John Todd. *Ocean Arks, City Farming: Ecology as the Basis of Design.* San Francisco: Sierra Club Books, 1984.

Tokar, Brian. *The Green Alternative: Creating an Ecological Future.* San Pedro: R. & E. Miles, 1987.

Toronto, City of. *Healthy Toronto 2000: A strategy for a healthier city.* Toronto: Board of Health, 1988.

Vancouver, City of. *Clouds of Change.* Vancouver: Report from the Task Force on Atmospheric Change, 1990.

On Community Empowerment

Bookchin, Murray. *The Rise of Urbanization and the Decline of Citizenship.* San Francisco: Sierra Club Books, 1987.

———. *Remaking Society.* Montreal: Black Rose Books, 1989.

Estes, Caroline. "Consensus," in *Home! A Bioregional Reader,* edited by Van Andruss, Christopher Plant, Judith Plant and Eleanor Wright. Gabriola Island, B.C.: New Society Publishers, 1990.

Friere, Paulo. *Pedagogy of the Oppressed.* New York: The Seabury Press, 1968.

Helman, Claire. *The Milton Park Affair: Canada's Largest Citizen Developer Confrontation.* Montreal: Véhicule Press, 1987.

Institute for Community Economics. *The Community Land Trust Handbook.* Emmaus, Pennsylvania: Rodal Press, 1982.

Johnson, Sonia. *Going Out of Our Minds: The Metaphysics of Liberation.* Freedom, California: Crossing Press, 1987.

Kotler, Milton. *Neighborhood Government: The Local Foundations of Political Life.* Indianapolis: Bobbs-Merrill, 1969.

Lee, Bill. *Pragmatics of Community Organization.* Mississauga, Ont.: Commonact Press, 1986.

The Mondrigon Experiment. BBC documentary film production. Horizon, 1980.

Starhawk. *Dreaming the Dark.* Boston: Beacon Press, 1982.

———. *Truth or Dare: Encounters with Power, Authority, and Mystery.* San Francisco: Harper and Row, 1987.

On the Culture of Communities

Brody, Hugh. *Maps and Dreams: Indians and the British Columbia Frontier.* Vancouver: Douglas and McIntyre, 1981.

Glavin, Terry. *A Death Feast in Dimlahamid.* Vancouver: New Star Books, 1990.

Gratz, Roberta. *The Living City: Thinking small in a big way.* New York: Touchstone, 1989.

Fawcett, Brian. *Cambodia: A book for people who find television too slow*. Vancouver: Talon Books, 1986.

Kuyek, Joan Newman. *Fighting for Hope: Organizing to Realize Our Dreams*. Montreal: Black Rose Books, 1990.

Lamoureux, Henri, Rober Mayer and Jean Panet-Raymond. *Community Action*. Montreal: Black Rose Books, 1989.

Lasch, Christopher. *Culture of Narcissism*. New York: W.W. Norton, 1979.

Melnyk, George. *The Search for Community*. Montreal: Black Rose Books, 1985.

Mumford, Lewis. *The Culture of Cities*. New York: Harcourt Brace Javanovich, 1938.

———. *The City in History: Its Origins, Its Transformations, and Its Prospects*. New York: Harcourt Brace and World, 1961.

Olmsted, Nancy. *Vanished Waters: A History of San Francisco's Mission Bay*. San Francisco: Mission Creek Conservancy, 1986.

On human needs

Berry, Wendell. *What Are People For?* San Francisco: North Point Press, 1990.

Ignatieff, Michael. *The Needs of Strangers: An essay on privacy, solidarity, and the politics of being human*. New York: Penguin, 1984.

Kneen, Brewster. *From Land to Mouth: Understanding the Food System*. Toronto: NC Press, 1989.

Leiss, William. *The Limits to Satisfaction: An Essay on the Problem of Needs and Commodities*. Toronto: University of Toronto Press, 1976.

Miller, Alice. translated by Hildegard and Hunter Hannum. *For Your Own Good: Hidden cruelty in child-rearing and the roots of violence*. Toronto: Collins Publisher, 1983.

Peck, Scott. *The Different Drum: Community Making and Peace*. New York: Simon and Schuster, 1987.

St. Anthony, Neal. *Until All Are Housed in Dignity: The Story of Project for Pride in Living*. Minneapolis: Bolger Publications, 1987.

Strange, Marty. *Family Farming: A New Economic Vision*. Lincoln and London: University of Nebraska Press, 1988.

Index

A

Aboriginal Centre   190, 194, 227
Aboriginal Cultural Society   224
Alkalai Lake   150

B

Bamberton   86, 87
Berry, Wendell   1, 135, 137, 158, 203, 229, 233
Bioregion   11, 75, 78, 84
Bookchin, Murray   35, 71, 107, 231, 232

C

Calmeadow Foundation   117
Cedar Riverside   48, 114, 120, 130, 186, 200, 207
Chipko   79
Citizens' Forum   37, 192, 223
Clouds of Change   72, 73, 232
Community supported agriculture   81, 160, 178
Core Area Initiative   142

D

DERA   120, 136, 197, 200
Dimlahamid   192, 203, 232

E

Environmentally Sensitive Policy Areas (ESPAs)   188
Evangeline, P.E.I.   122

G

Good Housing Foundation   184
Great Western Brewery   57
Green Guerillas   161

H

Habitat for Humanity   10, 49, 116, 165, 169, 201
Habitat Re-Store   49, 171
Heritage Land Trust   191

235

I

Inglewood 87
Inner City Voice 199
Institute for Community Economics 113, 117

K

Kensington market 185
Kingfisher Lake 61

L

LETS 52, 154
Logan Community 162

M

Milton Park 114, 127, 185, 200
Mission Creek Conservancy 189
Mondrigon 119, 155

N

Neechi Foods Community Store 225
New Alchemy Institute 88
New Dawn 120

O

Original Women's Network 226

P

Pittsburgh Historic Landmarks Foundation 184
Project for Pride in Living (PPL) 56, 116

S

Safe City Report 163
Seikatsu Club 80
SHARE community loan program 51
Shared Farmer project 161
Strathcona Chinatown 186
Street City 10, 165
Sudbury 46, 49
Sudbury 2000 105

T

Tall Grass Prairie Bread Co.   91, 160
The Forks   58, 189, 190, 191
Toronto' Harbourfront   77, 78, 188

U

United Hands   114, 124

W

Watershed Report   77
WEDCO   115, 193
Winnipeg Native Families Economic Development Corporation
    (WNFED) 225, 226
Women Plan Toronto   163
Women's World Bank   116

OTHER PUBLICATIONS AVAILABLE FROM THE CCSD

From the Roots Up: Economic Development as if Community Mattered
by David P. Ross and Peter J. Usher

The rash of plant and business closures across Canada illustrates the growing need for a new economic approach that recognizes the value of local community resources and community empowerment. This innovative work focuses on the importance of the "informal" economy and its role in building sustainable communities in North America.

Ross and Usher illustrate how the separation of economic and social problems in the "bottom-line" thinking of business and government can be replaced by a "social accounting," where smaller structures are developed closer to the community. They argue that by expanding the role of co-operative enterprises, small businesses, community development corporations, voluntary activity and household activity, more informal and democratic solutions to economic problems are possible. *From the Roots Up* explains why we need to revise our concepts of work and employment, our system of taxation and public finance, and our traditional perspectives on public issues.

    1986   194 pp. $15.00 (paper) $23.00 (hardcover)

New Age Business: Community Corporations that Work
by Greg MacLeod

Through case studies, the author presents "community development corporations" — autonomous business enterprises combining economic realities with a sense of social purpose — as a model for future economic growth.

    1986   96 pp. $9.95 (paper) $16.95 (hardcover)

Employment and Social Development in a Changing Economy
by David Ross, Guy Dauncey and George McRobie

Local, community-based economic initiatives may offer more opportunities for full employment than conventional business methods, says this report on the Canadian and British experience with this approach; methods of "humanizing" large mass-production technologies are also examined.

    1986   86 pp. $7.00

CANADIAN COUNCIL ON SOCIAL DEVELOPMENT

Advancing Social and Economic Security for all Canadians

Through research, consultation, public education and advocacy, the CCSD has since 1920 promoted progressive social policies and programs to enhance the quality of life of all Canadians. Our commitment to social justice, equality and the empowerment of individuals and communities directs our work.

WE NEED YOUR SUPPORT TO CONTINUE OUR MISSION

JOIN US

You will receive timely information and analysis on vital social issues through our periodical publications, such as our magazine *Perception*. You will also receive a 20 per cent discount on our books and preferential rates on conferences and workshops.

MEMBERSHIP CATEGORY:

__ Full-time student $20
__ Seniors, fixed income $20
__Individual $50
Organization:
Annual Budget
___ less than $200,000 $50
___ $200,001 to $500,000 $125
___ over $500,000 $200

PAYMENT:

__ Enclosed $ _____
__ Bill me $_____
       (organizations only)
__Visa No. _____
Expiry date _____
Signature

_____

Name		
Organization		
Address		
City	Province	Postal Code
Tel:	Fax:	
___Please send me a free copy of your publications catalogue.		

The CCSD is a non-profit organization registered under the Tax Act relating to charities.

RETURN TO: CCSD Membership Services, 55 Parkdale Avenue, P.O. Box 3505, Station C, Ottawa, Ontario K1Y 4G1